Military Leadersh
for Public Se

Military Leadership Lessons for Public Service

CHARLES SZYPSZAK

McFarland & Company, Inc., Publishers

Jefferson, North Carolina

ISBN 978-1-4766-6491-0 (softcover : acid free paper) ∞
ISBN 978-1-4766-2703-8 (ebook)

LIBRARY OF CONGRESS CATALOGUING DATA ARE AVAILABLE

BRITISH LIBRARY CATALOGUING DATA ARE AVAILABLE

On the cover *clockwise from top left*—Members of FEMA
Headquarters' Private Sector Division, Department of Homeland
Security; First Team welcomes new CO (official Marine Corps
photo by Cpl. Thomas Mudd); 112th Congress House of
Representatives Freshmen Class at the United States Capitol;
Massachusetts and California ANG units hoist TSP colors during
Frisian Flag (U.S. Air Force photo by Staff Sgt. Joe W. McFadden).
*The appearance of U.S. Department of Defense visual information
does not imply or constitute endorsement*

Printed in the United States of America

*McFarland & Company, Inc., Publishers
Box 611, Jefferson, North Carolina 28640
www.mcfarlandpub.com*

To a better understanding
that what makes someone
a good leader in the military
is what makes someone
a good leader in public service

When we assumed the Soldier, we did not lay aside the Citizen; and we shall most sincerely rejoice with you in the happy hour when the establishment of American Liberty, upon the most firm and solid foundations, shall enable us to return to our Private Stations in the bosom of a free, peaceful and happy Country.

George Washington to New York Legislature,
June 26, 1775

Table of Contents

Preface

Three careers ago I was immersed in learning leadership according to the United States Marine Corps. I was challenged with increasing responsibility and assessed for how well I applied what I was taught. As most veterans do, after several years I decided to try applying what I had learned in the military to the community, for me beginning with law school, then in a law firm, and later in academics. I thought that my experience would be welcomed in other leadership situations.

I also knew full well that I would encounter cynicism about having a "military mindset." I did not expect just how uninterested others would be in what I had learned about leadership—or that they would be guarded against and sometimes even hostile to it. I found that their perceptions were rarely based on any personal experience—very few of my contemporaries were in the military or had any direct connection to it in their families.

I learned that talking about my military experience as an example of how to approach decisions usually did not help convince others of the merits of my approach. If others mentioned my military background it almost always was jokingly—not as a source for their own inspiration. But I also found that the lessons I learned were transferrable regardless of what others thought. There were many experiences that proved this to be so. Two stand out clearly in my memory. The first was as an attorney in private practice. The other as an advisor to elected state officials.

As a practicing attorney I worked with many leaders in government, non-profit organizations, and businesses, and witnessed both highly effective and highly toxic leadership. I also saw this within my own professional organization, a law firm, in which I was among several directors who were about to become the next generation of leaders. Our senior colleagues charged us with developing a forward-looking business plan to help assure

1

us of continued economic success without abandoning the intangible features of the firm that shaped its identity, including a commitment to excellence, collegiality, and integrity above profit maximization. After a year of collaboration, including with an outside consultant who was an organizational behavior expert, we were excited to deliver an innovative proposal to restructure the firm into working sub-groups that would decide their own focus and operational principles, including professional development, risk taking, and reward sharing. When we presented the plan for approval to the firm's directors, I and my colleague who crafted the details asked our consultant what he thought of it. He surprised us when he said that the plan's details did not much matter. What really mattered, he said, was whether the firm's leaders could actually modify their behaviors in pursuit of a compelling mission. If we could do that, he said, we would succeed in overcoming the threats of selfishness and inertia, and prove to be an adaptable organization able to flourish in a competitive and changing environment.

The firm's directors approved the plan but we failed the test. We restructured and were energized initially. But less than two years later there was a backlash from some of the old guard over compensation, and the plan quickly unraveled. Those of us who developed the plan and put our faith in it soon left the firm. As I reflect on this experience and what our consultant taught us, I remember what I had learned in the military about what it means to be truly committed to a mission that is valued more highly than personal interests. This is easier said than done.

Another experience synthesized and reinforced in my mind something too easily disregarded about leadership, particularly in public service: mission commitment means putting service above self. It occurred in my work as an advisor to an association of elected public officials. Contrary to the popular impression that people who do the work of government tend to be uncaring bureaucrats, in my experience with these local government officials I found almost all of them to be honest and deeply committed to their public service mission. I saw a powerful example of their dedication when they were confronted with a change in the law that caused many of them personal turmoil because compliance conflicted with deeply held religious beliefs. Amid angry public accusations about their motives, what I saw and heard from them personally was deep reflection on their oath of office to follow the law. Those who could not reconcile their oath with their personal beliefs chose to resign rather than violate their commitment to the office. This was a stark reminder of something I had been taught well in the military: above all, leaders must be what they seem, even when it requires an act that carries a personal cost.

Looking back on the many difficult leadership challenges I have witnessed in various contexts causes me to wonder what mistakes might have been avoided if the lessons I had learned in the military were an explicit part of decision making elsewhere. The principles taught to me have proved to be adaptable to public service in all its forms. This truth is mistakenly disregarded both in leadership preparation and practice. Now I am part of a university program with a mission of preparing future public service leaders. Within such programs leadership is a focus of at least one course that the students must take, and the subject runs throughout other courses in the curriculum and in the professional development discussion. Throughout the program military leadership rarely is mentioned except dismissively as relying solely on formal authority and hierarchy. Military leadership experience is therefore deemed non-transferrable except perhaps to a limited degree in a crisis when a command structure is momentarily imposed, and then it must quickly be put back in its place when the crisis is over.

This bias in public service leadership surprises veterans. Probably most of what they did in the military entailed responsibilities similar to what is encountered in other public service—inspiring others to care about a mission that benefits a community, earning others' trust, supervising training and development, and making decisions about how to use limited resources. Veterans attended leadership schools, were mentored in leadership practice, and were regularly assessed for their actions and the performance of those whom they are charged with leading. When making a transition to other public service they know that they need to adapt their approach to an environment with different dynamics. They are justifiably frustrated when public service scholars and teachers seem oblivious that adaptability is how the military teaches leadership—not as a one-size-fits-all authoritarian style as many others incorrectly assume. Those who have served in the military also are likely frustrated when their learning is disregarded. The organizations they join lose valuable opportunities by not being intentional about tapping into it.

This book can help give context to military leadership veterans in a transition to other public service, including in government. It can also give insight to those in public service who do not know much about how the military teaches leadership. It concludes that there are, in fact, immutable leadership principles. Being mindful of them can better equip anyone for the challenges of leadership in public service.

CHAPTER 1

The Widening Gap

More than two million Unites States citizens are serving in the regular or reserve military. They left their families and communities in the prime of their lives for intensive training and strict discipline. They took an oath to follow the orders of their civilian government that can send them anywhere in the world, including into combat. Hundreds of thousands of them have college educations and are groomed for command responsibilities as officers. Most of those who serve will complete their duties honorably, having acquired the most intensive leadership training, mentoring, and experience available anywhere, and return to their communities seeking to apply what they have learned. But what they are likely to find among those who make decisions affecting public policy is not a welcome embrace for military training and experience, but rather a mistaken sense that it is not of much use in other public service. Most public policy shapers make this mistake, and the academic field that purports to teach them about leadership reinforces it.

A view that military experience is irrelevant to other public service is neither rooted in our history nor reflected in the general public's perception of who is best entrusted with others' welfare. The federal government executive was formed around the model of a military general who was instrumental in achieving independence—George Washington. During times of national crisis citizens at all levels of society have volunteered for the military as a matter of civic duty, and returning war heroes have moved into leadership in civil administration and in business. Still today, when the public is asked about the nation's various public institutions, a vast majority choose the military as the most trusted among them. The civil policy makers who dominate public life, especially the nation's lawmakers in Congress, are often mentioned as the least trusted.

Today, despite public clamor for more integrity in government, the military experience, which the public associates with integrity, is viewed as something that is properly confined to its own sphere, especially among those who influence policy in the media, academics, and special interest organizations. Few of today's policy shapers have served in the military or have had any direct connection to it in their families or social circles. This widening gap is cause for serious concern about good government. The military remains the largest and most intensive leadership laboratory. Its graduates bring great potential to other spheres of public service. This national resource should not be squandered with shortsighted views of the value of military training and experience. Nor should veterans be excluded from positions of civil authority by dynamics that render them misfits because their ideal of selfless service is deemed incompatible with a self-serving and cutthroat career path in politics.

National survival depends on an understanding of the military at all policy making levels. Yet decision makers become ever more disassociated and less directly well-informed about how the military functions or the challenges it faces. The halls in which future leaders are educated become less able to understand how policies affect service members, whose welfare and preparedness are both a pragmatic and a moral necessity. As those in control of public discourse increasingly see time in military service as a separation from citizenship rather than an integral part of it, our concept of who should be leaders, and what leadership entails, becomes unmindful and artificially shortsighted.

This gap between the military experience and other public service is mistaken. It emerges from lack of familiarity, is widened by unquestioning acceptance of false assumptions, and is reinforced by well-meaning but uninformed public service scholars. The two fields have far more in common than leaders in either tend to appreciate.

The Core of Public Leadership

Leadership in any context involves the exercise of influence by one person upon others. It can be associated with authority, as in an organization. Or it can be a natural dynamic, as within families and social groups. Even an organization that denies being hierarchical, which is the modern trend, must have some individuals who influence others in ways that determine the organization's success or failure. What it means to be a leader tends to be viewed differently in the three spheres of business, the military and other public service including government, non-profits, and charities.

There are some differences. But there also are fundamental commonalities.

Business leaders are distinctive in the sense that they primarily use their influence for profit in a competitive marketplace. How to achieve this goal must be part of how leadership is taught to business leaders in schools and promoted in academic and popular business literature. But there also is strong evidence that business leaders can achieve competitive success by employing leadership methods learned in the military. Former military officers attain chief executive officer positions in major companies at three times the rate of their representation in the male population.[1] Some highly successful companies such as FedEx, USAA, and Coca-Cola actively seek to hire former military leaders and integrate military leadership principles in their management.

Research provides insight into how military service can be very effective preparation for business leadership if understood and appropriately applied. For example, one study found that executives with Navy and Air Force experience tend to "take a process-driven approach to management; personnel are expected to follow standard procedures without any deviation," which allows them "to excel in highly regulated industries and, perhaps surprisingly, in innovative sectors."[2] Executives with an Army or Marine Corps background tend to "embrace flexibility and empower people to act on their vision. They excel in small firms, where they are better able to communicate a clear direction and identify capable subordinates to execute accordingly."[3]

A study by Korn/Ferry International found a correlation between six leadership traits emphasized in the military that also serve well in corporate leadership: "learning how to work as part of a team; organizational skills, such as planning and effective use of resources; good communication skills; defining a goal and motivating others to follow it; a highly developed sense of ethics; and the ability to remain calm under pressure."[4] There is a wealth of advice that can be found in publications by former military leaders about how to apply their learning and experience to management, as well as consultancies that advise enterprises and offer applied workshops.

Notwithstanding the value that many businesses find in military experience, studies show that there are important differences in the two fields. One study that compared literature on leadership in military and business environments revealed substantial differences in the factors identified as most important for effectiveness. Among the top five factors noted for the military are integrity and willingness to assume responsibility, neither of which was in the top five for business. Conversely among the top five for business are administrative skills, social skills, and task motivation and application, none of which make the top of the list for the military.[5] This reveals that although business looks at military leadership as a source of ideas that might be useful, the military more highly values matters of character—such as integrity and taking responsibility—that transcend operational success.

By contrast to business literature, advice about public service leadership does not explicitly borrow from the military experience. It tends to depart based on the obvious difference that government and other public organizations typically do not have a culture of authority and mission focus that prevails in military units. Emphasizing these differences obscures an essential similarity that should unify rather than separate how leadership is viewed in all of public service, both military and civil. They share the necessity of a commitment to service above self, which is symbolized by a solemn oath. This symbolism is not merely a corny relic of a bygone era. Its meaning is at the heart of public leadership.

In the military the oath is both inaugural and continual. By federal law someone who enlists must take an oath to "support and defend the Constitution," to "bear true faith and allegiance" to it, and to obey the orders of the president and senior officers "according to regulations and the Uniform Code of Military Justice."[6] All officers take the same oath to the Constitution but add that they undertake "this obligation freely, without any mental reservation or purpose of evasion," and to "well and faithfully discharge the duties of the office."[7]

The commitment made with these oaths remains conspicuous throughout military service. Those who take it for the first time are very conscious that they are surrendering some of their personal liberties to a cause, and it usually involves a compulsory tour of duty. The oath typically is given in a traditional and solemn ceremony, often preceded with introductory remarks about its meaning and importance. In some branches officers who give the oath are expected to give it from memory, further symbolizing that it is internalized by those who lead. It is on service members' minds when they are relocated or assigned duties that require them to be away from their families, and if they are sent to war. Violation of it can result in severe discipline and punishment.

Federal service also involves an oath. It is a ceremonial gesture in inauguration to high office. The president, members of Congress, judges, and others federal officials take the same or similar oaths as military officers. An oath also is part of state and local government service. Newly elected executives and legislators, judges, and elected and appointed local officials give an oath that expresses their commitment to public responsibilities including honoring the law. This is a significant step—a choice and a promise to put service above self. As professor of philosophy and public administration Mark Rutgers said, "Perhaps the most marked, traditional as well as symbolic expression for a special morality for public office is the requirement of the oath of office.... Underlying the oath of office has to be the notion that there are specific values for public functionaries that warrant the unique demand of an oath to begin with."[8] And certain responsibilities follow with the choice to make a commitment to these values. As Rutgers explained, "A public function brings with it special responsibilities that warrant asking the highest security and commitment a person can give. The reason being that a public office has a very special status, unlike any other office in society: someone is granted access to the most significant powers in society in the form of public authority and to the greatest economic means in society in the form of state powers."[9]

Some in public service give the oath with careful consideration of its meaning, fully intending to honor it. Unfortunately today more often its importance is deemphasized or ignored, especially apart from conspicuous public offices undertaken in public ceremonies. In practice the oath can become nothing more than an empty formality begrudgingly completed in the bowels of government offices. In some federal agencies new employees are gathered in conference rooms to repeat phrases that have little meaning to those who utter them, sometimes even by someone who does not speak the language. Treating the oath as nothing but a formality is a lost opportunity to focus attention on the responsibilities that accompany public service, including the responsibility to inspire others to something more important than just being an honest employee or effective manager of resources. As Rutgers warned, "there is a genuine danger of crowding out public values and attitudes if a legal perspective and managerial morale dominate ideas on public functions."[10] Joining the ranks of government and nonprofit organizations increasingly is seen as a choice made for career advancement, not involving a surrendering of self in service.

In government the "public values and attitudes" of which Rutgers speaks should involve much more than a promise to abstain from what is prohibited. John Rohr, a leading public affairs scholar, warns about a trend to view the oath merely as an instrument to discourage unethical behavior and increase organizational performance, rather than as an expression of a "moral commitment to the general interest, which outlines the distinctiveness of public service."[11] He wrote extensively about the interrelationship of constitutional principles and public administration and the importance that this be understood by those who enter public service. He stressed the important role of the oath as a reminder of this undertaking. He said, "Taking the oath ethically commits the public official to uphold the Constitution, giving autonomy to act as a guardian of the public interest. This includes a loyalty and integrity that can override a relativistic aim at efficiency or measured performance."[12] He further explained that the oath is "an initiation into a community of disciplined discourse, aimed at discovering, renewing, adapting, and applying the fundamental principles that support our public order."[13]

The extent that the notion of an oath no longer symbolizes thinking about leadership in public service is demonstrated by its absence from current leading textbooks on leadership in public organizations. Texts commonly discuss stewardship and service, but they blend these notions into generalized social aspirations rather than nonnegotiable personal obligations. For instance, one leading public administration leadership text notes that "the key element to administration leadership is its service or stewardship focus," but continues by framing "stewardship" as an environment "in which leaders are dedicated to responsiveness, openness, awareness of competing interests, the common good, and so forth in order to enhance the public trust."[14] Students are not likely to feel much weight of an undertaking with vague notions such as "the common good, and so forth." Neither is a public administration teacher assigning this reading likely to require students to reflect on the personal meaning of an oath.

The military shines a bright light on the meaning of a personal oath and its connection to the aims of leadership. Something is amiss when this foundation, which is shared with other public service, is fading from leadership discourse in public life. It is part of the fabric on which constitutional government is built and on which its promise relies.

Historical Foundation of Military Leadership and Public Service

The founders of the American form of government did not consider military leadership as a notion separate from civil leadership. They were inseparable. The founders' idea of how the nation's leader should act in the office of president was based on the model of the most prominent military hero, General George Washington. Other key figures also were experienced military leaders. Some of the country's early leaders first learned about leadership through military training and experience, such as Washington. Others applied leadership they had developed in their communities when called into military service. The first secretary of the treasury, Alexander Hamilton, was an aide to General Washington, served with him at Valley Forge, and led a key attack on a British outpost at Yorktown. He organized the Coast Guard. Henry Knox, the first secretary of war, was a general and commander of the Continental Army's artillery. The first attorney general, Edmund Randolph, was an aide to General Washington in the early part of the war, leaving to be Virginia's attorney general. James Madison, the principal author of the Constitution and Congress's first Speaker of the House, and Thomas Jefferson, the lead author of the Declaration of Independence and the first secretary of state, both were militia commanders responsible for its muster, though unlike most of the other early leaders they did not lead troops in combat. John Marshall, the preeminent Chief Justice of the United States, who was architect of the Court's early opinions establishing the principle of judicial review and defining the extent of the federal government's power, was an aide to Washington and served with him at Valley Forge. Nearly every key figure who conceived of the American idea of citizen service had direct and extensive experience with military leadership.

Though fully aware that a large standing army was a threat to republican liberty, the founders also knew the military was essential to national survival. Rather than separate military and civil service they sought to integrate citizenry and defense. They were careful to provide for a citizen militia in the constitutional framework. There is no question that they saw military and civil leadership as a single ideal of public service.

A lot has changed in the country since its founding. The federal government now fields a vast and powerful standing military of global influence with a budget that consumes a substantial part of the revenue. Military units patrol land, sea, space, and cyberspace, and forces regularly are dispatched to international conflicts and crisis relief. While the military is more omnipresent than it ever has been, those who lead it have largely become disassociated with civilian public service.

In some ways a separation of the military from civil administration was intended and has been appropriately preserved. The elected civilian representatives' supreme command of the military is a foundation of the American Constitutional system. The president, regardless of any military experience, is the commander-in-chief, and the military reports directly to the president's civilian officer, the secretary of defense. Only the elected representatives in Congress can declare war, and only the Congress can provide funding for the military to exist and sustain a presence in the world. The framers intended this civilian control to be a counterweight to the historic tendencies of generals to use their might to seize and keep political control, a tendency that persists in some parts of the world.

But subordination of the military to civilian control is a different matter than the separation of citizens with military experience from positions of influence in civil administration. That the framers did not intend this separation is evident from their own military experience. This view persisted in history, particularly during times of crisis. Three conspicuous examples show how until recently military experience was seen as something that was adaptable to the heavy responsibilities of other public service leadership: George Washington, Ulysses Grant, and Dwight Eisenhower.

George Washington is the obvious prime example. He was entrusted with supreme command when Massachusetts delegate John Adams rose at the meeting of the Continental Congress in 1776 and proposed Washington's appointment as commander in chief of the Continental Army in opposition to the British occupation. Adams argued that Washington, a man with "great talents, and excellent universal character, would command the approbation of all America, and unite the cordial exertions of all the colonies better than any other person in the union." Adams was right. Washington kept an army in the field despite what seemed to be insurmountable difficulties with enlistments, supplies, and pay, against a larger, better trained, more experienced, and better equipped opposing force. After years of struggle, in October 1781, Washington commanded a combined American and French force that encircled a 7,000-man British force, which effectively abandoned the British hope of compelling submission in the colonies. This was an astounding achievement against great odds.

Washington's leadership was even more singularly impressive after the war. In March 1783, at a critical point before formation of the new, constitutional federal government, General Washington spoke at a gathering of his subordinate military leaders in Newburgh, New York. Some of the officers were urging a revolt against Congress for failing to honor its promise to pay the officers and settle their accounts. As biographer James Thomas Flexner wrote of this critical moment, "This was probably the most important single gathering ever held in the United States. Supposing, as seemed only too possible, Washington should fail to prevent military intervention in civil government?"[15] Through force of example and appeal to higher virtues, Washington settled the course for transition to a federal republic of elected leaders. He warned the officers against agitators who were "sowing the seeds of discord and separation between the civil and military powers."[16] He told them not to lessen the dignity or sully the glory of what they had achieved in the war, and to detest those who disrespected the liberty for which they had fought and sacrificed. The uneasy officers were moved by Washington's appeal, and their abidance enabled the formation of a civil government based on a rule of law rather than force.

By the end of the war Washington had no rivals for power. He had the loyalty of the military's commanders and he had the most esteemed reputation among civilian authorities. Having no taste for autocracy, he surrendered his sword and command to Congress and headed home intending to leave public life. Learning of this act King George III of England, against whose forces Washington had led a victorious army, called Washington "the greatest character of his age."[17]

Washington's leadership proved to be indispensable in the creation of a stable national government. In 1787 the delegates at the Constitutional Convention unanimously elected Washington to preside. He kept a firm grip on the debates, quelling angry disagreements and urging compromise. He seldom spoke of his own views except to insist that the delegates stay and work together. The delegates respected him too much to let personal agendas prevail over collaboration. The convention's ultimate decision to have an elected single executive was influenced by the example Washington set as someone who could be trusted not to have royal ambitions. South Carolina delegate Pierce Butler reflected the framers' sentiment about Washington when he recalled that Washington's presence "shaped their ideas of the powers to be given to a President by their opinions of his virtues."[18] The Constitution defined the executive's powers in very general terms, leaving it to the former general to mold the office in the spirit of a republic founded on the idea of individual liberties. The Electoral College unanimously chose Washington as president.

Washington's model for the executive was one of limited government based on a rule of law and political compromise without personal ambition. During his self-imposed two-term limit he drew upon counsel from other head-strong leaders such as Jefferson, Hamilton, Adams, and Madison, to decide basic questions about the allocation of power and involvement in international affairs. He kept the federal government together and steered it away from what could have been disastrous entanglement in wars with England and France.

Washington's greatest frustration as president was the emergence of party conflict within his administration, which he saw as selfish. Secretary of the Treasury Alexander Hamilton and Secretary of State Thomas Jefferson deepened a political disagreement over the balance of powers between the centralized federal government and those reserved to the states, and over foreign relationships with Great Britain and France. Washington's vice president John Adams tended to align himself with Hamilton and in opposition to Jefferson. On many important issues Washington solicited the input from each of these great thinkers, urging them to keep their focus on what was best for the country. When Washington left office he warned that the developing factions were among the greatest threats to national survival. This tendency to separate, he said, "serves always to distract the public councils and enfeeble the public administration."[19] Appreciating individuals' natural tendencies to split into camps and pursue separate interests, he urged unity of purpose and restraint of self-serving partisanship. This was the same focus on service that he demonstrated so well as general, which enabled him to hold an army together under dire circumstances. History has shown that others too easily forget Washington's example and his warnings.

After eight years of service Washington eagerly surrendered his power to the newly elected president, John Adams. When Adams gave his inaugural address, Washington sat next to the vice president-elect, Thomas Jefferson. After Adams made his remarks Washington insisted Jefferson speak next, declining the offered reverence. Washington also insisted on following Adams and Jefferson as they left the room. His humility is unique in recorded human history. He was a man who refused to assume unlimited power others urged upon him. We need only compare his role in history to that of his near contemporary Napoleon, who turned his military successes into dictatorial powers that had catastrophic results for Europe and ended in his banishment.

Washington's example can teach much about leadership during times of crisis and transition. He had leadership traits and acted according to principles that were effective in both the military and in civil administration. Today many who enter public service will drive by a fitting reminder of him. The Washington Monument is across from the Pentagon and towers at the center of the national power. But it bears no depiction of the man, a lesson that leadership should be aimed at something more far-reaching and lasting than self-interest.

While Washington is the preeminent example of leadership that spanned both military and civil challenges, other prominent figures in history reveal that effective leadership in both contexts requires effective followers. One stark example is Ulysses S. Grant, who distinguished himself as a commanding general in the Civil War, but whose legacy in later service as president is largely remembered for the corruption and selfishness within his administration that frustrated his leadership.

As often is the case with military leaders, Grant came from humble beginnings. He arrived at West Point in 1839 as Hiram and became U.S. Grant when his appointment letter incorrected listed his name. As an officer he gained war experience in Mexico but resigned from the Army in 1854 and returned to civilian life to struggle with farming and working in a family store. He joined the Union Army when the Civil War began in 1861 and was quickly promoted based on his leadership in Missouri and Tennessee. His aggressive and direct style of leadership caused him to be nicknamed "Unconditional Surrender" Grant. He distinguished himself during the early part of the war as other Union Army generals were hesitant and ineffective, and he became a favorite of President Lincoln. Grant also became known for innovative and daring tactics that confounded other generals and surprised opposing forces. At Vicksburg, for example, he had his forces move along a rough route separated from a supply base, relying only on what they could collect in the field. Fellow general William T. Sherman openly questioned Grant for this unconventional tactic. Sherman later employed it successfully on his notorious march through Georgia and the Carolinas.

Grant was a decisive leader and did not think much of committees. He said, "I believe it is better for a commander charged with the responsibility of all the operations of his army to consult his generals freely but informally, get their views and opinions, and then make up his mind what action to take, and act accordingly."[20] At the same time he was admired for how he would delegate authority and entrust his commanders. As Grant's staff officer Horace Porter said of his commander, Grant "studiously avoided performing any duty which someone else could do as well or better than he."[21] M.D. Leggett, who also served on Grant's staff, recalled that he once heard Grant say "with a little impatience that he had less concern for an officer who was afraid to face the enemy than for one who hesitated in forming a judgment when he knew all the necessary facts. He said that the most cowardly officer in the command of troops was the one that was afraid of his own judgment."[22] Leggett also said of Grant: "He went where his duty took him, regardless of personal considerations."[23]

For leadership in post-war reconstruction the dominant Republican Party turned to Grant as president. Grant found himself distracted with corrupt schemes within his administration. His vice president accepted a bribe in a railroad financing scandal, which also involved Grant's younger brother. His chief of staff was involved in the infamous Whiskey Ring scandal in which liquor tax revenues were diverted to private uses.

Grant's frustrations occurred during a time of great turmoil. The country had been depopulated, much of its community leadership and workforce were lost, and large portions of the country were wasted from war. The southern economy was turned upside down and a large part of the population, though legally freed from slavery, was dispossessed and unemployed. Racism and regionalism persisted, and the unscrupulous saw opportunity in the social, cultural, and legal confusion. Grant's reputation suffered from the disloyalty of political appointees and the viscous manner in which his opponents and critics portrayed him. He was blamed for the corruption that he rooted out. He was portrayed as an alcoholic but there was no instance in which his performance was known to have been impaired by being under the influence.[24] These condemnations were mostly unfair and the product of those who wished to destroy his reputation for their own purposes. This unfairness that dogged Grant was most famously illustrated when President Lincoln, after being urged to dismiss Grant for drinking too much whiskey, said he wanted to know the brand, "because, if I can only find out, I will send a barrel of this wonderful whiskey to every general in the Army."[25]

Unfortunately for the country, Grant's leadership was squandered. He was surrounded by self-interested public administrators in whom he should not have trusted as he had been able to trust his military commanders. In his 1876 State of the Union Address, Grant acknowledged these mistakes, which he attributed to "the selections made of the assistants appointed to aid in carrying out the various duties of administering the Government—in nearly every case selected without personal acquaintance with the appointee, but upon recommendations of the representatives chosen directly by the people."[26]

Almost a century later the country again turned to a military hero in the aftermath of war. Dwight Eisenhower rose to supreme command due to his rare ability to inspire others to work together under the most difficult circumstances. His beginnings were humble like Grant's. He was commissioned in the Army after his graduation from West Point despite an academy physician's warning that he might be disqualified because of damage to his knee from torn cartilage and tendons suffered during exercises. This did not interfere with quick advancement in his career. In 1939, with a looming world war in two theatres, he returned stateside after serving on General Douglas MacArthur's staff in the Philippines to develop a program for training and equipping an Army that was to be multiplied in size, by 20 times, to five million. After the Japanese attacked Pearl Harbor he was called to Washington to be an assistant to Chief of Staff General George Marshall. Marshall was himself an inspirational leader known for entrusting his subordinates, and he recognized great ability in Eisenhower. Marshall's first assignment to Eisenhower was to think big and think about the question "What should be our general line of action?"[27]

Though Eisenhower sought a field command Marshall insisted that Eisenhower was more important to the national headquarters. Then when Eisenhower urged Marshall to assign a single commander to unify operations in Europe, Marshall finally agreed and told Eisenhower he was the man to execute it. His command of joint forces in Operation Overlord for the invasion of France was described by historian Stephen Ambrose as "the most coveted command in the history of warfare."[28] As Ambrose further explained, "Eisenhower's emphasis on teamwork, his never-flagging insistence on working together, was the single most important reason for his selection."[29]

One of Eisenhower's most remarkable leadership traits was his ability to work with powerful figures both within and outside the military. He had to account to President Franklin Roosevelt, British Prime Minister Winston Churchill, and Chief of Staff George Marshall, all of whom were themselves brilliant and charismatic leaders of immense achievement. He also had to gain the confidence and cooperation of other national leaders in the cooperative effort, including the unpredictable and domineering Soviet Union premier Joseph Stalin and French president General Charles de Gaulle. Within the military Eisenhower commanded generals who had aggressive and independent tendencies, such as the American general George Patton, who was known for unpredictability and irascibility, and British field marshal Bernard Montgomery, who was a brilliant but arrogant general who often expressed irascible impatience with Eisenhower. In the spirit of George Washington, Eisenhower kept these leaders working toward the same end by maintaining excellent professional relations with all in an honest, direct, and hard-working manner that exemplified a commitment to mission above self. Within the Army Eisenhower was also embraced by the troops, who gained strength from his unshakeable confidence and his ability to inspire sacrifice for the cause.

Eisenhower's reputation earned during the war led him to be elected president in 1952. During his campaign he said he intended to go to Korea and end the war there, and soon after he took office the fighting was stopped. He served two terms while the country underwent profound changes. He accelerated development of the space program and laid out a federal highway system. One public administration difficulty in which he demonstrated his exceptional leadership was the manner in which he handled the most divisive issue of his early presidency—Senator Eugene McCarthy's reckless accusations about communists in American government. Though Eisenhower himself was concerned about communist influence he deplored McCarthy's tactics and the way it turned Americans against each other. Rather than openly confront McCarthy as he was urged to do, and possibly further inflame the matter, Eisenhower could see that McCarthy would self-destruct and his influence quickly wane. He was right. McCarthyism is now a catchphrase meaning baseless political repression.

Though he was a career military officer Eisenhower's leadership perspective transcended that background. In his farewell address Eisenhower warned that "we must guard against the acquisition of unwarranted influence, whether sought or unsought, by the military-industrial complex. The potential for the disastrous rise of misplaced power exists and will persist."[30] That Eisenhower could see the risks to a free society from this development belies any assumption that someone who owes his career to military success would always promote military power even at the expense of peaceful civil interests. Of course Eisenhower was not the first president who had been a general to be concerned about the relationship of the military and civil government. Washington had said in his farewell address, "Over grown military establishments are under any form of government inauspicious to liberty, and are to be regarded as particularly hostile to republican liberty."[31]

These three examples from history show that national interests have been preserved and advanced with leadership derived from the military and applied to other public service. The same traits that caused these military leaders to be entrusted with the fate of an army at war were embraced in other aspects of public life during difficult times. But history also proves that successful leadership in public life requires adaptation and successful followership. Washington and Eisenhower, and especially Grant, experienced great frustrations, when others within and surrounding their administrations did not share the same mission commitment or integrity.

Separation

American presidents make weighty decisions about military force structure, leadership, and preparedness. They order service members into hostilities. Forty-three men have served as president. In addition to Washington, Grant, and Eisenhower, nine other presidents were generals: Andrew Jackson, William Henry Harrison, Zachary Taylor, Franklin Pierce, Andrew Johnson, Rutherford Hayes, James Garfield, Chester Arthur, and Benjamin Harrison. Presidents Kennedy, Johnson, Nixon, Ford, Carter, Reagan, George H.W. Bush and George W. Bush had some military experience. Kennedy, Johnson, Nixon, Ford and George H.W. Bush saw combat. For more than 55 years no general has been elected to the office.

One possible reason why no general since Eisenhower has become president is that the country has not faced a protracted conflict that galvanized the public around a military hero of the likes of Washington, Grant, or Eisenhower. But generals have played prominent roles not only in war but also in national and international commands, and they have had far more extensive leadership preparation than the politicians who have achieved the office. Their experiences suggest that in today's political system the nature of military command is likely not to be a road to the presidency. The paths of the country's most well-known generals have ended either because the generals became a focus of negative attention, failed to connect in popular contests, or chose not to subject themselves to the process.

Two generals who had presidential ambitions were Alexander Haig and Wesley Clark. Haig was the son of a lawyer. He graduated from West Point and served in Korea and Vietnam. As a general he was deputy to Henry Kissinger on the National Security Council and worked on extracting the United States from the war in Vietnam. He became chief of staff in the White House in the wake of Watergate, after which he was Supreme Allied Commander of NATO forces in Europe. He was so influential in his White House role that he was promoted from colonel to four star general without holding a major battlefield command.

Haig retired from the Army in 1979. His rapid rise continued when two years later President Ronald Reagan chose him to be secretary of state. He had experience with effective national command; he was known to have been making key decisions while in the White House when Richard Nixon resigned in 1974. When Reagan was shot in 1981, Haig infamously declared himself at "the helm," which others understood to be claiming to be the acting president despite constitutionally being the fourth in the line of succession. Haig's misstep when President Reagan was shot resulted in his rapid downfall. His rash announcement, and other public displays of irascibility and perceived arrogance, led to his dismissal by President Reagan in 1982, and Haig faded from national prominence. He ran unsuccessfully for the 1988 Republican Party presidential nomination, withdrawing after garnering only a small percent of the vote in the primary polls.

Wesley Clark also fell from national prominence quickly after an impressive ascent within the military. He was valedictorian of West Point and a Rhodes Scholar at Oxford. He served in Vietnam and was decorated for bravery when despite being shot four times he continued to direct troops in a counterattack. He became acquainted with national public administration as a White House Fellow in the Office of Management and Budget and worked on the creation of the Vietnam Veterans Memorial in Washington, D.C. He held several important commands and was recognized for developing new training programs and emphasizing technological innovation. He served in various leadership and coordination positions during the war in Bosnia and Herzegovina, and in 1997 became the Supreme Allied Commander for Europe. He commanded the bombing campaign in Yugoslavia. In 1999 he was rotated into retirement.

In 2004 Clark sought the Democratic Party nomination for president. He said he had been an independent his entire career but decided to seek the Democratic nomination because the party better aligned with his views on social issues. But some leaders within the party questioned his political loyalty. He also drew fire for giving qualified answers to debate questions, such as about support for the Iraq War Resolution. He made other clumsy statements that drew much attention, such as when discussing the space program he said that based on faith he disagreed with physicists about humans being able to travel faster than the speed of light. For a while he had substantial support in the polls, but he withdrew in 2004 as John Kerry's campaign pulled away. Since then Clark has been a consultant.

Both Haig and Clark sought the presidency but were unsuccessful. In recent decades there have been other famous military leaders who chose not to pursue the office. Two in particular seemed poised for success but never sought a nomination: Generals Colin Powell and Norman Schwarzkopf.

Colin Powell was born in Harlem, the son of Jamaican immigrants. He was commissioned in the Army through ROTC and was among the early military advisers sent to South Vietnam, where he was wounded by a punji-stick booby trap along the Vietnam-Laos border. During a second tour he was decorated for bravely rescuing members of his unit after a crash while he was aboard a helicopter. He later served as a brigade commander in the 101st Airborne Division. Even while in the military others recognized his potential for leadership in public administration, when he was awarded a White House fellowship and worked with the Office of Management and Budget, and later when he was an assistant to cabinet secretaries. He was national security advisor during the Reagan administration and was involved in the president's summit meetings with Soviet president Gorbachev that were instrumental in the dismantling of the Communist Bloc. In 1989, President George H. W. Bush appointed General Powell to be chairman of the Joint Chiefs of Staff. Powell led the development of the successful strategy for Operations Desert Shield and Desert Storm. He demonstrated an ability to appeal to both political parties when he continued as chairman of the Joint Chiefs in the first few months of the Clinton administration, and when during the following administration of President George W. Bush he served as secretary of state, having been unanimously confirmed.

Secretary of State Powell drew intense public criticism for his support of the invasion of Iraq in 2003. He was chastised for a speech before the United Nations Security Council during which he described an Iraqi weapons development program as justification for military action, relying on information provided by intelligence officials that proved to be wrong. He later acknowledged the errors in the information on which he had relied and became self-critical of his judgment and failure to follow his instincts. In 2004, he resigned as secretary of state. He surprised many when, still a Republican, he endorsed Democrat Barack Obama for election as president, supporting his policies on taxation and on ending military action in Iraq. Despite frequent mention in the media as a vice presidential candidate, he has not sought national elective office. Powell has described his reticence as a matter of personal choice made together with his wife, based on a lack of desire for campaigning and holding political office.

Norman Schwarzkopf, Jr., also was a very popular and publicly conspicuous military commander. He was a West Point graduate and later taught there. He served in the Vietnam War as an advisor to the South Vietnamese Army and as an infantry battalion commander. Schwarzkopf was highly decorated in Vietnam, including for courageously rescuing soldiers from a minefield. He quickly rose through the levels of command and served in the Invasion of Grenada in 1983. Schwarzkopf distinguished himself for his ability to inspire troops, and was critical of the Army's trend to emphasize technical knowledge at the expense of effective direct leadership.[32] In the late 1980s he took command of the U.S. Central Command and was charged with leading a response to the invasion of Kuwait in 1990 by Saddam Hussein's Iraqi forces. In the field Schwarzkopf led an international force of over 750,000 troops. During the operation he famously gave public press briefings that calmly and clearly explained the strategy and progress of a surprisingly swift and decisive campaign. He became a popular figure at the end of the quick war, nicknamed "Stormin' Norman."

Soon after Operation Desert Storm Schwarzkopf retired from the army and assumed a private life, until he died in 2012. He did not seek public office. He did not explain his choice publicly but his personality and approach to leadership suggest that he had little tolerance for the political grindstone. He probably felt that his rough-and-tumble style was more suited to leading the military in the field than to campaigning and public political life. He shied away from the kind of self-promotion that is associated with campaigning. His reticence may be best revealed by a quote for which he was famous: "It doesn't take a hero to order men into battle. It takes a hero to be one of those men who goes into battle."[33] He also revealed his sense of time and place when, at the close of his military career, he said, "I feel that retired general officers should never miss an opportunity to remain silent concerning matters for which they are no longer responsible."[34]

Several other successful generals who seemed highly qualified for public administration fell quickly from popular approval and any hope of holding high office. General David Petraeus, a West Point graduate with a doctorate in international relations and economics from Princeton, was internationally acclaimed for his command of the 101st Airborne Division in Mosul where he implemented a pacification strategy based on his doctoral thesis about counterinsurgency in Vietnam. His efforts in Mosul were frustrated when civilian leaders directed the exclusion of former Iraqi officers and soldiers, many of whom turned to armed resistance. He later called for a surge of troops and a more concerted effort to win support among the locals. In 2008 he was put in charge of the U.S. Central Command, which coordinates the military's operations worldwide. He later took command in Afghanistan. In 2011, Petraeus made his entry into civil public service when President Obama appointed him director of the Central Intelligence Agency. He resigned the next year when it was disclosed he had an extramarital affair with his biographer. In 2015 he pled guilty to sharing classified governmental information with her and he was fined and assigned to probation.

General Tommy Franks commanded American forces in the attack on the Taliban in Afghanistan in response to the 9/11 attacks. He also commanded forces in the 2003 invasion of Iraq and the overthrow of Saddam Hussein. He was criticized for decisions made after the fall of Bagdad, including the escape of terrorist leader Osama bin Laden, and Franks retired in 2003.

General Stanley McChrystal was highly regarded for his command in Afghanistan and his implementation of tactics that reversed the course of a deteriorating military situation. But his command lasted only a year. A *Rolling Stone* magazine article entitled "The Runaway General"[35] described offhanded remarks McChrystal made about his political leaders. McChrystal was reported as being surprised that the president seemed to know nothing about him when he was about to take a major command. He also was quoted as having made caustic remarks about the vice president during a question-and-answer session after a speech. McChrystal reportedly said the vice-president's counterterrorism strategy was "short-sighted" and would lead to a state of "Chaos-istan." He left the army and became a consultant and leadership instructor.

The record since Eisenhower raises serious questions about whether the kind of success that results in the highest leadership positions in the military can be a path for executive leadership in other public service. The nature of politics has fundamentally changed since the days when the soft-spoken, plain, and blunt Dwight Eisenhower could be elected president. A rise to the top of the political establishment seems to require a public persona precisely (and likely disingenuously) calibrated for the right combination of voter group appeals. Genuine field leaders may have distaste for the rabid media search for perceived personal flaws and suggestions of indiscretions. Also, a military leader is unlikely to have banked sufficient loyalties among campaign financiers. They are more likely to have achieved success with a frank and mission-centric approach and intolerance for distractions, traits that do not prepare someone well for the skills needed for fund raising and delivering only carefully formulated sound bites. While the country will survive if no other general becomes president as long other qualified leaders are elected, the disconnection between military leadership experience and other public service runs deep and is troubling. As the next section explains, the military is a fertile source of leaders who are prepared for service in the public interest.

Today's Military Leadership Experience

While high-level military commanders have for some time been largely absent from national civil leadership, the military remains the nation's largest and most intensive leadership training ground. Most service members spend several years learning how to lead and applying what they are taught in the field, and then leave the service looking to apply their learning and experience in their communities. The colleagues they join in other public service increasingly have little direct knowledge about this learning and experience. They can have false assumptions about the military, including about the diversity of the military experience and how leadership is taught and applied. A fuller understanding of the nature of this experience can lead to a less shortsighted view of military leadership and its application to other public service.

One main reason for a shortsighted view is that the percentage of Americans who actually serve in the military has been diminishing over time. Today there are about 1.4 million active duty members, and about another 840,000 serve in the reserves and National Guard. The Army is the largest branch with about 490,000; the Navy has about 326,000, the Air Force 311,000, and the Marines 132,000. The Coast Guard, which is part of the Department of Homeland Security but has training and experience similar to the military, has about 40,000. The raw numbers are large but they equate to less than one-half of one percent of the population. During World War II it was close to ten percent.

One likely misconception that results from lack of exposure to the military is having a simplified and stereotyped idea of the military leadership experience. But being in the military can be vastly different, including by branch culture, occupational specialty, and individual proclivity. There are military occupational specialties in all of the branches in which their practitioners could have similar leadership experiences. For example, each branch has officers who specialize as pilots, logisticians, personnel administrators, communications managers, and intelligence analysts. Units from each branch sometimes operate with a unified command. For example, the Army, Navy, Marines, and Air Force have units in the U.S. Special Operations Command, which have various reconnaissance, unconventional warfare, counterterrorism, rescue, and foreign military training functions. They include such renowned units as the Army Green Berets, Delta Force, and Rangers; the Navy SEALS and Underwater Demolition Teams; the Marine Raiders; and the Air Force Pararescue.

Despite many cross-branch similarities each of the branches organizationally has a different emphasis. Their initial leadership education is based on a model that reflects their core functions.

As the largest branch the Army must prepare for a major land war. It also has diverse specialties, many of which require mastery of technical skills as well as preparation for command of deployable combat units. The paradigm of an initial Army leadership assignment is as a platoon leader with command of an operational unit of 20 to 50 enlisted personnel in an infantry, artillery, or tank unit. In each case new officers are responsible for their unit members' welfare, discipline, training, and materiel, and they must be prepared to lead in combat. A junior officer will have a senior enlisted member who gives advice and works more directly with the enlisted personnel. Officers progress from these commands to being in charge of units of increasing size. At the culmination of a career an officer could be responsible for a complex organization with thousands of men and women.

Naval officers have a wide range of responsibilities for service on ships, submarines, and shore facilities, as well as with Navy air wings. Many of the specialties require advanced technical education and training, such as in nuclear power, naval engineering, meteorology and oceanography, and medicine. Navy leadership culture emphasizes the heavy responsibilities and strong traditions of command at sea. It often involves being in charge of communities and facilities similar to local governments. This can be one of 273 ships, including 10 aircraft carriers, 90 surface combatants, and 72 submarines, and air wings operating about 3,700 aircraft. A single ship can cost several billion dollars and have thousands in its crew and leading-edge power plants and weapon systems. Officers typically begin with command of a division, with responsibilities for a segment of equipment and operations and command of 12 to 50 enlisted personnel. As with the other branches the commands increase over time in size and complexity.

As part of the Department of the Navy, the Marine Corps shares much of the Navy's heritage and culture, including an emphasis on decentralized execution and independence of command. The Marines are organized into three divisions and three air wings, but the focus is on being able to deploy an integrated air-ground-logistics task force of any size under a single commander. Despite a wide range of occupational specialties, all Marines, including pilots, are initially trained to be infantry platoon commanders. This orientation emphasizes the Marines' traditional warrior culture and its focus on the primary consideration of enabling a rifleman to prevail in combat in any situation.

The Air Force emphasizes a culture of technical superiority consistent with its mission of being ready for warfare in air, space, and cyberspace. It depends on technical skills that can take many years to develop. It is organized into major commands that have functional responsibilities, such as global strike forces, cyber operations, space, and operational fighter, bomber, transport, refueling, training, and special operations air wings. Air Force officers' first assignments are likely to involve extensive skills or technical training, such as learning to fly. In their first field assignments they likely work in small units as part of a crew. With additional experience they will have command responsibilities for a crew and then larger units.

As part of Homeland Security the Coast Guard's focus is on seagoing domestic safety and security. In times of war, or upon the president's orders, it operates as part of the Department of the Navy and can be deployed to overseas combat zones. It is organized into area commands and districts. The Coast Guard operates cutters and other vessels and air-craft for search and rescue, port and coastal security, drug and illegal immigration interdiction, navigational aids, marine safety, environmental protection, and ice operation. Its culture emphasizes service to the public and working in small teams, and a willingness to take risks in extremely dangerous situations.

Almost half of the country's military force is in the reserve and National Guard. Most of those who serve in the reserve and National Guard units also work in civilian employment to which they can bring leadership experience as well as their ongoing learning in the service. Each of the branches has a reserve that is basically trained and includes mem-bers who have had extensive regular service experience. The actively drilling components of the reserve participate in weekend duty and annual two-week training exercises, in which they have ongoing leadership responsibilities. Many of these units are called into active duty and deployed, especially since operations began in Afghanistan and Iraq. There are about 300,000 drilling reservists in the combined forces of the Army, Navy, Marine Corps, Air Force, and Coast Guard. There are about another 230,000 in the individual ready reserve, who have previously served but are not part of a drilling unit but may be recalled to service. In addition, each state, the District of Columbia, and three territories have units of the Army National Guard and Air National Guard, a total of about 462,000, who respond to emergencies under command of governors but also can be called into federal service.

This summary of the structure, culture, and emphasis of the various branches shows that the variety of military training and experience is wide ranging. But there are commonalities important to understanding the value of this experience to the larger community.

Everyone who successfully serves a tour in the military will gain some leadership training and experience regardless of branch or specialty.[36]

Four out of five members of the military enlist without expecting command responsibilities. They begin their service at the most junior ranks—private (Army and Marine Corps), seaman recruit (Navy and Coast Guard), or airman basic (Air Force)—in an immersive training environment with instructors who teach discipline and responsibility and who model effective leadership. Soon even the most junior members will be assigned leadership roles within their units in which they must coordinate the activities of their peers. Within a few years enlisted members who perform well will be promoted to non-commissioned ranks and given small team leadership responsibilities. They will be expected to set an example of discipline and performance, teach basic skills, and give instructions in the field. With success the size of their units will increase, and those who remain in the service past their initial enlistments will be sergeants or petty officers with assignments as squad or division leaders. About 30 percent of the enlisted force achieves this level of responsibility. With added experience they will report directly to officers in charge of the units and give advice about discipline, training, and unit performance. Those who achieve the highest levels of the enlisted ranks, about three percent of the enlisted force, have leadership responsibilities within large commands and serve in administrative roles. They also mentor non-commissioned officers in training and combat environments.

Most who enlist in the military have at least a high school education. Some have a college degree when they join or earn at least some college credits during service. Those who achieve higher ranks are likely to leave service with extensive experience in supervising and inspiring individuals under challenging circumstances. They may also have developed advanced technical skills with such diverse things as operating or maintaining vessels, aircraft, heavy equipment, communications networks, or information technology, or they may become expert at such things as computer systems, foreign languages, law enforcement, or supply chain management. Non-commissioned officers have risen through the ranks with increased responsibility and likely have attended leadership training. Unlike officers they are not saluted or called "sir" or "ma'am," but they are alongside the junior enlisted members and tend to be highly respected. They likely leave the military with knowledge and experience equivalent to senior supervisors with the same functions in public service or business.

Those who become junior officers—second lieutenant (Army, Marine Corps, and Air Force) or ensign (Navy and Coast Guard)—receive well-developed leadership instruction and are evaluated for their leadership abilities in testing and observation, including in their performance as peer leaders within their training units. Career advancement passes through three distinct leadership phases. The first involves direct leadership, in which the officer is responsible for the training and performance of a group, such as an infantry platoon, ship's division, or aircraft crew. There are about 130,000 company grade officers (lieutenants and captains in the Army, Marines, and Air Force, and ensigns and lieutenants in the Navy and Coast Guard) who have direct unit commands, most of whom will not make the military a career. A new officer also will learn from advice coming from others with whom they serve in the field, in most units including from an experienced non-commissioned officer. They also are mentored by their own commanders, and typically serve in a unit with peers who may have slightly more experience.

Regardless of branch or assignment, early officer experience provides intense leadership education and experience in influencing others. A study by Korn/Ferry International, a leading executive placement firm, found that "the first 10 years in the military are really helpful in corporate life."[37] One reason: because officers in junior ranks "are in the front line with their charges and are exposed to the same dangers, they see firsthand how their actions directly affect their troops."[38]

Those who remain in service beyond the junior ranks become field grade officers (majors and colonels in the Army, Marines, and Air Force, and commanders and captains in the Navy and Coast Guard). There are about 90,000 field grade officers, many of whom are in charge of large organizations. They may have a command with several subordinate units that have their own commanders. Many of them serve for 20 years or more and then have a second career in such fields as defense industry consultants or in other business, and some work for the government, particularly in federal agencies. Most successful career officers leave the military at this level.

There are about 1,000 flag officers (generals in the Army, Marines, and Air Force, and admirals in the Navy and Coast Guard) in all the branches combined, about 37 at the highest grade with four stars. Promotion to general or admiral is advancement to strategic and planning responsibilities, often involving work with other branches and civilian leadership and agencies. Their promotions are most likely the result of battlefield success together with a reputation as an effective staff officer and the ability to work with external organizations. They progress through many leadership roles and may have responsibilities very similar to an executive in public service.

Veterans in Other Public Service

From the steady flow of trained and experienced leaders leaving military service, few enter into policy making positions in other public service, including in government.

In Congress there has been a trend of steady decline in members who served in the military. There are now 101 members who have this experience. Some served in the Korean War, the Vietnam War, the Persian Gulf War, Afghanistan, Iraq, and Kosovo, others during times of peace. Many of them were in the reserves or National Guard and several still are. By contrast, during the Vietnam War about three-quarters of the Congress had military experience.[39] Veteran representation is very disproportionately Republican.[40] This is troubling regardless of its cause. There should be no partisan affiliation between military service and national political leadership. Though parties may differ in their platforms about relative sizes of the military or its deployment, this difference should not be reflected in a disposition to serve in either military or civil leadership roles. George Washington, whose parting advice included a warning against splitting into factions, would shudder at the thought.

The other federal branches of government similarly have few military veterans. As of 2016 this includes only two members of the president's cabinet—Secretary of State John Kerry and Secretary of Veterans Affairs Robert McDonald. Most high-level officials followed a career path through elite law schools and political offices. Though many judges are military veterans, the U.S. Supreme Court, which ultimately interprets the Constitution and decides cases determining the extent of governmental powers and the nature of individual liberties, has scant military representation. A few justices had peacetime military experience—Justices Breyer and Alito were in the Army Reserve and Justice Kennedy was in the National Guard. No member of today's Court has had any wartime military experience. The last justice with such a background was John Paul Stevens, and he retired from the bench in 2010.

Veterans can be found in state governments but not at the highest levels. Most governors, who have legal authority to mobilize National Guard units, have no military experience. Seven of the 50 governors served, three of them in the reserves or National Guard. Only one governor—Terry Branstad of Iowa—served overseas during a foreign war.[41]

This sparse veteran representation in public policy-making positions looks even more bare when it is compared to the military and veteran populations overall. Of the 1.4 military personnel on active duty and

840,000 in the reserves and National Guard, about 366,000 are officers who are being trained and are gaining extensive experience in leadership under challenging conditions. There are more than 22 million veterans in the country, and hundreds of thousands of them held commands of men and women, ships, aircraft, distribution networks, technological systems, and installations with the infrastructures of large cities.[42]

Veterans are rarely found in public policy making positions but they are a major part of the rank-and-file of a functioning government. According to the U.S. Census Bureau, about 14 percent of those employed in public service are veterans, and "a veteran is more than twice as likely as a non-veteran to hold a job in a public administration industry."[43] Veterans are especially well represented within one segment of public service: federal agencies. More than 600,000 veterans are employed in the executive branch, about 30 percent of total employees.[44] They comprise a large segment of civilian employees in the Department of Defense and other defense activities, Veterans Affairs, Homeland Security, and Transportation, and many are employed in the Interior and Justice Departments and the General Services Administration.[45] Agency employers seem to particularly value military experience in the defense-related activities as well as in transportation, warehousing, and utilities, all of which are vital for manufacturing and commerce. Disproportionately few veterans work in education, healthcare, and social assistance.[46] Veterans get some benefit from the Vietnam Era Veterans' Assistance Act,[47] which requires covered federal government contractors and subcontractors to take affirmative action to employ veterans and enable their advancement, to list openings with an employment service, and to report veterans' voluntarily disclosure of their covered status.

University faculty also influence national public policy and how citizens view it, and today military veterans are largely absent from this environment as well. Universities with public service and policy programs rarely consider military leadership and experience as relevant to their teaching. College faculty predominantly describe themselves as "liberal"; more describe themselves as "far left" than as "conservatives."[48] This orientation and affiliation tend to be critical of recent American use of military force, disfavor military deployments, and favor cuts in troop levels and military spending. What students are likely to learn in the humanities and social studies is an emphasis on the horrors of war, its negative effect on combatants and their families, the failures of military adventurism, and the dangers of a powerful military-industrial complex. Students will read anti-war books and hear with admiration about anti-war protestors and movements. Increasingly historic military leaders and campaigns get at most brief mention and then the focus is on the negative. Most students will have teachers who are openly contemptuous of anything related to the military. Of course these are valuable perspectives to consider for any-one learning critical thinking; but the near uniformity of hearing this per-spective is a contributing factor to the widening gap between military service and public administration.

Even in academic environments that are explicitly non-partisan, stu-dents are not likely to be told there is much value in studying today's military. In the largest university-based local government training organ-ization in the country, at which the author is a member of the faculty, no one among the nine full-time faculty members who teach primarily in the public leadership program has had any military experience, nor do they involve the military or veterans in their teaching. At a faculty meeting one professor confidently told the author that there was nothing to learn from military leadership and students who are veterans have no knowledge or experience relevant to their need to learn about how to lead in public administration. The university of which the school is a part, which has 30,000 students, 3,700 faculty, and 8,300 staff, has only 15 faculty and staff who identify themselves as veterans on a list available to students after a campus-wide solicitation. This absence of veterans is typical within the academic community.

The increasing absence of the military from the places that influence and teach public policy has not gone entirely unnoticed. One astute observer is Mark Shields, a national political commentator who has worked on Democratic campaigns, and who served as an enlisted Marine. At a gathering of the powerful in Washington, while criticizing the national lack of attention to military developments that could lead the nation to war, he said: "This noisy, contentious city turned mute because almost without exception no Washington dinner party guest—liberal or conservative, Democrat or Republican—personally knows a single one of the 1.8 million enlisted Americans serving in our armed forces."[49] Shields also spoke about the typically shallow expressions of gratitude for military service. He said, "It is not enough just to 'support the troops,' especially when you would never consider having your own daughter socialize with those 'troops' you so vocally support."[50]

Authors Kathy Roth-Douquet and Frank Schaeffer illuminate the troubling nature of the growing gap between the military and other public service in their book *AWOL: The Unexcused Absence of America's Upper Classes from Military Service—and How It Hurts Our Country.*[51] Roth-

Douquet is an attorney who served in the Clinton White House and Department of Defense and knows the culture of the Capitol Hill elite. Her husband is a Marine officer who deployed twice to Iraq. Schaeffer is an author whose son chose to enlist in the Marines after graduating from an elite prep school. Their conclusion based on research and personal experience: "Members of the military are strangers to the upper classes. And it seems privileged folks want to keep it that way. They have consciously or unconsciously done all they can to avoid having anyone close to them become a member of the military."[52] The authors point out that as policy makers are more separated from the military, they are less likely to have a positive view of service and those who serve. As they note, "Analysis of why people choose to join the military shows that the single biggest factor is whether someone has a direct personal experience with someone they admire who is in or was in the service."[53] Those who have no such experience tend to adopt negative stereotypical views about those who choose to join.

Roth-Douquet and Schaeffer point to telling statistics about the relationship of the elite Ivy League schools and the military, beyond the obvious fact that faculty and students at elite universities loudly rally against any military presence in officer training programs or recruiting, which effectively prevents students who might be interested in the military from learning about opportunities. They note that "in 1956, 400 out of 750 in Princeton's graduating class went into the military. In contrast, in 2004, 9 members of Princeton's graduating class entered the services, and they *led* the Ivy League in numbers!"[54] Yet, as they point out, "paradoxically, the same individuals who may be moved to decry the fact that the military recruits more among less-advantageous groups still do their best to prevent those who are more advantaged from learning about service through on-campus representation," including in vocal opposition to recruiting and reserve officer training programs.[55] Schaeffer quoted an Ivy League–graduate friend whose husband and son both were Ivy League graduates. The friend, who is on the boards of influential environmentalist groups, acknowledged there might be "something valuable about military discipline," but noted she would be "horrified" if *her* son volunteered. With words she apparently thought would be helpful she told Schaeffer he should help his son, who joined the Marines rather than go to the Ivy League straight off, by considering what was missing in his life that led him to the military. She added, "If my son was about to do this, here is what I'd tell him: 'You should aim to work at the cabinet level.' I would say; 'If you want to serve your country, work to develop *real* leadership, to make a *real* difference. Why don't you work on one of those political campaigns?' I'd ask."[56] As Schaeffer characterized this attitude, it adds up to "saying no to military service and feeling morally superior for making that choice."[57]

The widening gap is therefore not merely a matter of demographics. It is also one of widely held attitudes. The vast majority of influential policy makers firmly believe that being in the military is irrelevant to the kind of public service and leadership that they have in mind. This shallow perspective has emerged in a vacuum.

Impressions of the Military

When people have very different backgrounds they are likely to misunderstand each other's perspectives in some significant ways. Veterans leaving their military community after years of service know they will have to learn a new perspective and adjust to civilian employment. But they may reasonably expect that their supervisors and colleagues will value abilities developed in the military, including leadership traits and methods. In this they probably will be disappointed. They are likely to find false stereotypes about what they learned and what they did, and mistaken assumptions that their training and experience are of little use outside the military.

Misunderstanding about the military experience is a natural result for the many who have had no personal involvement in it and little interaction with those who have. This is especially true in public policy making circles in which veterans make up such a small portion of the population. Without first-hand exposure impressions are probably based on what is portrayed in the media. One source is recruiting advertisements, but these are snapshots that give little insight into the real experience. The military aims these portrayals at young people who are potential recruits. The advertisements logically try to appeal to a sense of adventure and challenge. So they stress how *different* life is in the military compared to everyday life. It seems joining the military means going to faraway places and doing dangerous things. Even when stressing opportunities to learn skills transferrable to civilian employment, the message is that these skills are learned in an experience that cannot be replicated in normal life.

The public is unlikely to get a fuller or clearer perspective about military service from other conspicuous sources including the media. Bad news dominates—conflicts and casualties, especially situations gone wrong. Operations are reported with sensational headlines and images. Many successful operations are never known—not just clandestine strikes and raids. Routine operations that most in the military predominantly experience go unreported because they seem of no interest to the public. No one hears about the everyday successes providing security, delivering disaster relief, stabilizing local governments, carrying on diplomatic relations with other countries' armed forces and within their communities, and a myriad of other actions that require nuanced leadership approaches and give valuable experience.

Those who are unfamiliar with the military will likely instead get the impression that military service means traumatic experiences. This can be seen clearly in the most successful films about war, which typically depict military leaders as brutal and psychotic. There is not much box office appeal in a fulfilling military career or undramatic combat experience. Consider the films with the greatest box office success. *Platoon* depicts a massacre of families in a Vietnamese village, rampant drug use, and a good-versus-evil struggle to the death between non-commissioned officers. *Full Metal Jacket* first depicts boot camp as so brutal that it causes a recruit to go on a psychotic rampage and murder the inhumane drill instructor. It then follows cynical Marines as they are consumed in a senseless and chaotic war, including a scene in which a helicopter door gunner guns down fleeing women farmers while laughing. The Vietnam-era film *Apocalypse Now* shows war as a hellish experience in which its participants descend into primitive bestiality. In *The Deer Hunter* soldiers are debased into drug-induced suicidal matches and destructive personal relationships. Both in film and in the highly successful television series, *M*A*S*H* celebrates the cynicism of doctors and their staff who saw no sense in war or Army regulations. *American Sniper* depicts a Navy SEAL as militarily skilled and heroic, but his experiences corrupt his human values and render him unable to return to a normal life. Even in the rare film that develops a character in combat in a positive light, the plot usually will emphasize horrific bloodshed that forever scars the survivor.

Modern film, television, and literature rarely depict those who serve in the military as enriched by it. Writers and producers do not paint a picture of personal growth through leadership, discipline, and a sense of fulfilling a patriotic duty. Such experiences, while common for veterans, have little box office appeal, and their portrayal would not contribute to expressing the kind of anti-war or anti-establishment sentiments for which the entertainment industry typically aims. This highly selective and extremely negative orientation toward military service contrasts sharply with how those who oppose war or military service are depicted—they are usually shown to be courageous, sincere, and endearing characters. The same is true about public portrayals and perceptions of kinds of public service that some choose rather than the military. Service in the Peace Corps, for example, is likely to be viewed within public administration and academics as noble, culturally enlightening, and "a life-defining leadership experience," as the Peace Corps puts it.[58]

For the vast majority of veterans the prevailing public depictions are unfamiliar. Most occupations in the military are not combat related. Many are identical to occupations in the civilian community. Someone is just as likely to train to drive a vehicle, maintain complex machinery, build computer networks, cook, police a community, or fly a plane as to prepare for direct combat. About 40 percent of the today's service members have not been deployed to a combat area and those who have are more likely than not to have finished their tours without being shot at or shooting at someone. Among those who have been in direct combat their experiences vary widely, from horrific to momentary. Their reactions to the dangers and aftermath are as varied as people can be. Some remember combat as thrilling and do not seem adversely affected; some are disabled by trauma; others have vivid and troubling memories but are able to incorporate them into leading normal lives. The myriad of possible experiences and reactions contrasts sharply with the stereotypical images projected to the public eye.

An obvious contributor to perceptions about the military is someone's attitude toward wars that political leaders call upon service members to carry out, particularly for those who oppose it. To attribute war making decisions to individual members of the military is unfair. Service members have their own varied reactions about whether wars they are ordered to fight are justified. The oaths they took to follow the orders of their civilian leaders are not contingent on agreement with the rationale for those orders. Some individuals do object and some refuse and suffer the consequences. But the vast majority of service members do not tie their obedience to agreement with policies. They are justifiably unsettled when they are personally criticized or degraded for their obedience, or made to feel as if their willingness to carry out orders was foolish. There is more than a little irony in blaming a service member for doing something that only the civilian leadership could cause.

Ignorance about the diverse backgrounds and abilities of those who serve in the military also results in mistaken assumptions about the intellect and interests of service members. Those who pride themselves in their higher education achievements may assume veterans comparatively have had a narrow education and are shallow thinkers. Veterans know this is not so. Everyone in the military has at least a high school education or its equivalent, and most have some higher education they either completed before joining or are undertaking as part of continuing education while in service. Academic progress is considered in assignment and promotion. Presumptions of narrow education or limited intellect are wildly inaccurate with respect to officers, who come from a wide variety of colleges and have a wide range of majors and advanced degrees. Many are very knowledgeable about history, political science, and classical and modern literature. Many have science or engineering degrees. Graduates from the Air Force Academy, for example, can receive a highly regarded science and engineering education including in air and space fields, and many Navy officers have advanced degrees in such fields as nuclear engineering. In all branches those officers who have advanced into the higher grades most likely will have attended lengthy leadership programs as well as have completed at least one graduate degree. Most veterans remember having had colleagues who were remarkably intelligent and well-read compared to most others they will encounter after the service.

Many veterans remember that some of the smartest people they ever met never wanted to go to college—surprising to many who did and were never immersed in an organization with those who did not. They also remember serving with others who have an amazing range of talents and interests. In virtually all military units there are individuals who are into motorcycles and others who are into chess, some read literature and others science fiction, some listen to country and others to rap or classical. Someone usually can sing beautifully and someone else can dance like a professional; someone is expert at fine wood work and someone else loves tattoos. Just as the intimacy and stress of living and operational conditions can bring out conflict, they also bring out the best in talent and the most expressive in interests. Someone who has not served may see only the uniform and the uniformity it represents, while those who have served recall learning about many unique and surprising personalities.

Veterans' own views about how the military experience affected them also can vary as much as individuals vary in their personal traits and reactions to diverse experiences. Despite variation there are some traits that veterans commonly take beyond the service, which may also contribute to misunderstandings because they are not so common among civilian counterparts. For example, a veteran is likely to be punctual—even early—both going to work and meeting deadlines. Punctuality and promptness are of course virtues in any organization and can contribute to success. But the degree to which veterans tend to exhibit this behavior can be off-putting to those who are used to a more laissez-faire approach to timeliness and productivity, as is notoriously common in public service. Veterans also tend to work independently. As training and health consultant Alison Lighthall wrote about student veterans, "They are self-sufficient; they will only ask questions when they cannot find the answers themselves."[59] She also observed, "Veterans do not see themselves as victims. Ever. Victims are people who feel no control over their lives and perceive themselves as being at the mercy of others."[60] Others in the organization may joke about traits such as these rather than try to emulate them, attributing them to an inability to adjust to the "way things are done" in civilian life.

These are some of the ways in which assumptions about the military based on available information divorced from real experience can cause a mistakenly narrow view about who serves and what they can do. The gap between perception and reality continues to widen. Assumptions about military experience feed into a mistaken perspective that military leadership is fundamentally different from leadership in other public service.

Different Languages

Our perspectives about each other and about the world are shaped within the framework of the cultures in which we have been raised and in which we live. When our cultural influences are very different we can have very different perspectives. This applies to how we think of leadership—what it means, how to develop it, and how others will react to us when we are in positions of influence. Someone's vocabulary—the words and how they are meant—reveals much about cultural perspective. How certain words and phrases related to leadership are used also illuminates the gap that is widening in public service between those with military experience and those without it. The following dozen words and phrases, which are often used with potency, are a sampling of such contextual differences: patriotism, mission, responsibility, service, honesty, sacrifice, heroic, diversity, comradery, work-life balance, following, and leadership.

Patriotism. Service members are immersed in a patriotic culture. Many of them cite love of country as a reason why they joined. They salute the flag and sometimes wear one on their sleeve. Without any embarrassment they honor patriotic traditions, march in parades, and speak of duty, honor, and country. Military service culture does not abide disrespect for national values of liberty and democracy. After leaving the service most veterans continue to have a patriotic spirit and to be overtly expressive of it. Many display flags at their homes, are members of veterans groups whose mission is to honor the country and its traditions, and participate in patriotic holiday and memorial celebrations.

Overt patriotism may strike others as naïve or unenlightened, especially in subcultures immersed in cynicism about traditional values. Many who campaign for public office get attention by stressing what is wrong with the community or the country. Many in influential public policy positions admire other cultures rather than their own—European, Asian, African, or anything other than what is traditionally American. They do not consider criticism of things American as unpatriotic, but rather as self-reflective and honest. A bumper sticker that can be seen in academic communities aptly expresses this sentiment when it says, "Dissent is the highest form of patriotism."

Mission. The essence of military leadership is focus on accomplishing a mission. Often the mission can clearly be visualized and its accomplishment measured, such as by capturing a key location or rendering a particular enemy force ineffective through destruction or capitulation. It also can be deployment to a particular place or achieving a particular state of readiness. In all cases leaders are expected to keep the mission paramount in their decision making and in the exercise of influence. Leaders strive to define the mission clearly and communicate it throughout the unit. Part of military culture is enthusiastic commitment to the mission regardless of whether you would choose it yourself.

Public service tends to refer to "mission" in an aspirational sense and usually with broad reference to a greater good that is beyond any real measure of progress or accomplishment. For instance, one city government states this as its mission: "The city partners with our community to deliver excellent service, and plans for the future while preserving, protecting, and enhancing the quality of life." Another government organization, a state employment agency, states its mission this way: "To promote economic growth and stability by delivering and coordinating workforce services to include: policy development; job placement services; temporary income support; workforce information; and transition and training services." Generalized and immeasurable statements of this sort, which are subject to infinite personal interpretations, can be a useful reminder about the organization's direction and emphasis. But it is not an objective on which decisions and effort can be focused in the same sense as how the military envisions a mission.

Responsibility. One of the first lessons learned in initial military training is to take responsibility not only for one's own actions but also for the actions of everyone else in the unit. Recruits and officer candidates are taught that a failure by anyone in the unit is a failure for all. In training the military uses group accountability to make this point; typically everyone does punitive exercise or loses a privilege if any member of the unit fails, regardless of individual performance. This teaches the importance of teamwork and paying attention to others who need help or encouragement for improvement, as well as the unacceptability of putting yourself first and blaming others. A military leader does not escape accountability by pointing out that a failure was due to the error of a subordinate in the unit. The leader must take responsibility for not adequately training and supervising, and commit to attend to the corrective action needed to avoid a repeat.

In contexts other than the military "responsibility" usually has a different sense, referring to decision-making authority. Someone who is "responsible" for something is in charge of it and can give direction. When something goes awry the focus is likely to be either on external factors or on faults attributed to particular individuals. Political bodies and many others in government divide into camps and blame each other rather than shine a light on their own shortcomings and work together toward a unified goal. They may feel a sense of personal vindication as long as they can point a finger elsewhere. Such behavior is anathema in the military.

Service. Service in the military means surrendering some personal liberty, doing what you are told, and going where you are told. Some service members join intending to make it a career, others when they find that at the time the military suits them better than any other option. But "joining the service" has always meant leaving a civilian life behind and postponing whatever other opportunities might have been available. Most spend extended periods away from their family, including from a spouse or partner and children. It sometimes means being away when important things happen in the family, such as the birth of a child. It also involves serious personal risk. Those who join know they will do dangerous things and may be sent into combat and wounded or killed.

Many in public affairs also value the commitment to service above self that it represents. But generally the notion of "service" has a more amorphous meaning than in the military. It may be used to describe a career path, rather than a relinquishment of control at personal cost. Common terms used in public affairs reflect this expansive view: someone who is an elected or appointed official may enjoy a relatively high salary, perquisites, and influence, yet describe the work as "public service." Public service career paths also often entail adventure and influence and lead to lucrative opportunities in other fields. Someone elected to federal office is likely already to be, and continue to be, very wealthy.

What may be most striking about the different ways in which the notion of "service" is considered is the way many in policy making positions, and those seeking them, look at military service. Chief Judge Dennis Jacobs of the U.S. Court of Appeals for the Second Circuit wrote that in some parts of academe "military service is not credited as public service for purposes of scholarship funding or preferential admissions—though official statements may say otherwise.... I believe it is easier for a law school applicant to claim the credential of public service for having done voter registration in a cemetery than for a stint in the Navy."[61] This prejudice against military experience is particularly ironic to veterans who spent their time doing the very things that others describe precisely as public service, such as putting themselves at risk in an effort to bring democracy and stability to other parts of the world, or bringing relief and delivering emergency supplies to a disaster area.

Honesty. The importance of honesty is a dominant theme in both military and other public affairs leadership. For decades leadership theory has emphasized that trustworthiness is not only a desirable personal trait but also something that inspires others to work together for a common goal. In the realm of military leadership training the notion of honesty takes on another feature that is not as often discussed or explicitly practiced in public affairs more generally. This is the notion of being honest with others about shortcomings.

Those who have had leadership experience in both military and other public service should notice a stark difference in frankness in response to difficult questions. The military teaches that subordinate leaders at all levels are expected to communicate disagreement to their commanders about the desirability of direction they are given, in an appropriate way and at the appropriate time. In expressing disagreement or feedback they are expected to be tactful and whenever possible be supportive and inspiring. Leaders are also taught that after a decision is made with which they disagreed they still must enthusiastically carry out their orders. The same honesty principle applies in the development of subordinates. Military leaders are expected to be swift and frank in noting failures among subordinates and to give specific direction about how performance can be improved, both for the good of the unit and for the individual's personal development.

Military leadership training does not encourage argumentative attitudes or hurtful criticism. Of course not all leaders adhere to these principles and some are defensive or vindictive against those who express disagreement. But leadership training explicitly focuses on combatting this tendency. Military organizations even build in mechanisms with this in mind, such as having within the unit an enlisted member at the highest rank—a sergeant major, master chief, chief master sergeant or similar position—whose function it is to solicit frank complaints from the ranks and share them with the commander without attribution.

Public affairs leadership theory also applauds open discussions about organizational issues and transparency in decision making. Committee and organizational meetings commonly involve invitations for expressions of disagreement and complaints, but these tend to be opportunities to "vent" so as to give the appearance of consensus. "Positivity" is emphasized. For instance, some consultants advise group members never to say "yes, but," instead always to say "yes, and"—"because," they advise, "when you apply 'Yes, and' to life, people feel heard, valued and supported. It creates collaboration in times of conflict and engagement in times of trouble."[62] Another approach, called "appreciative inquiry," urges "unconditionally positive questions that strengthen and eschews criticism, qualification, and negation."[63] These tactics may be well intended and cause many participants to feel more comfortable in meetings, but creating the pretense of agreement can obscure the realities of the decision making process. Making agreement and support preeminent also can suppress the kind of frank discussion that the military stresses as an essential part of a focus on mission accomplishment, and leave those who have concerns fearing that they will be cornered and dissociated unless they aim to be perceived as always a cheerful team player.

Sacrifice. Sacrifice involves forfeiture—giving up something valued for something beyond the self. In a religious ritual a life or possession may be relinquished as a gesture of piety. Members of a community sacrifice for a cause by donating effort or valuables. A necessary aspect of sacrifice is that there is no expectation of an equivalent exchange. Those who join the military enter a culture in which sacrifice is a cultural imperative. Personal pursuits are postponed or foregone; training includes anticipating the possibility that death may occur in accomplishing the mission. Deployments usually involve extended absences from families. Those who are in for a career will repeatedly leave for extended periods, and their families are left with their absences and needing to pick up full caretaking responsibilities. Service members actively consider that they may have to give all for their unit and country. As James Toner, a professor of international relations and military at ethics at the Air War College wrote, "The essential character of the military ethic is based upon the conviction that there is something worth living for and perhaps dying for that is more important than one's own skin."[64] Those without military experience may be shocked when they hear someone in the service unflinchingly say that "family comes second, after service." It is a well-understood cost for those who wear the uniform. Many who leave the service do so because they do not want to continue to carry this burden, or do not want their families to bear it, beyond their initial tour of duty.

Some in public service share the same notion of sacrifice as in the military. Police and correctional officers, emergency responders, child welfare professionals, and many others who do difficult work take risks that likely are inspired by ideals beyond personal interest. There can be a different notion, however, among many who influence public policy. Today, when those who are in public affairs speak of sacrifice, they may be referring to a career path with pay that is less lucrative than might be available elsewhere. Public organizations typically have long-timers who have settled into comfortable careers with an eye toward a pension and an attitude that they are not paid enough to be expected to do more than is already comfortable to them. While the choice of a public service career may have real monetary disadvantages, the trade-off is of a different order than how the military views the sacrifices that they are prepared to make willingly.

Heroic. "Heroic" when used in the military usually describes acts of bravery at grave personal risk. When the word is used in commendations it signifies acts that go beyond what can fairly be expected of a normal person. For example, former senator and presidential candidate Bob Dole received the Bronze Star for heroism in Northern Italy during World War II, when, despite being severely wounded, he attempted to rescue a radioman under enemy fire. Senator and presidential candidate John McCain received the Distinguished Flying Cross for heroism when he continued a bombing pass over North Vietnam after his aircraft was severely damaged. In Italy during World War II former senator Daniel Inouye directed his platoon through a hail of fire up a treacherous slope and neutralized two machine gun nests. Despite being severely wounded he continued to direct his platoon until enemy resistance was broken. He received the Congressional Medal of Honor for heroism. The military pays tribute to individuals such as these who acted in extraordinarily selfless ways.

In public service "heroic" is often used to describe someone who has persevered, such as from a tragic loss or from something systemic. The term may be used to honor or hold someone out as an example for others to emulate, such as for being a good teacher or a caring parent. The term "hero" also is used to refer to outstanding sports figures. Those who inspire others through determination, effort, and achievement are worthy of recognition and emulation, and they may very well have done things that are heroic. But to use the term "heroic" whenever something is laudable is to use it in a sense different than how it is meant in military culture.

Diversity. Today diversity and multi-culturalism are dominant themes in public service. The military population is more integrated than the general population in many ways. About one-third of the enlisted members are non-white; more than 18 percent are African American. About one-quarter of the officer corps is non-white; 17 percent are African American.[65] As a study of diversity in the military population concluded, African Americans are drawn to the military "as a more color-blind employer than they are likely to find in the civilian labor market."[66] The fastest-growing ethnicity in the military is Hispanic, surpassing ten percent,[67] an ethnicity that is grossly underrepresented in many public spheres. An aspect of diversity with which the military continues to struggle is opportunity for women and constraints on their advancement, which are due to a combination of factors including views about appropriate combat roles, experience, and personal prejudices. Still a growing percentage of the armed forces are women—they make up between 14 and 20 percent in the branches other than the combat-leveraged Marine Corps, of which women comprise six percent.[68]

The military is more tolerant of open religious expression than other public spheres. Institutionally it has always provided religious support to service members, who face severe spiritual and moral challenges. Military chaplains include ministers from a hundred faith groups including Jewish and Muslim. They provide religious ministry and support in their own faiths, facilitate the religious requirements from all faiths, care for service members and their families including those subscribing to no specific faith, and give advice to their commands in ensuring the free exercise of religion. Most in the military are Christian but in a smaller percentage than in society, in part reflecting the diminished religious orientation of younger generations that comprise the military. Service members are used to their commands making opportunities available for religious observance and study, and references to God, prayer, and worship are common without objection. Veterans find a stark contrast in other public employment, where many in charge find any references to religious practices—especially the most common, Christian faith—to be inappropriate and offensive in the abstract. Concerns about violations of the First Amendment Establishment Clause have greatly diminished the presence of expressions of faith in public spheres, even though 70 percent of Americans describe themselves as Christians and many practice other faiths.

As a result of its composition and its culture, the American military experience therefore is different than most other environments in the way in which its members are immersed in a population comprised of individuals of different races, ethnicities, and religions, and from various geographic and economic backgrounds. Unlike many communities that strive to be diverse such as on college campuses, those who join the military are not able to self-segregate. The nature of military service compels recognizing authority and cooperating with each other regardless of race or other innate characteristics. Military leaders tend to ignore the kinds of innate individual characteristics that cause separation and have plagued American society. They can see that such differences should have no bearing on someone's abilities or trustworthiness. Everyone wears the same uniform. They share the same challenges in training, living conditions, and dangers. Many will serve side-by-side with others who come from unfamiliar backgrounds and regions, in a way that those who do not serve are unlikely ever to experience. Most people who have served recall being very close to someone from a very different culture. The military has its share of interpersonal conflict resulting from prejudices and other human failings. It continues to have challenges in ensuring equal opportunity and representation, especially in the officer corps. But most service members experience an environment that does not distinguish in opportunity based on race, ethnicity, or religion.

Public service does not share the military's approach to diversity and inclusiveness. Rather than leveling differences in innate characteristics and background there tends to be an emphasis on them as a way to overcome under-representation or to promote multiculturalism. Being the member of a particular race, ethnicity, or sexual orientation can be a factor in selection and promotion, and deemed a qualification to be representative of a group having similar characteristics. Members who do not have the characteristics associated with a targeted status are urged to think about the experiences of others, so they can be more culturally informed and sensitive. Regardless of the long-term social implications of these approaches, the extent to which the conversation in today's public organizations centers on differences tends to highlight rather than level them, which can overshadow a focus on the traits that are truly related to mission accomplishment.

Camaraderie. Supervisors should recognize the value of coworkers getting along. Studies show, and common sense confirms, that workers in an organization are more productive when they like and trust each other. Organizations typically encourage and reward collegiality and provide opportunities to interact informally in break rooms, at celebrations and holiday parties, and in organized social and cultural activities. Mutual respect and collegiality also lead to better retention, which can save the costs and disruption of searching for and hiring new employees.

During service members of the military experience a unique kind of camaraderie. They tend to describe relationships with their fellows effusively with such terms as a "family," "brotherhood," or "band of brothers." For Marines the sentiment is embodied in the notion of *semper fi* that conveys a sense of a lifelong dedication to the Corps and all who have served in it. They do not refer to themselves as an "ex-Marine" because "once a Marine, always a Marine." In all branches bonds formed in training, in duty assignments, and in combat often are unforgettable and unrepeatable. Those who have served bravely in combat often say that what motivated them was their love for the others in their unit and feeling it unthinkable to let them down. Combat veterans who complete their deployments or are evacuated because of injury often express a feeling of being compelled to return to their units regardless of risk. Legends tell of severely wounded warriors who left a hospital against instructions to return to their fellows on the line. Those who are uninjured often express a sense of guilt for being lucky while their fellows were wounded or killed.

Journalist Sebastian Junger, who has been embedded with combat units including at the hotly contested Restrepo outpost in northeastern Afghanistan, explained why a combat veteran who has returned to civilian life might have preferred being with his colleagues in war. Junger said, "I think what he missed is brotherhood.... Brotherhood is different from friendship.... You will put the safety of everyone in your group above your own. In effect you're saying, 'I love these other people more than I love myself.' ... Think about how good that would feel.... And then they come back home and they are just back in society like the rest of us are. Not knowing who they can count on. Not knowing who loves them, who they can love. Not knowing exactly what anyone they know would do for them if it came down to it. *That* is terrifying."[69] Veterans rarely find this same sense of fellowship in other lines of work.

Work-Life Balance. The military trains for missions the success of which may depend on effort that is at the limits of human courage and endurance. From the beginning service members are pushed so they prove to themselves that they can perform physically and mentally under stress far beyond their previous comfort levels. Even with everyday tasks such as maintaining their quarters and personal effects, trainees learn to strive for perfection. Some programs intentionally put trainees in chaotic and exhausting conditions to screen for those who are able to perform at their limits, in a simulation of the strains of combat. Career assignments entail increasingly heavy responsibilities that often involve heavy collateral duties. Even when in garrison workdays can be 12 hours or longer. There is no apology for these expectations; everyone knows they must do whatever is in the "needs of the service" regardless of burden or inconvenience.

Most other public service environments are not preparing for anything like combat and their members do not sign on for high stress in training and work assignments of the sort involved in the military. Work hours and workloads must conform to employment laws and workplace customs. Increasingly expectations also involve alternatives such as part-time schedules, extended leaves, and the ability to work from home. Employers may seek competitive advantages by portraying their work place as "family-first" or as enabling employees to determine the "work-life balance" that is most comfortable to them. This culture can result in boundaries for what is considered "busy" or "at capacity" that would be unrecognizable in the military. A veteran is likely to be surprised by this culture, needing to recalibrate effort to avoid creating hard feelings from co-workers about being annoyingly "hard charging" and frustration from not being recognized for effort that is disproportionate to others.' But many veterans also succeed due to their comparative hardworking ethic combined with being accustomed to completing assignments ahead of time in a manner that exceeds expectations.

Following. Obedience is part of military culture, both as a legal obligation according to the Uniform Code of Military Justice, and as a reflexive practice deemed essential to survival in combat. Combat may require following orders instantly even when their logic is unclear at the moment, and service members know that they may be required to do things that will go against their natural instincts. Basic training aims to instill a habit of not just following orders but doing so enthusiastically. Failure to follow enthusiastically results in disfavor or demotion; the most senior officers can see an end to their careers for being critical of decisions that affect them. But contrary to common misconceptions, following in the military also requires exercising independent thought, and when appropriate, expressing concerns about decisions or a state of affairs. It also involves understanding that when a decision has been made you must do everything you can to implement it and influence others to act in the same way.

The word "obedience" is not heard within civil public service except derisively. The word "following" is most likely to be used in a very different sense than in the military. It tends to mean being a supportive member of a team. As strange as it sounds the notion of following can be turned on its head to mean holding *leaders* accountable. As one popular public service leadership textbook puts it, "followership" theory "tends to emphasize the importance of followers in critically and fairly evaluating formal leadership performance. Followers not only can change leaders who are elected, but also can topple leaders by lack of support, open resistance, and even sabotage."[70] Veterans tend to be surprised by how public service organizations empower individuals to feel they may withhold their consent to direction given, and how much depends on voluntary cooperation and consensual "buy-in" rather than faithful adherence to a chain of command.

Leadership. Service members are immersed in a culture in which leadership is always on everyone's mind. All are expected to have and improve traits and abilities that enable them to be effective influencing others, and to pass what they develop in themselves on to others so that they too can become effective leaders. There is constant observation, mentoring, and evaluation. Performance and fitness is measured not only based on individual achievements but also the performance of units. This notion of leadership is both aspirational and real; it is aspirational because there is always a model of effective leadership toward which everyone is expected to strive; it is real because feedback is relentless and specific.

Of course leadership also gets attention in other public service especially among those who have significant organizational responsibilities or are in the position of influencing public policy. Some share much the same kind of responsibility as military leaders for accomplishing a mission. But there is no unified or persistent notion of what it means to be a good leader within public service generally, and there rarely is any systemic leadership development, mentoring, or evaluation in an organization. The word "leadership" may be used to describe something that makes no sense from a military perspective. A committee that completes its charge may be thanked for its "leadership" for doing what it was asked. An effective local government finance officer may be commended for "leadership" in working through a challenging budget. In some public service scholarship, and within some public service organizations, catch phrases include such oxymoronic things as "everyone is a leader" or "lead from behind." While apparently intending to encourage achievement it also can be sophistry that equates group participation with leadership. Such linguistic devolution blurs the reality that real leadership involves carrying the heavy burdens of being entrusted with responsibility for others' performance and welfare. To do this well requires much effort, self-discipline, and sometimes making decisions that will not be applauded.

Unfamiliarity Can Breed Contempt

Of course a military career is not a prerequisite to being an effective public service leader. But public service in the broad sense suffers if a class of very experienced leaders who might take leadership roles instead follows a well-worn path to monetarily lucrative consultancies with private companies, as seems to have become the logical choice. History also suggests that military officers may be effectively excluded from conspicuous posts based on standards that do not seem to be applied to others. Political candidates, elected officials, and even presidents have gained and held offices despite the same kinds of mistakes that have abruptly ended a military career and further service. This is an unfortunate outcome if the nation's most intense and comprehensive leadership preparation is no longer a viable path to the highest offices. But the disconnection between the military and other public service is much deeper than just concern about who fills the highest offices. Why does it matter so much?

This book argues that leadership as taught in the military is based on immutable and experientially proven principles that apply equally to all public service. In other words, everyone can learn from the military experience and apply it to be a more effective leader. But most people in a position of influence in public service today know very little about this experience except for false or simplistic stereotypes and assumptions, and as a natural result they see it as relevant only to an authoritarian and hierarchical organization. The next chapter explores how these stereotypes and assumptions underlie public service leadership scholarship, which instead offers kaleidoscopic alternative perspectives moving as far away in approach from the military as possible.

Of course seeing military leadership as irrelevant to other public service promotes an attitude of discounting veterans' leadership experience and ability. Associates and fellows at influential consulting firms, Capitol Hill interns, political campaign organizers, non-profit staffers, and new lawyers from top law schools joining major law firms are most likely to see those who chose the military as having little chance for success in the world of power politics and influence. Not surprisingly the public service academic programs that teach the politically inclined aim their lessons at those who would never consider wearing uniforms or taking orders. Faculties rarely include veterans, and their instruction does not include anything having to do with the military, except perhaps critical analysis of the use of force in international affairs.

The disconnection between public policy makers and the military necessarily also has an impact on citizens' perception of their leaders' ability to make decisions about security and the military's deployment, which are of vital national importance and involve risk to the lives of the many who volunteer for service. These decisions profoundly affect many other aspects of national life including individual liberties, the federal budget, and the economy. Those who make these decisions should be in the best position possible to understand the military, those who serve in it, and those who are affected by their service.

No policy decision is more important than sending the military to war. Even if not a matter of national survival, wars profoundly affect lives and communities. Sound public policy requires that civil leaders only commit military forces when it makes sense to those who serve and to others affected by it. The Vietnam War experience showed how questionable motives can tear apart a society and cause national turmoil. The same is true about decisions not to deploy the military; this should not be a matter of shying away from a dip in the popularity polls when there is unreasonable longer-term risk from withholding action. Decisions made in the years leading up to World War II showed how timidity can have grave consequences. The public's view of a leader's decisions will be affected by what the public perceives to be the motivation behind them.

Of course military service is not a prerequisite to the public's acceptance of a civil leader's legitimacy. The president as commander in chief has a secretary of defense and the Joint Chiefs of Staff to give advice about military preparation, capabilities, and deployment. Presidents without military backgrounds have been highly effective leading during war. Lincoln, who was commander in chief during the nation's most destructive war, joked about his brief military experience in the Illinois militia, and Woodrow Wilson and Franklin Roosevelt were not in the military but were highly effective commanders during the world wars. The more open question is whether the nation is best served when the path to civil leadership seems entirely separated from military service. Lincoln, Wilson, and Roosevelt took office in a society in which civil and military leaders were familiar with each other and all part of a public service community. Each of these presidents had personal connections to the military. To mention a few, Lincoln's eldest son Robert Todd joined the Union Army during the war; Woodrow Wilson's eldest daughter Margaret volunteered to perform at Army camps during World War I; and Roosevelt's eldest son James won the Navy Cross as a Marine officer in World War II. Parents' deep concern for the welfare of a military in which their children serve in wartime cannot be seriously questioned.

Ironically a national leader's war-making legitimacy, regardless of military experience or connection, is least likely to be openly questioned by those who must take the risk: the military. History proves that the critical component of sustained civilian control of the military is *the military's* commitment to this principle, and fundamentally the American military has never raised serious doubt about its commitment. They have continually put themselves at risk in far off places even when no one back home seems to care. Community support for military action can rest on a conditional ground, particularly if there seems to be disagreement between the president's decisions and the recommendations of senior military officers. There is serious reason for concern when there is public cynicism about the leadership's military deployment decisions. As sociologist Charles Moskos said, "Citizens accept hardships only when their leadership is viewed as self-sacrificing."[71] This can be questionable when leaders are elites who do not put themselves or their families at risk in the actions they undertake.[72]

The public also should be concerned about the perspectives of those who make national policy for veterans programs. Basic justice and fairness require that those who have been willing to put their lives at risk be cared for when they return, especially those who have been disabled and their affected families. This responsibility has not been hedged in rhetoric but the record of fulfillment is disappointing and inexcusable. Uproar over revelations highlighting failures in federal veterans' affairs, particularly in health care for veterans, disappears from discourse as quickly as it arises. As the policy makers become more distant from the military experience they also will become more distant from being able to feel the reality of the challenges that veterans face and why meeting them is imperative in a just society.

Important policy decisions that affect the military's readiness and the service members' well-being must be made regardless of whether the nation is at war. Some of these decisions are ongoing, such as the size of the force, weapons and equipment, housing and installation facilities, compensation and benefits, deployment and service time requirements, weapons and equipment, and housing and installation facilities. A real understanding of the military may be especially important for decisions that affect the forces irreversibly. Two such issues that have been under scrutiny recently are the policies on sexual orientation and the status of women within the military.

While political pressure has mounted for changes to policies of exclusion based on sexual orientation, military leaders have urged political leaders to work with them on a careful and measured approach to change that does not overshadow the ongoing necessity of unit cohesiveness and readiness. Sensitivity to concerns unique to the military environment is essential in achieving this goal. The same is true for the status of women. The military has urged political leaders to be careful about sweeping changes in the assignment of women to combat roles. A recent experience shows that there can be considerable tension in differing perspectives between military and civil leaders. The Marine Corps is highly leveraged toward combat and has been slower than other branches to open front line roles to women. In 2015 the Marines completed an experiment studying how women react during typical ground combat skills tests. Groups comprised solely of males, and some of mixed genders, went through exercises in an infantry company setting. The experiment found that all-male units performed better than mixed-gender units in most tactical areas, and that during the tests women suffered a higher rate of musculoskeletal injury than men. Almost simultaneously with release of the study, Secretary of the Navy Ray Mabus, a Harvard lawyer who served two years in the Navy, gave a public statement discrediting the study as using flawed methodology and exhibiting prejudicial thinking.[73] Maybe the secretary's statements are an honest and informed assessment, or maybe they are a predictable political defense of an administration's policy choices. The fact that a civilian leader with authority over the Marine Corps would immediately and publicly discredit the command's study casts doubt on whether the public should trust the information it is being given. This kind of conflicting vision could undermine the public's faith in decisions that are made about policies that are in the political limelight, including those that fundamentally affect national defense and the military's readiness and deployment.

The public is naturally skeptical about important decisions their political leaders make and the explanations that are given for them. Polls show that the public views the military in a more trusting light than civil leaders. Part of this perspective must reflect a reality that the military is built on integrity as a central tenet. Former generals and presidents Washington and Eisenhower were and remain models of ethical behavior. Their understanding and commitment to truth were evident in the way they viewed military power with caution despite having had supreme command in the field. Though the military community has its flaws, integrity remains the central focus in leadership development and accountability. A service member's word is bond, and the rules do not allow for tolerating even slight breaches.

This is not to say that service members never violate trust; they do, but these acts conflict with military culture, especially by comparison to modern political life in which public perception of honesty is measured with a "fact-checking" percentage and plenty of room for error. Research shows that veterans carry their culture of integrity beyond their military service when they join communities with different values. A study of chief executive officers in business who have served in the military showed that chief executive officers with military experience are less likely to be involved in corporate fraud than those were not in the military.[74] It showed that former military CEOs have more conservative investment policies, particularly in research and development, and their companies perform better under stress. The study concluded, "One potential explanation for our findings is that military men learn how to make decisions in extreme conditions during combat,"[75] which prepares them to function well in distressing situations. The study also concluded that these "findings are particularly significant in light of the steady decline in corporate America of CEOs with military backgrounds in the past 25 years. The reduction in the supply of executives who have conservative investment policies, are less prone to fraud, and are plausibly better equipped to navigate through times of crisis may be detrimental for firms if these skills cannot be easily provided to individuals through alternative sources, such as MBA programs."[76]

Like executives in business, public service leaders need to make sound investment decisions, combat fraud, and be prepared to lead during times of crisis. Ethics is a recurring theme in scholarship about leadership in public service. Commonly cited landmark works emphasize its importance in building public trust in representatives and officials, such as the writing of John Gardner, former Marine and secretary of housing and urban development.[77] Some more recent leadership theories, such as "servant leadership," similarly emphasize ethical responsibilities. But these writings do not purport to offer guides for instilling an ethical culture within an organization. Meanwhile public service leaders are increasingly seen in the public as self-promotional and shady, and the public's trust in them continues to decline. Public service would benefit from a spillover of the foundational emphasis on integrity in military training and leadership, something that becomes increasingly difficult as the gap widens between those in policy making positions and those with military experience.

CHAPTER 2

Leadership as Taught

Some people seem to be born leaders. But there is too much need for good leadership in society to leave its presence to nature's whims. The military is fully aware of the vital importance of effective leadership throughout an organization, and determined to cultivate it. When selecting officer candidates, recruiters screen for potential as best they can, but they know not to presume that someone's natural potential will be realized. So officer training schools teach leadership theory in the classroom, model it during training, and put candidates in peer roles in which they are challenged to take responsibility for their units' performance and held accountable for how well they are able to direct and inspire others. In officers' career development beyond this initial screening and training they will have progressively heavier leadership responsibilities giving them an ever-broadening range of experiences. Later they will have more formal leadership schooling and be constantly mentored by their seniors and evaluated for their own performance and the performance of those under their charge. Throughout someone's career the military aims to be an immersive and relentless learning laboratory.

Public service spreads too widely for its leaders to be expected to have the kind of comprehensive leadership screening and continuous development that are integral in the military. The vast majority of government managers and elected and appointed officials and others who work in public service will not have had a structured leadership education or be supervised in its practical application. But anyone with leadership responsibilities—and any organization in which they work—could benefit from methodical leadership development, certainly more than hoping that experience will be instructive and natural talents will emerge. Some scholars and consultants within the public service field have recognized this reality. Through research within public organizations they have developed and presented various theories about the nature of effective leadership. Aspiring and working public leaders can learn from this research and these theories in university coursework and professional development seminars. But they also can climb the ladder of influence without paying any attention to it.

We might reasonably expect that public service leadership education would incorporate and complement the military's extensive and proven approach to leadership thinking and development. We might also reasonably expect that public service employers would recognize that there are many highly capable military veterans interested in service who have had valuable training and experience and who are ready to share it with their colleagues. Of course the military experience is unique in some ways and this must be kept in mind, including the obvious difference in the nature of a military leader's formal authority and expectations about obedience. But these differences should not obscure fundamental similarities in leadership pledged to public service, whether it is in the armed forces, government, or other public purpose organizations.

Neither should the differences between the military and other public service be exaggerated by the uninformed. Contrary to the popular impression that the military cultivates an authoritarian, strident, and inflexible approach to leadership, it aims to develop leaders who can appreciate the complexities of any given situation, account for individual strengths and weaknesses, and understand the need to develop trusting relationships that will inspire others. Contrary to the popular impression that all the military is all about war fighting, most military leaders have had responsibilities that do not involve combat and these responsibilities can be the same as those found in other types of public service. They may involve such things as managing supply chains, delivering emergency relief, maintaining buildings and grounds, providing security, or governing communities that are in upheaval. But despite these commonalities, the scholars who lead the public service leadership field of study seem to feel compelled only to distinguish military leadership from other public service, rather than incorporate it. This stiff-arm can leave veterans wondering why no one values their experience, and it can leave emerging public service leaders with a confusing kaleidoscope of theories about leadership and little useful advice about how to do it in practice.

The following summarizes how leadership is taught in the military and in other public service. These two fields exist in separate camps and seem to have little occasion to consider whether they really do think about leadership in fundamentally different ways.

Military Leadership Education

The military has long had the most well developed training ground for leadership. Today's academies, university-based officer training corps units, and other officer training programs have a mission of identifying capable individuals who have the moral character, intellect, physical fitness, self-discipline, and motivation for service associated with leading in the most challenging of circumstances. They teach about leadership and put candidates into situations in which they must organize, direct, and inspire others. Graduates of entry-level programs get immediate additional formal education and training for their specific occupational specialties. Later, those who continue with military careers will pass through several more stages of educational gateways that address the challenges of leadership within larger commands and in collaborative multi-branch and multi-agency roles. Military leaders will be closely mentored in their development in all phases, and their performance will be continually evaluated with explicit and detailed feedback, both supportive and critical. In this progression, growth is a prerequisite to advancement; those who do not show continued development will be separated. The following description of the various stages of this process illustrates that the military is a rich source of experiential evidence about leadership development. There is much that could be emulated.

The military has always had leadership education programs for those who prepare to become officers. In the modern military officers are expected also to have the general education of a college degree. Formal preparation combined with university education for some began with the founding of the Military Academy at West Point in 1802. A distinguishing feature of an academy education is that leadership preparation is part of an immersive experiential culture. Students must learn about leadership in the classroom, but they also get hands-on experience as part of a student corps in which they serve in peer leadership positions. They hold various billets during the school year and in summer training phases with active military units. They learn about being in charge and about following those who are.

West Point enrolls about 4,400 cadets preparing to be Army officers. It is highly selective; fewer than nine percent of over 15,000 applicants are admitted. Eighty-five percent of the cadets are men, but West Point actively seeks to recruit and integrate women. Racial minorities make up almost 30 percent of the cadet population. The naval services counterpart, the Naval Academy, also known as Annapolis, was created in 1845. It has a student body similar to West Point's but prepares its candidates to be officers in the Navy and Marine Corps. The Air Force has an academy aimed at preparing its career officers, founded in 1954 in Colorado Springs. The Coast Guard Academy, founded in 1876, in New London, Connecticut, is the smallest of the five federal service academies, with 900 candidates. The Merchant Marine Academy was established in 1943 in Kings Point, New York, during World War II. It is operated by the Department of Transportation and prepares licensed mariners but also incorporates leadership training for possible military naval service. All of the academies integrate academic and experiential education, which is reflected both in their faculty and curricula.

The academies offer a variety of majors and concentrations from which candidates can chose, but all available majors are in some way deemed related to leadership and service. West Point has a broad curriculum in sciences, natural sciences, social studies, humanities, and engineering. Leadership is among the required course work with two courses, *General Psychology* and *Military Leadership*. West Point also offers a major in *Leadership Development Science*, drawing on theories and principles from organizational behavior, psychology, and management. This major considers leadership not only in the military but also in other settings including industrial, retail, non-profit, research and development, consulting, and academic settings. The West Point faculty also integrates leadership study in courses such as behavioral science, which includes analysis of leadership dynamics at individual, group, leader, organization, and environment levels.

Coursework at the Naval Academy is heavily science, technology, engineering, and math due to the Navy's technical needs. But leadership is taught throughout the curriculum. As part of the required coursework, first-year students take a course *Preparing to Lead*. After their first year, midshipmen may choose from among several leadership electives, such as *Ethics, Human Behavior, Leadership Theory and Application, Psychology of Leadership*, and *Communicating as a Leader*. The Air Force Academy, which also emphasizes science and engineering, has leadership-related courses such as *Honorable Living, Respect and Responsibility, Leaders in Flight Today*, and *Character and Leadership*. Its Department of Behavioral Sciences and Leadership offers as many as 20 different leadership courses. At the Coast Guard Academy elective courses related to leadership include *Moral and Ethical Philosophy, Leadership/Organizational Development/Change*, and *Diversity and Leadership*. The Coast Guard Academy also has an Institute for Leadership, which is committed to leadership development by "organizing and understanding the progressively complex and challenging activities designed to mold leaders of character over the 200 week Coast Guard Academy experience." The U.S. Merchant Marine Academy has a similar curriculum, including required courses in naval leadership and in ethics.

This summary of academy leadership courses shows that officer education is not narrowly focused on combat roles. Academy course work covers leadership topics also found in public service leadership programs, including such things as an overview of leadership theories and personal style self-assessments. However, many of the academy instructors have far more extensive field leadership experience than would likely be found elsewhere, and they integrate what they have learned in practice into their teaching. Candidates in these programs also have a uniquely wide range of other course options that emphasize various aspects of leadership, such as examples from history, the relationship of character and leadership, organizational leadership, and negotiation for leaders. Sometimes the coursework focuses on specific leadership situations, such as a course at the Naval Academy on engineering leadership that studies technically complex or industrial environments that require a combination of technical expertise, organizational understanding, and personal influence. Other times leadership is viewed from a very general perspective, such as in consideration of ethics, psychology, or organizational behavior.

Much of the direct leadership learning in officer preparation comes from outside the classroom while being part of a student corps in which candidates hold increasingly responsible leadership roles. Candidates begin with indoctrination and instruction on basic discipline and military skills and observe upper class students and instructors performing in leadership roles. As they advance in class year candidates are given leadership assignments within their units that require them to inspire their juniors and teach the discipline and skills they have learned themselves. They have assignments that require them to ensure members of their units function according to training and academic expectations. They are assessed in their leadership performance both by their senior classmates and by their faculty instructors. They also get feedback from their peers. By the time they graduate they likely will have been involved in challenging situations in which they had to address performance or discipline problems. In short, the leadership education is immersive. As Colonel Larry Donnithorne wrote in *The West Point Way of Leadership,* "From the very first day, cadets find themselves submerged in a cauldron of experiences, which are frequently complex and fast-paced.... But *every one of these experiences, every aspect of every day of the cadet's training, is designed to teach leadership."*[1]

Reserve Officer Training Corps units on many campuses offer another route to an officer's commission for those who are not admitted to an academy or who prefer a more regular college experience. Some ROTC candidates get full scholarships for up to four years in exchange for their post-graduation service commitment. A majority of the officers in the Army, Navy, and Air Force are commissioned from an ROTC program. Naval ROTC has an option for a commission in the Marine Corps provided candidates complete a separate Marine officer candidate school during the summer before their senior year. All ROTC students complete the college degree requirements and also take courses in which they learn basic military skills, fundamentals of leadership, and other topics related to their branches.

Leadership development is a significant part of the ROTC curriculum. For instance, Army ROTC programs offer courses like *Introduction to Army Leadership, Applied Leadership Theory, Team Dynamics and Peer Leadership,* and *Ethical Decision-Making.* Students participate in military drills, exercises, and other organizational activities in which they have progressively greater leadership responsibilities, and their performance is evaluated. Completing an ROTC program also involves summer leadership experiences. For instance, the Army's *Summer Leadership Development and Assessment Course* is a five-week summer program at Fort Knox, Kentucky. Navy midshipmen complete a summer experience with duties as an enlisted member of the fleet, and another as a junior officer. The Navy also requires participation in a summer training course that introduces candidates to aviation, submarine, surface warfare, and Marine Corps training. Candidates choosing the Marines must complete an intensive officer candidate school in Quantico, Virginia, between their third and fourth years.

These officer accession programs are supplemented with officer training authorized at "senior military colleges," which include The Citadel, Virginia Military Institute, Texas A&M, and the University of North Georgia. The training programs at these institutions are similar to ROTC but more immersive. Another route to a commission begins at a military junior college, which enables students to become commissioned officers in the Army Reserve through a two-year early commissioning program after which they complete a bachelor's degree before serving on active duty. The military curriculum at the junior colleges is the same as at four year ROTC programs, with heavy emphasis on leadership development and military training, along with summer training. There are five military junior colleges: Georgia Military College, Marion Military Institute, New Mexico Military Institute, Valley Forge Military Academy and College, and Wentworth Military Academy.

The third primary route to an officer's commission, in addition to the academies and ROTC, is through each branch's officer candidate school. A majority of Marine Corps officers obtain their commissions through the OCS program. Most OCS candidates have completed their bachelor's degree. Some were noncommissioned officers and deemed qualified for a commission upon completion of their college degree. OCS is an intense and fast-paced experience that about one-third of the candidates do not successfully complete. The Army's program, for example, is 12 weeks conducted in three phases. During the first phase candidates are immersed into Army culture and discipline, trained in basic land navigation and tactics, and complete classroom studies on basic Army topics. The second phase emphasizes application of skills, concepts, and knowledge including a field leadership exercise with various unit command responsibilities that involve decision making, planning, and supervising. The final phase emphasizes leadership and professionalism. Army OCS also includes an academic curriculum that highlights leadership through readings like *Leadership: The Warrior's Art*,[2] which portrays soldiers who learned the values of leadership in the military and how they applied those values to the civilian world after service. OCS in the other branches similarly progresses from basic discipline and military skills through application of leadership in assigned roles. In Navy OCS, for example, the candidates in the final phase are involved in the initial training of newly arriving candidates.

Regardless of point of entry the first step in an officer's career path is completing an intensive indoctrination phase that is unique to the military. Every person entering into service as an officer undergoes initial training that both screens newcomers for leadership ability and prepares them for leadership responsibilities. Each branch has its own leadership culture and prepares officers for the particular needs of that branch. But they also have fundamental similarities. Each instills disciplined behaviors and an understanding of the branch culture. Each also has a program of physical training and fitness testing, academic coursework and testing on basic military subjects including organizational structure, communications, ethics, and leadership principles, and assignments and assessment for leadership potential. Though much is learned in the programs, to a large degree successful completion also reflects preparation. Physical training improves conditioning but candidates must arrive with sufficient readiness in strength and endurance to keep up and be able to pass the tests. Candidates with a solid academic background are unlikely to find the academics too difficult except for the challenge of studying while under physical and mental stress. Meeting the leadership challenges, including in peer roles, also likely will reflect how well the candidate already understood the need to be decisive, reliable, and tactful. Someone is unlikely to succeed in officer training without have an already well-developed drive to take on personal challenges.

To assess whether candidates have the make-up and maturity to succeed as leaders, instructors create situations to see whether candidates can keep their focus and make decisions under stress. The Navy and Marine Corps, for example, initially create a sense of chaos and frustration with rapid-fire demands and redirection. Candidates must demonstrate an ability to persevere despite confusion and failure, keep their composure, and be supportive of their unit colleagues. As training progresses candidates are given leadership assignments that require them to anticipate how to prepare their units for activities and prioritize among competing demands. They must be able to give clear direction that inspires spirited cooperation. For example, a typical challenge used in practical leadership training is an activity in which candidates take turns being in charge of a small group that is given a seemingly impossible goal, such as moving a barrel through a maze of hazards with random tools and no apparent solution. Candidates are not graded so much on task accomplishment as they are for their ability to direct a coordinated effort without becoming frustrated or alienating the unit with confusing, inept, or repellent directions.

A distinctive aspect of the peer nature of military leadership training is the group training environment that involves both personal and collective responsibility. The stresses of training make cooperation imperative, and individuals develop a real, mutually supportive bond that cannot be fully appreciated without the actual experience. Nathaniel Fick, a Dartmouth classics graduate, Marine Corps officer, and author of *One Bullet Away*, offers this reflection on his initial training: "The one thing keeping me going was being part of a group, knowing each mistake made my comrades a little weaker. Group punishment, shunned in most of American society, was a staple at OCS. Platoons fight as groups. They live or die as groups. So we were disciplined as a group. The epiphany struck one morning ... as I locked my body in the leaning rest—the 'up' pushup position. Sergeant Olds put the whole platoon in that posture while he berated a candidate at the far end of the squad bay for having scuffs in his boots. The message wasn't in Olds's words; it was in recognizing that this wasn't about how much we could take, but about how much we could give."[3] Much of the candidates' success in these kinds of situations depends on the relationships they have been able to build with their peers; those who have proved to be trustworthy and committed to unit success will have support when they need it. Candidates learn well that they must stick together under the worst of circumstances.

After commissioning all military officers continue leadership education that further develops their knowledge and skills. For example, in the Marine Corps all officers attend The Basic School, a six-month intensive leadership development and tactical education program. All Marine officers—even future pilots and lawyers—learn the skills of an infantry platoon commander and how to mentor, train, and develop Marines in a small unit. Officers in the Marines and all other branches attend follow-on schools that prepare them for their occupational specialties, such as infantry officer school, flight school, naval surface warfare officer school, or intelligence school. These specialized programs focus on equipment, tactics, and knowledge that are peculiar to a role within the branch, but they also reinforce and refine general leadership principles and how they apply to the members of units within the specialty.

Throughout their training new officers learn about aspects of leadership that are particular to the military, such as how to give orders and administer discipline through exercise of formal authority. But this is only a part of their initial development. They quickly learn that reliance on formal authority is shortsighted and they must be able to lead with genuine concern, support, and encouragement, and most of all through example. A large part of this learning is experiential and comes through the nature of their early leadership assignments. In peer leadership positions they have the trappings of authority associated with temporary roles, but in reality they must depend on their colleagues' voluntary cooperation. The immersive peer leadership experience is an aspect of military officer training that likely is unappreciated by those who have not been through it. Exceptional performance depends on building a bond of mutual support. The student peer leader must trust that student subordinates will do their best, and those who are given peer direction must trust their peers to be competent to make unselfish decisions with the unit's best interests at heart. Those who attempt to rely only on authority are likely to encounter difficulty in their roles and suffer damage to their relationships. This experience is a unique incubator for learning how to lead in situations that will be encountered in other walks of life where there is no formal line of authority on which to rely.

Another aspect of military leadership development that most likely is not understood by those without the experience is that the need for the cooperative approach learned in training continues into initial field assignments. A newly assigned officer likely will have the least experience in the unit, and this is well understood especially by salty veterans. Of course the military instills respect for all officers—it is legally required by the Uniform Code of Military Justice and the penalties for disrespect or disobedience are severe. But everyone also is fully aware that new officers have limited practical knowledge and effective leadership in the field must be learned through experience. The officer's development is aided by the guidance of non-commissioned officers who have established influence and credibility with the unit. Wise junior officers form an immediate trusted relationship with these NCOs that enables the officers to be guided without undermining their authority within the unit. Initial officer leadership training stresses the importance of this relationship and provides advice about how to cultivate it. Officers often remember their first senior NCO relationship as a defining part of their leadership development, in which they learned the many different ways in which someone must lead and the difference between theory and reality.

Officers' initial training and first assignments are the most immersive period of leadership development. But those who remain in the service beyond the several years of initial commitment will undergo additional formal leadership education at transitional phases in their careers. The second stage is likely to be a command and staff college, which includes the Army Command and General Staff College, the College of Naval Command and Staff, the Marine Corps Command and Staff College, and the Air Command and Staff College. These programs are aimed at field grade officers who are advancing from direct small unit roles to command of larger units with subordinate officers, or to staffs with functional responsibilities such as operations, logistics, administration, communications, or intelligence. The curriculum is focused on operational strategy but also includes leadership development and ethics. For example, the Marine Command and Staff College requires courses like *Leading Forces*, *Human Behavior*, and *Moral Decisions*, which draw upon leadership philosophy. As another example, the Air Command and Staff College offers a course on *Leadership and Warfare* that guides officers in establishing effective leadership through crises. Along with the professional military development program at these schools, students can be eligible for a master's degree, such as in *Military Operational Art and Science* with a concentration in leadership.

Career officers will pass through a third phase of formal leadership education. The war colleges—the Army War College, Naval War College, Marine Corps War College, Air War College, and the National War College—are the senior structured professional military education programs. A typical residential program takes one year to complete and can result in a master's degree. The curriculum spans leadership theory, self-assessment, and development of self-improvement goals. Courses are taught with a perspective that the students will have senior leadership responsibilities, and some studies focus specifically on how to lead in such an environment. For example, the Army War College has a core course in strategic leadership that examines the leader's role in aligning an organization's climate and culture with a strategic vision, how to synthesize leadership skills in an interagency, intergovernmental, and multi-national environment, and approaches to leading through change. Ethics is a recurring theme in these programs. For example, the Air War College offers an elective: *Right, Wrong, In-Between: Philosophy and Ethics for Senior Leaders.* Participants in these advanced schools also will complete assessments to reflect on their personality attributes and identify areas in which they will want to focus their self-improvement programs. Unlike the assessments that are common in preparatory college programs, participants in senior military colleges will be able to draw upon years of direct leadership experience when considering their own strengths and weaknesses.

Senior leadership studies include topics that typically are part of leadership studies in public service, as well as perspectives from business and industry management. Participants also are exposed to the perspectives of enrolled officers from other branches and other nations. An example of how these programs look at leadership in the broadest sense is the recurring use of Jim Collins' best-selling book *Good to Great: Why Some Companies Make the Leap—and Others Don't.*[4] Based on a comparative study of American publicly traded companies whose historic cumulative stock returns were at or below the general stock market return, and those that beat the market by a wide margin, Collins found that successful organizational leaders focus on their manager's character attributes. As he says: "People are your most important asset turns out to be wrong. People are *not* your most important asset. The *right* people are."[5] These conclusions affirm the military's emphasis on aligning unit members with the mission, rather than the other way around. Collins notes that this conclusion confirms the approach of the Marine Corps, which "recruits people who share the corps' values, then provides them with the training required to accomplish the organization's mission."[6] The other branches also teach about what Collins found in successful business organizations. For example, the Coast Guard's policy is to search "for people who have a predisposition for strong leadership," because "every member of the team must be able to contribute to the cause. They must be able to perform multiple tasks, and they must become leaders in whatever position they may hold. Internal training alone cannot meet these objectives. Therefore, it all has to begin with the selection process."[7] Findings in Collins' research into successful companies also reflect other points of emphasis in the military, such as the importance of confronting the hard facts, focusing on a simple and well understood core mission rather than trying to be the best at everything, having a culture of self-discipline in which managers keep focused on their responsibilities, and using technology selectively as consistent with the mission rather than for its own sake. With these kinds of readings senior military leaders are exposed to material that deepens their leadership knowledge and expands their perspective about what is effective in various contexts.

These schools and programs combine into a well-developed, systematic approach to continuous learning and reflection for officers, who from the start and throughout their careers are expected to be leaders of increasingly complex and diverse organizations. But officers are not the only leaders in the military. Everyone soon has some direct leadership responsibility for others, beginning with small teams. Junior enlisted members are mentored in their leadership by non-commissioned officers, and as they advance they will attend leadership training courses within their commands and at service schools. For example, Marine NCO courses, like the ones at Marine Corps University in Quantico, Virginia, prepare corporals and sergeants to be small unit leaders so that they can lead physical training sessions, drills, and inspections. The Air Force NCO Academy at Air University in Montgomery, Alabama, devotes a quarter of its curriculum to leadership studies with more than 50 hours of classroom instruction on such things as negotiation, discipline, and continuous improvement. The Coast Guard and Navy have programs that teach similar subjects with an emphasis on the kinds of enlisted leadership responsibilities that are common in their branches. The formal training progression in all branches culminates in educational opportunities for senior NCOs, such as multi-week programs that offer courses in leadership philosophies, organizational behavior, and professionalism. The Navy's senior enlisted academy, for example, focuses on organizational leadership with a curriculum that includes organizational behavior, leadership, communication skills, and professionalism. Students attend with senior enlisted personnel from other countries, and courses are often taught with Socratic engagement and facilitated group discussions.

The military's approach to leadership development emphasizes everyone's responsibility not only for personal growth but also for actively developing leadership in others. Each branch shares the premise that organizational success depends on continuous development of leaders at all levels. This is a necessity in the armed forces; leaders usually hold a particular command for only a few years and must be constantly thinking about succession. They also know that in combat every unit leader is a target and at risk of being wounded or killed, and the unit's success in accomplishing the mission depends on the ability of subordinates to take the initiative and continue the fight. So every commander is expected to percolate leadership experience and give continual, constructive feedback on how to improve. They also are expected to find opportunities for their subordinates' leadership growth through enrollment in schools and programs and in career planning. How well this responsibility toward others is met is an integral part of performance evaluations.

This summary of the military's approach to leadership development shows that contrary to the popular impression that the education and training is rigidly doctrinal and authoritative, they are multi-faceted, broad, and deep. At the same time, as the following describes, the military's approach to leadership is based on core principles and expected leadership attributes that give aspiring and accomplished leaders a strong foundation aimed at keeping them from getting lost in a relativistic fog.

Military Leadership Principles

Military leadership is distinctive in the extent to which commanders may rely on formal authority and strict obedience. Everyone in the military has been taught the seriousness of having to follow direction and why it could matter in combat. Disobeying a lawful order or disrespecting an officer is a crime under the Uniform Code of Military Justice, punishable with severe penalties. But everyone also understands that effective leadership involves much more than relying on the legal force of being able to give orders. Relationships must be built that will withstand the stresses and chaos of combat.

This broader view of military leadership is reflected at the core, in how it is defined. For example, the Army doctrine defines it as "the process of influencing people by providing purpose, direction, and motivation to accomplish the mission and improve the organization."[8] This intertwines several important aspects of leadership that transcend use of authority; it involves *influencing* others, not just telling them what to do. This influence is exercised by giving a purpose and direction and by *motivating* them to want to act together toward these ends, which requires respect for them as individuals and as members of a team.

The military accordingly stresses that the relationship between the leader and those to be led is a matter of both mutual trust and mutual respect. It teaches that leaders must sometimes make difficult decisions and therefore must always remain professional in their relationships— leaders should *always* act as leaders. Losing sight of the proper nature of the relationship can distort the decision making process, cause jealously and a sense of unfairness within a unit, and raise questions about the integrity of decisions that affect individuals within the unit. Reflecting these risks the Uniform Code of Military Justice prohibits romantic and personal financial arrangements between officers and enlisted and between others in chains of command, and violation can result in punishment under the Uniform Code of Military Justice and discharge from the service. The ability to build and maintain trust and respect is an important part of leadership development and assessment.

The military's definition of leadership connects influence with the purpose of accomplishing a mission. The aim of this influence is therefore not satisfying the personal needs of the unit members, nor is it orienting the unit toward some higher social goal apart from accomplishment of the mission. The definition also instructs that leaders should not be short-sighted in their mission orientation. Mission accomplishment is connected to the longer-range goal of organizational improvement. As the Army leadership manual says, "Leaders demonstrate stewardship when they act to improve the organization beyond their own tenure. Improving the organization for the long-term is deciding and taking action to manage people or resources when the benefits will not occur during a leader's tour of duty with an organization."[9]

The military is aware that leaders can lose focus on long-term organizational improvement, which can result in what it calls "negative" or "toxic leadership." Examples of toxic leadership include self-centered behavior, abusive tactics, and emphasis on short-term demonstrations of achievement rather than long-term organizational welfare. Toxic leadership frustrates individuals and endangers the organization. The military understands that its leaders sometimes function in isolated positions in which authority can be abused. The Navy, for example, is very direct about this risk for ship captains. An officer can be summarily relieved of command for misconduct, a significant event, unsatisfactory performance over time, or loss of confidence in ability to command. The Navy has a policy of being very public about such command failures and the disciplinary action and the circumstances that led to it. During one year the Navy publicized that 20 senior officers were relieved of command of their ships, bases, or units for such things as improper behavior, misuse of funds, improper civilian hiring practices, and loss of confidence. It also publicized that four executive officers and eight senior enlisted sailors were relieved of their duties. This approach is personally harsh to those involved, but it sends a clear signal to everyone that in the Navy responsibility follows command and there are severe consequences for failures to meet these expectations.

While the military aims to keep leadership aimed at mission accomplishment and organizational wellbeing, it does not foolishly pretend there is only one approach that always works. Its doctrine explicitly recognizes that different circumstances may call for different approaches. These situations are sometimes called "conditions of leadership." Leaders use formal leadership due to rank or position. They also must develop informal leadership abilities through such attributes as setting an example, taking initiative, and applying special expertise. Military leadership teaches that no one approach is likely to be sufficient for all leaders because they must adjust to uncertain and often uniquely complex environments. At the higher levels, for example, the Army teaches that leadership is often based on skills that do not involve direct authority but rather effective use of negotiation and consensus-building skills.[10] Leaders are taught to try to understand their own personal strengths, work to improve their weaknesses, and align their approaches with varying styles and conditions in the environment in which they must lead.

Describing effective leadership as situational runs the risk of giving the impression that there are no specifics that can be taught about how to do it well. The military equips leaders for success with more than sweeping aspirations. Based on experience it identifies important attributes and competencies for which an effective leader should strive. It also stresses that leadership is complex and must be exercised in an infinite variety of circumstances that require applying these attributes and competencies to different extents and in different ways. For example, the demands of leadership vary with the level of responsibility. In small unit contexts the weight of leadership demands are felt in direct relationships; leaders must be examples of integrity and proficiency. With increasing responsibility such attributes and competencies as judgment, knowledge, and keeping the members of the organization informed take on added weight. But there are specifics that can be learned and remembered.

The Army uses a "leadership requirements model" that identifies attributes and competencies for which a leader should strive. It groups desirable leadership attributes in three categories: character, presence, and intellect. Character is at the center of it all, and character is a matter of integrity. As Army doctrine states, "The Army relies on leaders of integrity who possess high moral standards and are honest in word and deed. Leaders are honest to others by not presenting themselves or their actions as anything other than what they are, remaining committed to truth."[11] In Colonel Donnithorne's outstanding reflection on Army officer education in his book *The West Point Way of Leadership*, he writes about how West Point teaches cadets to "go to extremes in matters of principle. One must become comfortable risking everything—one's career, one's life—to keep principles alive. Leadership requires this kind of commitment on a daily basis, not just when one is in a crisis."[12] The second group of attributes, focused on presence, emphasizes the importance of a leader's demeanor, words, and actions, which set the tone for subordinates especially under duress. The third group of attributes, comprising intellect, emphasizes the importance of a leader's study and the ability to solve problems.

In Army leadership doctrine leadership competency involves influence within the command as well as the ability to influence others beyond the chain of command, such as in relationships with unified action partners. There are three categories of competency for action: leading, developing, and achieving. Leaders are expected to be competent in building trust, setting an example, and communicating an understanding about needed action and the reason for it. Army leadership competency also involves creating an environment to encourage self-improvement and the development of others to become more expert and more responsible. The competency of achievement requires personal responsibility for accomplishing tasks and missions on time and according to established standards.

The military illustrates desirable attributes and competencies with abundant and conspicuous models from history. These examples are studied in training, they are ever present in symbols and monuments, and they are passed on through storytelling in training and in the field. For instance, the manual *Leading Marines*[13] includes historic and modern examples to illustrate the Corps' leadership doctrine. Marines are taught about the many heroic individuals who gave of themselves for others, symbolized poignantly by the iconic Joe Rosenthal photograph of the flag being raised under fire on Iwo Jima—which does not depict faces, only undaunted courage and determination. Service members in all branches are inculcated with a sense of personal responsibility for upholding tradition, and they are empowered with the force of collective devotion to that high standard.

As in the Army, Navy and Marine Corps leaders are expected to strive for certain attributes in themselves. The naval services call them traits and describe them as built on three "core values": honor, courage, and commitment.[14] Honor is the foundation of character that includes ethical and moral behavior, uncompromising integrity, respect for human dignity, and respect and concern for each other. It involves doing the right thing even when not being watched. Courage is the mental, moral, and physical strength "to do what is right in every situation, to adhere to a higher standard of personal conduct, to lead by example, and to make tough decisions under pressure."[15] Commitment includes discipline for unit and self, concern for others, and a determination to achieve a standard of excellence.

The Navy and Marine Corps have succinct statements of desirable leadership traits that uphold their core values, which are the foundation of their leadership education and evaluation.[16] As the Marine Corps says unwaveringly, "Each trait is important, and the lack of development in one or more of the traits makes for imbalanced and ineffective leaders."[17] The articulation of these traits reflects what all the branches essentially value in leadership development. They are:

Bearing. Bearing is a product of carriage, appearance, personal conduct, and tone. Leaders are expected to look, talk, and act like leaders, which includes setting an example of strength, self-discipline, and dedication to duty. With their example they inspire others to do the same including when under stress.

Courage. Leaders must have physical courage that enables them to act in dangerous conditions and to be able to make decisions in chaotic circumstances despite personal risk. They also must have moral courage to do the right thing when facing challenges, including the prospect of criticism or personal disadvantage.

Decisiveness. Leaders must make decisions promptly and give direction clearly even in chaotic circumstances. They seek the advice of others but do not await agreement or approval when the circumstances demand action. A decisive leader knows there can be greater risk in confusion and inaction than in initiation. Responsible decisiveness includes a readiness to recognize that a prior decision needs to be modified as circumstances develop.

Dependability. Leaders are not expected to be infallible but they must be trustworthy, do their best, and always be loyal to their units. Dependability breeds dependability; effective leaders can expect subordinates not only to carry out their missions faithfully but also to be ready to assume greater responsibility if circumstances require.

Endurance. Military leaders work to develop the mental and physical stamina to prevail in combat by having the capacity for withstanding stress, fatigue, hardship, and pain. Their hours and workloads can be extreme. Leaders are expected to be able to set an example in stamina that strengthens the resolve of those within their command. This includes not only physical fitness but also working hard in routine duties and professional development.

Enthusiasm. A leader has a can-do attitude and gives an optimistic best effort that inspires others to do their best. Complaining is contagious and cancerous. Leaders do not talk behind others' backs and do not allow personal disagreement with a course of action impede their performance of it once the decision has been made. Units have the best chance for success through individual earnest effort and suffer in capabilities and morale with anything less.

Initiative. Contrary to what many might assume about the military due to its clearly defined hierarchies, leadership doctrine stresses that individual initiative at all levels is expected especially in situations that do not allow for waiting for direction from a senior commander. Initiative is interrelated with decisiveness. It includes adapting when the situation changes rather than blindly adhering to a plan.

Integrity. Integrity is the core of leadership. The same notion is embodied in terms such as character and honesty. Integrity is a matter of intent, not appearance, as expressed by the Latin phrase *esse quam videri,* or "to be rather than to seem." A leader's word must be impeccably trustworthy, as must the genuineness of the leader's actions.

Judgment. Judgment is the ability to assess information, weigh the possible solutions, and make sound decisions. Good judgment requires knowledge, open mindedness, and a realistic sense of self. It is something that can be developed with learning, experience, and reflection. An ability to remain calm under stress is essential for reliable good judgment.

Justice. Justice involves administering rewards and punishments meritoriously and consistently. This applies not only in decisions made in disciplinary action but also in assignments and promotions. Leaders must sometimes make unpleasant decisions. Unit morale suffers from perceptions of favoritism or unfairness.

Knowledge. This trait involves professional military knowledge but also more general knowledge about the world and human behavior so that sound decisions can be made. It also involves a commitment to continuous learning and self-improvement.

Loyalty. Leadership requires loyalty at many levels, including to the oath of service, to the branch and its traditions, to seniors and subordinates, and to fellow service members and veterans. Marines express this value with their cherished motto *semper fidelis*, or "always faithful." Veterans of all branches tend to remember the loyalty they felt to their colleagues as a powerful force, especially in combat.

Tact. Tact pertains to being intentional about how something is said as well as what is said. Contrary to a stereotypical image of an intimidating drill instructor angrily shouting at recruits, beyond initial indoctrination training leaders are expected to communicate in a way that respects and emboldens others and creates a sense of cooperation in a noble cause.

Unselfishness. Unselfishness in a military leadership sense is dedication to mission accomplishment. It is not unthinking martyrdom. The military teaches that units have the best chance of success if every individual gives all. Being able to count on each other even at grave personal risk liberates selfless courage.

Marines are taught to remember these 14 leadership traits with the acronym JJDIDTIEBUCKLE.

* * *

The Marines and Navy refer to "leadership principles" to provide foundational guidance about actions that leaders are expected to take.[18] In early officer training the statement of principles is meant as a guide for interactions and as a tool for self-evaluation and self-improvement. The following is how the sea services express these principles, but it also is similar to how the other branches view them:

Know yourself and seek self-improvement. Leaders continually evaluate their own strengths and weaknesses. They strive for a clear understanding of themselves and group behavior and try to learn how best to deal with situations they are likely to encounter and how to approach unexpected situations. Self-improvement is not an occasional event; military leaders are regularly assessed in their development and they are expected to have an ongoing self-improvement plan that prepares them for increased responsibility.

Be technically and tactically proficient. Leaders must be highly competent in basic military skills and in their occupational specialties to understand their units' capabilities, train appropriately, and make sound decisions about deployment. Basic military skills expected of all leaders include an ability to understand the demands of the branch's core functions. For example, the Marine Corps requires everyone, whatever their specialty, to learn basic infantry skills and to regularly meet standards for small arms marksmanship. Specialty skills—such as flying a plane, conning a ship, or analyzing a threat—also require continuous improvement. As leaders gain advanced specialty skills they are expected to pass them along to their juniors.

Know the members of your unit and look out for their welfare. Leaders are expected to realize that individuals have unique abilities and personalities and may react differently to challenges even in an environment that stresses uniformity and adherence to regulations. Leaders are expected to take an interest in the individual welfare and professional development of all their unit members. Each of the branches has traditions that reinforce these tenets. For example, the Navy has the tradition of a "mast" at which the ship's captain is available to hear concerns directly from the crew members without their fearing retribution. A Marine tradition that symbolizes a primary concern for the welfare of the troops is that officers eat last when the unit has a meal. By this officers are reminded about the preeminent importance of their troops' welfare, and troops are reminded that officers care about them.

Set the example. Leaders are expected to set standards by personal example in ethical behavior, appearance, attitude, and physical fitness. This requires considering how words and actions will be perceived by others. Leaders strive to inspire others and should not expect the members of their units to do things they are unwilling to do themselves. Setting a good example also requires being genuine and acknowledging mistakes.

Keep the members of your unit informed. Members of a unit who are informed about a situation are better able to understand the desired ends and accomplish them. With knowledge they are also better able to carry on without direct personal supervision and to exercise initiative to find better solutions to deal with unexpected developments. Leaders are taught to communicate instructions in a clear and concise manner, and to give a chance for questions to be asked and concerns to be expressed. Leaders check on progress periodically to confirm the assigned task is properly accomplished.

Make sound and timely decisions. Leaders must analyze a situation using the best available information and make sound decisions based on that estimation. They do not delay in the unrealistic hope that a perfect solution will appear or everyone will give their unqualified endorsement. The military emphasizes that leaders make the best possible decisions based on what is known, seeking and considering advice if possible, and then going forward, while being prepared to revise the plan as necessary. Leaders gain respect by acting decisively and correcting mistakes immediately.

Train the members of your unit as a team. Leaders train the members of their units to operate as a team, taking into consideration individual abilities. Individuals are expected to share their knowledge and experience with each other with an overall goal of organizational effectiveness. Leaders ensure everyone knows their responsibilities and learns to trust each other always to do their best even if at personal cost.

Develop a sense of responsibility in your subordinates. Leaders show they are sincerely interested in their subordinates' professional development. They assign tasks and delegate authority in a way that promotes mutual confidence and respect among the leader and the unit members. They give feedback that honestly acknowledges success and encourages improvement.

Seek responsibility and take responsibility for your actions. Leaders actively seek out challenging assignments for their professional development and they take responsibility for how their actions contribute to mission accomplishment and how they affect others. They also are responsible for all that their units do or fail to do and cannot escape this responsibility by attributing it to others' failures. If something goes wrong they reflect on what they could have done differently. Leaders are willing to accept justified and constructive criticism.

* * *

This particular description of leadership traits and principles is drawn from Navy and Marine Corps doctrine. The other branches may state them slightly differently but the essence is the same.

The Air Force, which due to its core function more than the other branches has an institutional focus on technical superiority, strikes similar themes in its doctrine. It defines leadership as "the art and science of motivating, influencing, and directing Airmen to understand and accomplish the Air Force mission in joint warfare."[19] As with the other branches, the Air Force's statement combines a mission focus for leadership within the context of a relationship between leaders and the led. It calls this simply "people and mission." The Air Force summarizes the underpinning of its view of leadership in three core values: integrity, service above self, and excellence. These core values encompass the leadership traits of integrity, loyalty, selflessness, professional ability, energy, emotional stability, decisiveness, and humaneness.[20] The Air Force also teaches that leadership involves three actions: influence, improvement, and accomplishment.[21] Leaders act decisively to influence their subordinates by creating a vision of the desired end-state and tailoring their behavior to motivate them to achieve that vision. Leaders employ education, training, and challenges to foster improvement of the unit and its individuals, and to develop subordinate leadership ability. These descriptions are harmonious with how the other branches talk about leadership.

Also similar to the other branches the Air Force teaches that leadership can be viewed as occurring at three levels: tactical expertise, operational competence, and strategic vision. As an airman progresses to higher leadership levels the emphasis shifts from personal, to team, to organizational competencies.[22] At the personal level Air Force leaders are expected to focus on developing their technical expertise and demonstrating leadership to others by the way they perform their duties. Junior officers typically influence others with whom they work directly, such as with crews. At the next level leaders are more likely to have command responsibility over a team and therefore must more thoroughly understand operational capabilities and be able to integrate people and their capabilities into coordinated efforts. At the organizational level there is more of an emphasis on branch functions and being able to operate within joint, multinational, and interagency relationships.[23]

Among the branches the Coast Guard's core operational responsibilities are most similar to those of civilian public service organizations. Its units often function within civilian communities. These responsibilities include maritime policing, border security, search and rescue, and emergency response. In its leadership development the Coast Guard approach is similar to the other branches. For instance, it integrates tradition as a core aspect of leadership. As Coast Guard doctrine states, "Honoring history and tradition instills several elements that benefit any organization" including giving purpose, fortifying long-term decision making, enhancing strength and character, and motivating and inspiring.[24] Similar to all branches the Coast Guard identifies character as a fundamental premise that captures several leadership traits. It "involves the concepts of high ethical conduct, moral behavior, honesty, integrity, trust, and doing what is right, not just what is easy."[25] The Coast Guard also stresses that character

requires respect, "which is one of the least talked about but most important values in leadership."[26] Respect involves caring about shipmates. It
also involves respect for authority, and this is related to a commitment of
devotion to duty, which the Coast Guard describes as "the moral obligation
to place the accomplishment of assigned tasks before individual needs,
considerations, or possible advancements."[27]

Like the other branches, the Coast Guard tries to address tendencies
that naturally develop to impede effective leadership. For example, it
teaches that an organization's leaders must pay special attention to what
is called "the frozen middle," which is comprised of "the middle managers
who, technically, run everything. And yet, ninety-nine times out of a hundred, they are the people who are the most resistant to change."[28] To overcome this impediment the Coast Guard works to ensure that these middle
managers—senior enlisted chief petty officers and chief warrant officers—feel empowered to communicate with commanders and encouraged
to speak up when they see something wrong.[29] The Coast Guard's relation-
ship-based approach also teaches that leaders should develop caring relationships, promote the team over self, sponsor continual learning, take
responsibility for teaching new employees about the organization and the
importance of teamwork, and be inclusive in decisions about change and
clearly communicate purpose.[30]

Another approach that the Coast Guard uses to counter a natural
tendency in organizations is what it calls "giving the field priority." The
military has learned through experience that operational units must feel
empowered to act unconventionally in response to changing conditions,
and not have to wait for an organization-wide decision making process to
run its course. A top-down-only approach stifles needed change. A recent
example of this reality was shown in Persian Gulf combat, where troops
in the field devised make-shift armor plating to protect their vehicles from
improvised explosive devices long before the Department of Defense procurement process supplied an improved standard vehicle. The Coast
Guard and the other branches teach that organizational leaders must
actively take steps to create a culture for a sense of empowerment to try
new things. This requires leaders to demonstrate their interest and support
even when the change is unsuccessful. One reason why organizations are
slow to change is the leaders are not familiar with the conditions on the
front. One way to address this, the Coast Guard explains to commanders,
is "instead of anchoring yourself at headquarters, get out in the field and
visit the troops," and "consult field personnel before new policies that will
affect them are planned and implemented."[31]

The military also teaches that leadership entails direct responsibility for the development of leadership in others. As the Army puts it, leadership development is a "deliberate, continuous, sequential, and progressive process,"[32] and leaders must always feel invested in the leadership progression of the members of their units. Feeling responsible for others' development is necessary as a practical matter to prepare for combat because leaders, especially in small unit commands, are vulnerable enemy targets and the unit's success often turns on the ability of others to step in under fire and carry on. Whatever the operational condition, organizations function best when individuals at all levels take a personal interest in embodying leadership traits and acting according to leadership principles. Commanders therefore should always be observing the leadership behavior and potential of the members of their units, mentoring them by example and advice, and assigning increased responsibility over time so the learning can be applied.

Responsibility for leadership development involves both formal and informal means. It occurs in structured programs, with operational experience, and with self-development through study, readings, and discussions. For example, the Army's field manual includes leadership development activities with indicators of strengths and weakness and ways to focus on improvement. To develop others leaders are encouraged to "provide honest feedback to others, discussing strengths and areas for improvement. Effective assessment results in an individual development plan designed to improve weaknesses and sustain strengths."[33] The steps to achieve results include designing a development plan collaboratively, encouraging subordinates to take the lead, agreeing on the required actions to improve leader performance, and reviewing the development plan frequently and modifying it as necessary.[34] Performance reviews include assessment of how well commanders are fulfilling this responsibility for members of their units.

This summary shows that the military's approach to leadership is comprehensive, beginning with a memorable definition of what it is, giving clear guideposts for its embodiment, and setting expectations for a culture of its continuous development. This approach is a product of a deep, experienced-based understanding of the importance of leadership throughout an organization.

Public Service Leadership Education

Until recently leadership theory was studied at universities only indirectly within fields such as history, philosophy, and political science. History includes study of the traits and actions of influential figures. Students will learn about the distinctive leadership approaches and achievements of people such as Caesar, Joan of Arc, Cromwell, Washington, Lincoln, Gandhi, King, and Mandela. Those who study ancient philosophy will learn what great thinkers such as Plato, Sun Tzu, and Machiavelli said about how leaders should behave. In political science students consider the nature of power and the appropriate ends of its exercise. From these and other interdisciplinary perspectives much can be learned about leadership, but few university students, outside of ROTC and other military training programs, had the opportunity to take a course that focuses on what leadership means to them and how they can develop it in themselves.

Leadership as a subject has become part of some graduate programs in fields such as psychology, education, or business. Within public service programs leadership as a field of study has expanded within the past three decades. There now is a significant body of academic research and publication. Much of this work has been spent making an argument amid ongoing disagreement about what is even meant by leadership as a concept. As a leading textbook put it, "After decades of dissonance, leadership scholars agree on one thing: They can't come up with a common definition for leadership.... The bottom line is that leadership is a complex concept for which a determined definition may long be in flux.... In the past 60 years, as many as 65 different classifications have been developed to define the dimensions of leadership."[35] Without agreement on what leadership means the approach to teaching it within academic programs tends to be kaleidoscopic. It asks questions without purporting to give clear answers that can serve as guidance for leadership in practice.

The master of public administration degree is aimed at preparing leaders for public service. Variations on this degree include a master of public service, public affairs, or public management. A master of public policy focuses more on policy research and analysis than the other related degrees. There are about 185 accredited programs in the field enrolling about 12,000 students.[36] About 35 percent of the graduates will join the government, mostly state and local, and 21 percent will work for non-profit organizations.[37] Programs in public administration typically include one course devoted to the study of leadership. Compared to other professional fields—such as master of business administration or master of education programs—the course is taught with less of an expectation that someone will be immediately faced with direct leadership responsibilities. In fact the degree itself is not seen as necessary professional preparation, and there are no obvious tangible rewards for getting it. Few government employers will cover the tuition, and most who already hold public service positions would expect no return on investment with a salary increase or promotion.

Relative enrollment numbers show how little a role public administration degrees play in professional preparation. In the country annually more than 350 thousand masters' degrees are awarded for business and education, and only 44 thousand for the various masters of public administration or social services degrees.[38] The relative infrequency of getting the degree can be seen by comparison to the number of employees in these fields. There are more 2.7 million employees in the federal executive branch and more than 90 thousand in state and local governments. Public service leaders actually are more likely to have a professional degree in law or a master of business administration than a public administration degree. Consequently, unlike the military, which prepares all of its leaders with an immersive education, in public service leaders' formal leadership training is more likely to be informal and sporadic.

Those who do have the opportunity to study public service leadership in a graduate program, or who otherwise become familiar with the academic literature in the field, will encounter thinking that is very different from a military education. Montgomery Van Wart, who is a leading scholar in public service leadership and author of a widely used textbook on the subject, and his co-author Kevin O'Farrell studied courses offered in the field and found that they have four goals.[39] Naturally the most common feature in such courses is an overview of the major public service leadership theories.[40] This is also the dominant content of the most widely used textbooks. Students will be able to describe the progression from studying "great men" to more recent theories such as "transformational" or "servant leadership." Often students in these classes are assigned to groups and make presentations on what they see as the strengths and limitations of each theory.

A second common component of public service leadership education that Van Wart and O'Farrell identified is exercises intended to inform students about how they view their own personalities and "leadership styles."[41] A common exercise of this type is completing the "Myers-Briggs Type Indicator," or MBTI, which draws on psychological theories about personality types and the preferences for relying on sensation, intuition, feeling, or thinking.[42] As co-developer Isabell Myers put it, "The essence of the theory is that much seemingly random variation in behavior is actually quite orderly and consistent, being due to basic differences in the way individuals prefer to use their perception and judgment."[43] The student chooses a point on a scale indicating a preference for such things as being organized or spontaneous, shy or outgoing, and responsible or flexible. The responses generate a score between extraversion-introversion, sensing-intuition, thinking-feeling, and judgment-perception, and this combines into a characterization as one of 16 personality types. For instance someone may get a result of being "ISTJ": introverted, sensing, thinking, and using judgment. The idea is that with such feedback about preferences students can better see how they might interact with others and affect an organization, and with this perspective they can focus on strengthening their weaknesses.

There are other methods for students to obtain this kind of feedback about their preferences based on the information they give about themselves. For example, another is a "Leadership Practices Inventory" that James Kouzes and Barry Posner created based on their popular "Leadership Challenge."[44] Students complete self-assessments and ask their seniors, peers, and subordinates to answer questions about them, called a "360 degree assessment." For example, a question asks about how comfortable someone is with the statement: "I set a personal example of what I expect from others," or "I find ways to celebrate accomplishments." The program produces a profile that purports to measure the frequency of the student's specific leadership behaviors. It gives scores that rate such things as how well the subject treats others with dignity and respect, sets a personal example, talks about future trends, seeks out challenging opportunities, develops cooperative relationships, and praises others for a job well done. The scores are used to create charts that show the relative frequency in which the listed positive behaviors are demonstrated in the answers.

Van Wart and O'Farrell reported that these commonly used self-assessment activities for defining personal styles or preferences are not regarded as among the most successful leadership teaching methods in public service courses.[45] One obvious reason for the limited utility of such exercises in academic settings is that the students completing them typically are basing their self-images on experiences that have not involved the kinds of leadership responsibilities for which they are being prepared. Also, someone can answer questions in a way intended to confirm a self-image rather than get objective feedback. Another limitation is that the assigned preferences are expressed in binary terms that do not reflect the complexity of human behavior and circumstances. Many people, for example, can be either extraverted or introverted depending on very particular circumstances; some of the strongest leaders were shy in their personal lives but not when making decisions about official responsibilities.

Another exercise frequently encountered in public service leadership education is aimed at causing students to reflect on their disposition toward certain behaviors in group settings. For this some leadership consultants favor Edward de Bono's "six thinking hats," in which individuals must act out various roles in discussions based on the color of the hat they are given to wear during the exercise. With a white hat the subject focuses on facts; with a black hat on being the devil's advocate and looking for danger; with a yellow hat on optimism; with a red hat on emotion and intuition; with a green hat on creativity; and with a blue hat on controlling the group's process.[46] Participants then reflect on their tendencies and how they affect group communication and productivity. Segregating communication approaches into these categories is supposed to generate a more balanced discussion. It is also supposed to enable individuals to simplify their thought processes by being able to recognize differing perspectives and switch the way of thinking to suit particular situations. De Bono calls this "lateral thinking." In a leadership context an understanding of the technique can encourage individuals to think more broadly and consider alternative perspectives. But it can also encourage disingenuousness that will endanger a leader's integrity and trustworthiness if taken to mean a leader should be anything but honest and genuine. The danger is most acute when the importance of integrity is not otherwise stressed.

Public service leadership instructors also often ask students to incorporate self-assessments into a "personal vision" of leadership. In this process they may be required to keep a journal of reflection about their engagement with the course content and exercises. Or they may be required to generate a "development plan" that describes short and long-term actions that the student will undertake to improve leadership practices. In most cases such an exercise will occur without the context of significant leadership experience; usually students necessarily reflect on their interactions with classmates. Participants in these kinds of exercises typically report that they benefit from being encouraged to think about their tendencies and how these could affect their leadership relationships. Most have difficulty envisioning how to translate such reflections into a development plan in the abstract. Ironically, the type of graduate student who is most likely to have had significant direct leadership experience is a military veteran. But veterans are also likely to be told that their experience is peculiar to the military and not relevant to public service.

Another common goal of public service leadership courses that Van Wart and O'Farrell identified are readings and discussions intended to give students an understanding of a public leader's ethical responsibilities.[47]

This often is addressed within the context of the study of various leadership theories, many of which emphasize the importance of public trust in national leaders. Students also may have case study discussions in which they talk about ethical dilemmas. For example, a student may be asked to consider being a recently appointed public official who expects to be presented with a major proposal that the student considers to be unwise. The student is asked to consider the ethical implications of working with other discontented officials to place conditions on the proposal that will doom it to failure. Or even more generally students may be asked to debate a question such as "do worthy ends ever justify questionable means?" The discussion typically includes extreme statements and sharp disagreements. Rarely are students advised that there is any right or wrong approach.

To complete the categories of common goals in public service programs Van Wart and O'Farrell identify developing "students' practical knowledge, skills, and abilities through class discussions and activities."[48] They report that practical training receives the least attention of the common program goals, and not much evidence is available about how it can be done effectively in an academic setting. The authors found that schools tend to rely on activities such as critiquing leadership models or role play. These kinds of activities may help students think about the various aspects of leadership but they do not generate specific guidance for how to do it. For instance, one syllabus for a course purporting to give practical guidance had the following description: "The art of leadership focuses on the creative and artistic way in which leaders utilize concepts of time, space, and energy in their 'performance' and in such elements of leadership development as concentration, improvisation, aesthetics, expression and communication, discipline and practice."[49] Such ethereal imagery is probably going to dispel any sense students may have had that they understood leadership. It is not as likely to increase their comfort about knowing how to deal with real challenges. Another syllabus informed students that the course will enable them "to critique leadership and other theories and models—what makes sense and would work for them."[50] Engaging in such critique and self-selection could broaden knowledge but it also could be dangerous false comfort if it forms predispositions within a vacuum of experience.

Other scholars also have noted the difficulty of teaching leadership in a university classroom setting. An article analyzing public service teaching approaches noted the reality that "being told about leadership" does not help students "to fully apprehend what is involved in leading."[51] As a best possible substitute the authors of this article proposed "a realistic experiential environment" including simulations and role play. To keep the exercises from seeming too artificial they urged that students should be asked to think through problems together with limitations on time and resources.[52] Putting such constraints on fictional discussions may be a good idea to show students choices need to be made, but the consequences of those choices necessarily are artificial. Classroom role plays and simulations also cannot give someone a sense of what it takes to make difficult decisions that involve a real cost to the decision maker and to those affected by it. Leadership skills are most needed when handling what is uncomfortable and unpleasant. Motivational speeches, prizes and congratulations, and team building exercises are valuable but they are the easy part. What is difficult are such things as an uncomfortable conversation with someone who is not performing, choosing between costly alternatives with real costs, or regaining trust when something has gone wrong. Only by living through such experiences does a leader learn the importance of facing up to the truth, focusing the organization on working together, and building and keeping trust. This is difficult even to describe to students who have not yet had direct personal leadership experience. Effective leadership can only be learned and measured in the context of real human relationships and over the course of time.

Whatever value university programs can provide to their students as an introduction to leadership, even this preparation will not have been afforded most with leadership responsibilities in public service. However, some of the themes that run through university course work can be encountered in professional development workshops. For example, the federal government offers leadership training opportunities including the Office of Personnel Management's courses for executives. Topics include collaborative leadership, supervisory development, leading organizations, and leading change. For example, in a course called *Learning to Lead*, students study different styles of learning and thinking and how a personal style may be modified to work more effectively with others, strategies for overcoming impasse, and concepts of employee motivation and engagement. The Office of Personnel Management also runs a *Leadership Education and Development* (LEAD) program, which offers several certification levels aligned with executive core qualifications. Five courses are required for a certificate, offered at several locations nationally and internationally. The five leadership levels are project or team leader, supervisor, manager, executive, and professional leader. The material focuses on leadership competencies and self-assessments. After completing five courses, participants submit a capstone paper detailing lessons learned and describing at least one example of application back on the job. Other courses emphasize such things as self-improvement, communication, and effective collaboration techniques.

Managers in major federal agencies tend to have access to some kind of leadership development program. A point of focus is concern about managers' ability to motivate and develop their workers. For example, since 1968 the Federal Executive Institute has offered leadership training programs and workshops. A four-week *Leadership for a Democratic Society* program for senior career federal government executives includes study of personal leadership, transforming organizations, policy in a constitutional system, and the global context for executive action. As is common the program includes self-assessments and facilitated peer consultations. The Institute also develops targeted leadership programs for particular agencies, and multi-day programs focusing on individual skill development as well as organizational enhancement. Common study material, such as *The Trusted Leader: Building Relationships*, by Terry Newell, Grant Reeher, and Peter Ronayne,[53] draws on the notion of a leader who acts with integrity, listens to dissent, involves others in decision making, and works to build teams.

Public administrators in state and local government also may have opportunities for continuing education in leadership topics at academic institutions. For example the University of North Carolina offers a 40-hour *Public Executive Leadership Academy* to give city and county managers, their assistants, and key department heads an opportunity to learn more about themselves as leaders and to gain skills to lead and manage change in their communities. In learning teams the participants design a project for regional, community, or organizational change. Participants also work on a personal leadership development plan that incorporates feedback from faculty and colleagues. Throughout the country such programs offer opportunities for officials to exchange experiences with other officials and to undergo self-assessments similar to common elements of a master of public service curriculum.

Although courses and workshops such as these exist for leadership education in public service, no formal training is required or expected for entry into responsible positions or for promotion or continued service. Leaders must therefore mostly learn through experience. Ray Blunt, a public service leadership scholar and consultant, and a graduate of the Air Force Academy, noted that in public service "systematic approaches to developing future leaders are rare."[54] Instead leadership development must predominantly occur through challenging job assignments and learning from others' examples. Blunt added that someone in public service is very fortunate to get to work within an organization with job conditions that allow for training in workshop and operational settings and that have supervisors who set personal examples of effective leadership.[55] Blunt notes that such conditions are "counter to the way that government managers typically develop—within their functional, operational, and geographic 'stovepipes,' and through training programs attended by individuals—'largely serendipitously.'"[56] Blunt also observed that in the best organizations leaders assume personal responsibility for developing other leaders at all levels of the organization.[57] Montgomery Van Wart, author of a leading public service leadership textbook, also noted the importance of in-practice leadership development. He said, "While part of leadership is the result of formal training, it actually may be the smaller component. Experience is likely the more important teacher. In the extreme, this position states that leadership cannot be taught, but it can be learned."[58]

The rarity of systematic leadership development in public service has manifested in infamous failures within government. Consider the example of an independent commission's findings after studying leadership at the Veterans Administration. It concluded that a "lack of a comprehensive approach to leadership development and a complete lack of formalized succession planning results in an inability to identify potential leaders and prepare them to assume their future roles."[59] The Veterans Administration is not alone among public organizations in having a leadership development vacuum. Yet leadership training opportunities are more readily available within federal executive agencies than in the innumerable other government offices at the state and local levels and in public interest organizations.

Public service's hit-and-miss approach to leadership development, compared to the systematic and relentless education, mentoring, and evaluation in the military, is in some ways easily understood. Public service involves a more diverse array of roles, responsibilities, and career paths. But rather than see this as a reason to disregard the military experience it should cause public service policy makers to borrow from the essence of what has proved to be successful within the military. It also should lead to a readiness to embrace the learning and experience that veterans can bring and share within the broader public service community. But as the next section will explain, public service leadership scholars increasingly have instead cabined military leadership, mistakenly viewing it as having nothing worth sharing in other public service contexts.

Public Service Leadership Theories

Public service leadership theory tends to focus on the desirable ends of leadership, particularly in influencing national policy. Academics develop their descriptions of effective leadership based on surveys into perceptions within and across organizations. Some of the most influential scholars can draw on personal leadership experience they had in government, and occasionally someone has had military experience, but they too tend to describe leadership on a large scale rather than in its direct application between individuals. They also tend not to try to articulate any sort of immutable leadership guidelines about *how* someone influences others to accomplish an organizational mission for fear of seeming too rigid or unpalatable to those who stress the relativity of leadership approaches.

This approach is markedly different from the military's concern with providing guidance to leaders who are preparing for command responsibilities. This difference makes sense in some ways. The public service field has a wide variety of leadership situations and organizational cultures. Obviously public administrators cannot draw upon some aspects of the military's repertoire because the organizations in which they function will not have similarly well-defined formal authority or shared immersive training experiences. Understanding that civil service does not afford its leaders opportunities for learning about leadership of the sort that the military provides, public service thought leaders once looked to the military experience for insight, understanding that at its core effective leadership is the same: influencing others to accomplish a mission that puts public service above self-interest.

One way of teaching about leadership that was once common in both the military and other public service fields was studying the examples set by great leaders. Public administration leadership scholar Montgomery Van Wart observes that "the nineteenth century was dominated by the notion of the 'great man' thesis" with which a "core belief is that there are only a few, very rare, individuals in any society at any time with the unique characteristics to shape or express history."[60] For many years now viewing leadership through such a focus has been roundly criticized and discarded among academics. Figures once held up as examples to emulate are studied now as much for their flaws and shortcomings as for their virtues and achievements. Historical accounts of them are criticized for omitting the complex circumstances that led to a figure's notoriety and the essential contributions of others. In the modern view leadership has come to be seen not as the act of an individual's influence but rather as a collaborative group process. While correctly complementing the understanding of leadership dynamics, this deconstructive emphasis that now prevails taints the inspirational value that once was found in the example of rare individuals who led through difficulties. This is especially so for military figures such as Washington and Eisenhower who are associated with an increasingly distant past. Discrediting the notion of individual influence in history and modeling does not apply in all contexts, however; some known for being leaders in bringing about social change, for example, are lionized in modern culture.

The evolution of public service leadership theory also has distanced itself from the core of military teaching that there are identifiable and desirable traits and teachable leadership principles. This has not always been true. Some highly regarded public service leadership scholarship reflected an understanding and appreciation of military leadership learning. John W. Gardner's book *On Leadership*[61] is often mentioned as a classic in public affairs leadership. A former U.S. Marine and secretary of health, education and welfare, he decried the lack of effective leadership in the country and the absence of any meaningful approach to remedying the problem. As he said, "Why do we not have better leadership? The question is asked over and over. We complain, express our disappointment, often our outrage; but no answer emerges."[62] The solution to this problem, he argued, was not just having better leaders at the top; it was having a culture of leadership running throughout society. As he said, "To emphasize the need for dispersed leadership does not deny the need for highly qualified top leadership. But our high-level leaders will be more effective in every way if the systems over which they preside are made vital by dispersed leadership."[63] Public affairs leadership literature generally affirms his emphasis on the necessary trust between leaders and their followers, or as Gardner preferred to call them, constituents. Less often carried forward are the ways in which his writing adapted military leadership to other public service contexts and gave emerging leaders practical guidance based on the tenets that apply to both.

Gardner defined leadership as "the process of persuasion or example by which an individual (or leadership team) induces a group to pursue objectives held by the leader or shared by the leader and his or her followers,"[64] which is reminiscent of the military's definition. In his studies of effective leadership he was truly integrative, considering in the same vein leaders such as Gandhi, Jane Addams, Churchill, Caesar, and Eisenhower. Rather than simply describe leadership, he identified desirable attributes while acknowledging that they are not all present in every leader and the importance of each depends on the situation.[65] His list showed the cross currents of his experience in both the military and in the federal government. He taught that leaders must be trustworthy, courageous, adaptable and flexible, intelligent, able to exercise good judgment-in-action, technically competent, understanding, skilled in dealing with people, and willing to accept responsibility. Gardner also observed that strong leaders are driven by a need to achieve and they follow unbeaten paths to do it. And they must have confidence. He said, "It requires confidence to take the risks that leaders take, and confidence to handle the hostility that leaders must absorb."[66]

Writing more than 25 years ago, Gardner described a trend he saw in public affairs to avoid the hard work of cultivating leadership attributes. As he said, "Today the aspirant to political office is likely to seek out quite early the advice of a professional image maker. If funds are available, there begins an elaborate process of information management and behavior modification designed to place before the voting public something other than the real man or woman who seeks the office."[67] No one can seriously argue that the path to success has turned back toward substance since Gardner wrote these words.

Gardner stressed the importance of leadership development at more than just the highest levels. He advised, "Our thinking about leadership development for the nation must be broadly based and necessarily involve very large numbers. That is not at all what people have in mind when they say they need more and better leaders. But given the dispersed leadership so essential to the vitality of our society, we have no choice."[68] He urged parents, schools, colleges, and off-campus public service to teach leadership and provide opportunities linked to instruction and counseling.[69] He certainly would agree that the modern military—which aims to develop the same attributes that Gardner said comprised leadership in a broader sense—is a leadership training ground that should play a central role in achieving broad and diverse leadership within society. He would not find much evidence that this rich source of knowledge and experience is valued in public service more generally.

Some aspects of Gardner's work still are mentioned in public service leadership texts, especially his insightful characterizations about leaders' inspirational functions.[70] But his value-laden description of desirable attributes that mirrored military leadership experience has faded from the public service literature and from the classroom. A wave of scholars and consultants emerged in the 1970s during the Vietnam counter-culture turbulence symbolized by the corrupt failure of the Nixon Administration. The new breed of leadership theorists, who are now the staples of public service leadership education, had backgrounds and academic preparation that focused on cultural change. Influential author James MacGregor Burns was educated as a political scientist at Harvard and ran for Congress as a liberal Democrat from Massachusetts. After Watergate he wrote an influential book equating leadership with causing change. Robert Greenleaf, another influential author, retired after a career working at AT&T and urged leaders to devote themselves in service of the greater society, which he argued leads to personal spiritual growth. He was influenced by one of the favorite novelists of the 1960s counter-culture, Herman Hesse, in particular *Journey to the East*, which portrayed a spiritual quest.[71] Authors of the most commonly used public service leadership textbooks, Montgomery Van Wart and Peter Northouse, are post–Vietnam academics. None of these public service thought leaders since Gardner, as intelligent and well-spoken as they may be, had any military experience and they showed that they had a jaundiced view of how it affected people. In their work they made clear that they see the approach to leadership in their field of public service as necessarily something fundamentally different from what they see as the historic error of drawing from military experience.

One of the most influential writers in modern public service leadership theory is Douglas McGregor, a social psychologist trained at Harvard. He became highly influential through his work published in 1960 on what has become known as "Theory X and Theory Y." McGregor argued that leaders must understand what they believed about others and the assumptions they make about others' motivation. Someone who ascribes to "Theory X," McGregor said, is authoritarian and focuses on performance, and sees humans as tending to want to avoid work. Someone who ascribes to "Theory Y," he said, focuses on social needs as catalytic motivators and organizes conditions to address needs for self-esteem, self-fulfillment, and fellowship.[72] McGregor advised using this perspective for self-awareness and being better able to relate to others. He rejected what he said was a failed tendency within American management to think in Theory X terms, which he largely blamed on the military. He said, "The conventional principles were derived primarily from the study of models (the military and the Catholic Church) which differ in important respects from modern industrial organizations.... [I]f there are universal principles common to all forms of organization, it is now apparent that they are not the ones derived by classical theorists from the Church and the military."[73] McGregor thereby not only urged a quarantine of the study of "military models" that he assumed to be wrongheaded "conventional principles," but also equated them to an orthodox religious belief system rather than see them as a proven, experience-based, nuanced, and continually evolving approach.

The binary perspective for which McGregor's Theory X and Theory Y has become known has become embedded in the curriculum. A more explicit and sweeping departure from ideas associated with the military took hold in the 1970s, a principal proponent of which was James Macgregor Burns, in particular for the formulations in his 1978 book *Leadership*.[74] According to Burns, experience and study about leadership had so far left it one of the "least understood phenomena on earth."[75] He urged that leaders should be judged "by actual social change measured by intent and by the satisfaction of human needs and expectations."[76] Reflecting the popular call for social change in the era and the discrediting of conventional approaches, Burns characterized leadership as either "transactional" or "transformational." Leaders, he said, are "moral agents" who should "shape and alter and elevate the motives and values and goals of followers."[77] This is what he called "transformational leadership." According to Burns leaders should strive to unite others in collective pursuit of higher social goals. They should look beyond trying to cause others to act in any particular instance with promises of rewards, which he called "transactional leadership," because, consistent with McGregor's view of human motivation, it falls short in addressing the true needs of individuals as part of a society.

Along with urging a refocus of leadership studies on what are deemed to be higher social goals, public service in principle discarded the leadership attributes approach developed in the military and incorporated into Gardner's writing. Public service scholarship portrayed efforts to define leadership traits as fruitless because a short list of desirable traits cannot be applied across all situations and therefore, the argument goes, it becomes useless. As Van Wart wrote, "Without situational specificity, the endless list of traits offers little prescriptive assistance and descriptively becomes little more than a laundry list."[78]

As Van Wart wrote in his summary of the evolution of public service leadership theory, after conventional wisdom was rejected, "The next major thrust was to look at the situational contexts that affect leaders in order to find meaningful patterns for theory building and useful advice."[79] In this effort behaviorists proposed "an antidote to the excessively hierarchical, authoritarian styles,"[80] with a dismissive tone that gives a taste of the inclination to see military leadership as in a category of its own and otherwise irrelevant. Peter Northouse's textbook on *Leadership* described the "skills approach" of identifying desirable attributes and competencies as "intuitively appealing" because "when leadership is framed as a set of skills, it becomes a process that people can study and practice to become better at performing their jobs."[81] He criticized the approach when used in public service because, he said, it involves so many components that it "becomes more general and less precise in explaining leadership perform-ance."[82] He noted that the skills approach "was constructed by using a large sample of military personnel and observing their performance in the armed services."[83] He put distance between the military and other public service as he sees them when he warned, "Although some research suggests that these Army findings can be generalized to other groups, more research is needed" to determine whether this is so.[84] In such a way students looking to lead in public service are being told that they should put aside teaching developed through the most extensive and tested envi-ronment, and with which many leaders have been trained, until there is "more research."

These characterizations pay no heed to the military's experience find-ing that there are fundamentals that have proved to be associated with effective leadership in widely varying circumstances. It also dismisses guideposts to which developing leaders have turned time and time again in making hard decisions in leadership situations. Consider, for example, the notion of integrity, which has been a centerpiece of military leadership training and leader accountability. Studies consistently show the preem-inence of a leader's example to the ethical behavior of others within the organization.[85] The need for personal legitimacy has been central to all public service teaching, including by those who call for transformational leadership. Someone who is perceived as duplicitous and unreliable will be unable to inspire others to follow direction in difficult circumstances. The same is true for other leadership traits that have always been empha-sized in the military. For example, courage is an essential characteristic for any leader who is attempting to lead others through challenges. Anyone who has had leadership responsibility knows of the importance of such attributes, the importance of which is not diminished by the possibility that others can think of a different way of putting it or of other desirable attributes.

Research done in public administration confirms that attributes stressed in the military but usually unmentioned in public service lead-ership teaching—including personal integrity, courage, dependability, and decisiveness—are associated with admired leaders. In their multi-million copy selling book *The Leadership Challenge*,[86] which is commonly assigned in public affairs leadership education, James Kouzes and Barry Posner describe an investigation they made of thousands of business and government executives about the values, traits, and characteristics most valued in leaders. Respondents were asked what they sought in someone they were willing to follow. Integrity, or honesty, was the most commonly noted characteristic of an admired leader, and dependability and courage are also high on the list.[87]

Despite most scholars' rejection of the so-called trait or skills approach to leadership, the compelling need for some such guidance for decision making and personal development has not always been fully resisted. In his current textbook Van Wart did not purport to look to the military for any guidance but he acknowledged that there are "leader characteristics that are particularly susceptible to refinement."[88] He identified several categories of desirable abilities: communication skills, social skills, influence skills, analytic skills, technical skills, and a proclivity for continual learning.[89] He stressed that a leader must be skilled at communications and consider the importance of clarity. He departed from the military's emphasis on being direct, however, when he advised competency in strategic approaches in one-to-one communication, such as "learning to 'pace' your communication partner" by trying "to appreciate his/her style in the communication process."[90] He also recommended developing social skills as "a major pillar of the leader's skill set," which, he said, when strategically aimed can lead to "personal power."[91] For "influence skills," he suggested several "strategies": "legitimating tactics" that emphasize conformity with policies, "pressure tactics" that demand, "exchange tactics" that involve trading favors, "rational persuasion" that relies on facts and logic, "consultation" that involves a "target" in developing a plan, "emotional appeals" based on rousing others based on shared values, "personal appeals" based on loyalty, friendship, or compassion, and "friendliness," which is "the use of affable behavior or praise, or the provision of unrequested assistance, in order to increase responsiveness to future requests and orders."[92] Being supplied with this cache of influence methods could be understood by students as encouraging insincerity and manipulation to influence others, an approach that military leadership training would characterize as toxic. Some of the other useful characteristics on Van Wart's short list are more reflective of desirable attributes emphasized in the military, such as analytical skills that enable leaders to draw on their memories, distinguish among options, deal with cognitive complexity, and tolerate ambiguity, and technical skills to understand the work and earn the respect of those doing it.[93]

Within public service leadership education such occasional mention of leadership attributes is easily lost in the heavy emphasis on broader social goals. One theme that has received considerable attention is the notion of what has been called "servant leadership." According to Robert Greenleaf, who is the author commonly cited as the spokesperson for this theory, leadership "begins with the natural feeling that one wants to serve, to serve first. Then conscious choice brings one to aspire to lead. That person is sharply different from one who is leader first.... The difference manifests itself in the care taken by the servant-first to make sure that other people's highest priority needs are being served."[94] Servant leadership theory therefore does not reflect an emphasis on service in the sense employed in the military and as symbolized in the oath that unifies the military and other public service. Nor does it echo the military's emphasis on mission accomplishment. Rather it "focuses on the behaviors leaders should exhibit to put followers first and to support followers' personal development. It is concerned with how leaders treat subordinates and the outcomes that are likely to emerge."[95]

The concern for others that underlies servant leadership is a necessary aspect of any effective leadership in public service. In a sense it also reflects the truth that a leader's ability to inspire others depends on demonstrating sincere commitment above personal gain. Servant leadership goes further to urge an orientation that leaders should use their influence for some greater good as determined by the followers. As a leading textbook describes it, "the long-term outcomes of putting others first include positive social change and helping society flourish."[96] In this way the approach becomes essentially a call to social service, as demonstrated by the type of questionnaire that is typically used in servant leadership orientation to give feedback to a leader within an organization. It asks about such basic leadership matters as an understanding of the organization and its goals, concern for developing subordinates, honest and ethical behavior, and knowledge about whether something is wrong at work. But many other questions aim to assess an orientation toward accommodating others' personal interests—talking to them on a personal level, knowing of their personal problems, and caring more about their personal success than the respondent's own success. Other questions seem to raise social goals above organizational mission, such as asking about the extent to which the respondent is involved in community service or understands the importance of "giving back to the community."[97] The feedback received from this assessment reinforces certain behaviors deemed socially valuable. It also shifts the focus away from leadership aimed at accomplishing a mission as the organization may define it.

Public service benefits from teaching that encourages community service and commitment to improved social conditions. It also benefits from a reminder that effective leadership requires caring about the welfare and development of those who are led. But something else is needed in leadership education to prepare someone to lead others effectively in performance of organizational responsibilities. Leaders must sometimes make decisions and give direction that has nothing to do with desirable social change. They also must sometimes make decisions that do not suit the personal preferences of others in the organization, such as the ultimate decision to discipline or dismiss an individual.

Other than feeling the weight of emphasis on caring about others and promoting change, students of today's public service leadership theory have difficulty taking away any clear messages or guidance about how to be an effective leader. Some who explicitly note confusion within the field may go so far as to present yet another theme of their own. For example, Martin Chemers, a social psychologist and author of *An Integrative Theory of Leadership*,[98] acknowledges that "a common criticism of contemporary leadership research and theory, both from within the leadership area and from other organizational theorists, has been that the literature is fragmented and contradictory. A lack of both coherence across theoretical approaches and reliable empirical findings is said to characterize the field of leadership studies."[99] After surveying the field, his analysis results in a conclusion that effective leaders must do three things: "project an image of competence and trustworthiness," "establish a relationship with followers that guides, develops, and inspires them to make meaningful contributions to group goals and the organizational mission," and "mobilize and deploy the collective resources of self and team to the organizational mission."[100] Rather than break new ground, this rephrases how the military has always framed leadership, though the military gets no mention. Chemers' book lists several hundred works with theories and empirical findings, but does not make a single reference to a military leadership publication. He looks back only as far as theorists writing after the 1960s, and describes the era before then as suffering from "the sparse yield of the trait and behavioral approaches."[101] This aptly illustrates how a student of today's public service leadership theory would not know the military had anything relevant to say on the topic. And a military veteran would be made to feel no better off in leadership learning for having served.

Learning Leadership Across the Gap

Academics achieve success in their fields by being distinctive. To get their credentials they must produce a lengthy dissertation that makes an "original contribution to scholarship." For notoriety they must publish and speak about findings that upset conventional ways of thinking. There is little prestige in academics for speaking an old truth. Unsurprisingly since the 1970s public service scholars, coming to age in an environment in which the dominant view protested the military's influence in society, have written and taught about leadership in a way that belies the idea that military experience is transferrable to other fields of public service.

Meanwhile in their segregated sphere the military has continued to refine its approach to defining and developing effective leadership. The refinements incorporate new learning about human behavior, the changing nature of service in an increasingly global and technologically oriented world, and the diverse responsibilities with which military leaders are now charged by civilian leaders. Much of this evolution mirrors change in public service. In fact in important ways roles are intertwining or even crossing over; military leaders are increasingly involved in such traditionally civil functions as emergency relief and local government administration, and civil administrators must prepare for terrorist attacks, combat gang warfare, and respond to failures in vital infrastructure.

Change requires refinement but not necessarily abandonment. The military must understand this as it seeks to incorporate its centuries of experience from which proven principles have emerged as guideposts for difficult decision making and personal development in today's world. Experience, old and recent, should similarly be incorporated into the education of public service leaders. But based on what most public administrators are likely to see, which rarely involves exposure to the military's approaches, they have little reason to believe that they too can benefit from this learning. Veterans of the military, many of whom have applied the approach in diverse circumstances, are likely to be told that they should leave their learning and experience at the base gate. Instead they will be immersed in a prevailing view that military leadership is alien to other public organizations and there is nothing to learn from it. As a consequence, in practice everyone is left with no real reference point for making hard leadership decisions or dealing with difficult leadership situations. In its place they are told in various ways about the need for self-reflection and the importance of supportive relationships and promoting social change. While there is value in these lessons, they do not equip leaders for making decisions to influence real people to accomplish the organizational mission.

Those who are entering public service without a military background should not be assumed to be unwelcoming of any rich source of leadership guidance. If given the opportunity to consider the reality of military leadership principles and experience they can see their value. The author witnessed a resounding example of this with an elective course he taught in a master of public service program: *Military Leadership and Public Administration*. The topics included a study of leadership as taught and demonstrated in the services and how it translates to leadership in the government and non-profit sectors, and issues concerning the transition of military leaders to civilian management and leadership roles. Some of the students were experienced active duty military officers, others had no military exposure. Reading assignments included background on the realities of military service, branch military doctrine, public service leadership theory, and case studies involving mayors in crisis situations and local government leaders dealing with competing demands for attention and resources. Guest speakers included commanders from ROTC units who spoke about leadership development. All of the students embraced the material and noted its unfortunate absence from the core public service curriculum. In an anonymous course evaluation one student commented on both the value of the material and its relevance: "The readings, case studies, and guest speakers were all very helpful in understanding military leadership and how it relates to public administration. Thanks to the course, I came to understand that military leadership is a distinct kind of leadership, but one that lends itself well to public administration problems." Another summarized what is missing from the usual program: "I went into this class with a very narrow view of how the military operated, and I feel as though I'm leaving with knowledge everybody else in our program should have. The military is barely (if ever) mentioned in other classes even though it is such an enormous piece of the public sector. Not only do government agencies interact with the military, those of us going out into the world will very likely be working with veterans at some point. After taking this class, I feel much more equipped to work alongside those who have served in the military."

Public administrators should resist joining the chorus of discrediting the application of military principles. They should realize that this wealth of knowledge and experience has mistakenly been ignored, and that if they want to learn about it they will need to do it on their own. They should also realize that there are many veterans looking to serve in government and communities with knowledge and experience and a well-developed and nuanced approach to leadership. Veterans have much to share including invaluable insights about how to lead that are especially timely and relevant to a field that depends on the same core commitment to service.

CHAPTER 3

Leadership Under Fire

Military leaders prepare for the worst. They train in exercises intended to test what they can be expected to do when their units are attacked, suffer casualties, and lose communications. Some in public service have primary duties that involve preparation for war-like conditions. Emergency management, a well-developed field informed by experience and research, involves learning how to anticipate and respond to dangerous situations. Other civil leaders, who are not emergency managers by profession, also may find themselves in charge during a crisis situation. If they do, their leadership abilities will be severely tested.

Some civil leaders know to expect certain kinds of emergencies on their watch. This is especially true in regions that are vulnerable to disastrous conditions caused by hurricanes, tornadoes, earthquakes, or wildfires. But as the old Yiddish proverb goes, "We plan, God laughs"; even if we expect we might experience an emergency, and plan for what can reasonably be foreseen, we can never fully anticipate the nature and scope of what will happen. Leaders in regions that do not expect natural disasters also may find themselves in situations that threaten the community. We see reminders of this reality in the fortification of public buildings since the truck bomb attack in Oklahoma City in 1995. More recent events have thrust civil leaders into situations involving destruction and dangers of unprecedented proportion. The mayors of New York and New Orleans knew their cities were vulnerable to emergencies, and they had management teams working on contingency plans. But neither the mayors nor anyone else reasonably could have anticipated the havoc that 9/11 and Hurricane Katrina would cause.

We might be tempted to say that effective leadership in any crisis is an innate characteristic that cannot be learned. Certainly some people perform better under stress than others, in public leadership as in war.

But no one in public service can afford to dismiss crisis leadership as something purely magical. Those who would have to lead in a crisis should be as ready as possible in case such a situation arises. One way of preparing, which has always been part of military training, is to study how others have acted during crisis situations and consider what seems to have made them more or less effective. Three individuals and the deadly situations in which they found themselves provide fertile ground for such study, one of whom was a professor in military command and the other two civil leaders with no military training.

Joshua Chamberlain was in command at Little Round Top at Gettysburg as the Confederate Army aimed its assault at his unit to turn the tide of the critical battle. Rudy Giuliani was mayor of New York City when terrorists flew planes into the World Trade Center on 9/11. Ray Nagin was mayor of New Orleans when the city was raked by high winds and rain from Hurricane Katrina and tens of thousands of residents were stranded as much of the city was submerged in flood waters. While each of these men faced unique circumstances, in important ways they faced similar leadership challenges, and reflection on their decisions and actions can give valuable lessons. Understanding the leadership they exercised in crisis requires considering their backgrounds and demonstrated attributes before they were called upon to lead under fire.

Lieutenant Colonel Joshua L. Chamberlain and Gettysburg[1]

Military leaders who have not yet tasted battle logically wonder how they will hold up if they come under fire. They know battlefield simulations alone do not prepare someone for the confusion and horrors of actual battle. Certainly Joshua Chamberlain could not have expected what he would do when his unit faced annihilation at Gettysburg.

While growing up in Maine Chamberlain studied Latin and Greek and learned to love classics like Homer and Thucydides. He pursued his intellectual interests at Bowdoin College, in Brunswick, from which two of the country's greatest writers had graduated—Nathaniel Hawthorne and Henry Wadsworth Longfellow. He was said to be a shy speaker, which was related to a speech impediment that caused him to stammer when using certain consonants. He nearly fainted when he gave an oration at commencement. After graduating from Bowdoin he went to the Bangor Theological Seminary. Instead of pursuing a life in the ministry for which he had prepared, he returned to Bowdoin as an instructor in logic and natural theology, and also tutored freshmen in Greek.

A few years after Chamberlain joined the Bowdoin faculty the Civil War began. He watched as students left to join the Union Army to fight against the army of the seceding southern states. Many students in Brunswick joined the service during the war. Many of Chamberlain's fellow teachers saw this as a waste of youth, and they did not support faculty interest in joining the units being formed in Maine. Chamberlain strongly believed in national union and was drawn to military service when he heard of the Union Army's defeat at the First Bull Run and of President Lincoln's call for volunteers.

Chamberlain volunteered for service and the state's governor appointed him a lieutenant colonel in the 20th Maine Infantry Regiment, to be second-in-command of a unit that had nearly 1,000 volunteers. He served in the same unit with his youngest brother, Tom. Joshua Chamberlain was then 34 years old, older than the regimental commander, Adelbert Ames, a 26-year-old West Point graduate and regular army officer. But Ames was battle hardened. He received the Medal of Honor for his actions at Bull Run for continuing to man artillery guns despite his unit being overrun. Most of those recruited into the newly formed unit had as little military experience as Chamberlain when they marched south toward the fighting. While at camp along the way the newly commissioned Chamberlain studied manuals on infantry tactics. He underlined and made marginal notes in a textbook written by a French engineer officer, Nicolas Edouard Delabarre-Duparcq, about the moral effects on soldiers of quickly switching from a defensive to offensive posture in battle. This knowledge would be important when at Gettysburg Chamberlain's unit seemed about to be overwhelmed by advancing Confederate troops.

At Fredericksburg Chamberlain had his first experience commanding under direct fire. His unit was in position near the Rappahannok River where Union troops were unsuccessfully advancing on Marye's Heights. When Chamberlain's regiment was ordered to advance under fire and take down a high board fence, the men hesitated. It was their first battle. Chamberlain led the way forward through gun fire, asking his men "Do you want me to do it?" They followed his example and rushed forward to clear the way. Chamberlain's men continued to advance toward the high ground, past four fallen lines of prior attackers, but night fell as they reached the enemy and exchanged fire. They spent the night on a bloody battlefield, listening to moans and calls for help, with Chamberlain himself sleeping next to two corpses for warmth and protection. The Maine soldiers held their positions the next day as the Union army regrouped from its unsuccessful assaults. They had gained valuable experience for what was to come. Ames and Chamberlain were both recognized for their bravery under fire. Later reflecting on his actions, Chamberlain said: "An officer is so absorbed by the sense of responsibility for his men, for his cause, or for the fight that the thought of personal peril has no place whatever in governing his actions. The instinct to seek safety is overcome by the instinct of honor."[2] The next June Chamberlain was promoted to colonel and given command of the regiment, after Ames was promoted and sent to a larger, brigade command.

Within days Chamberlain's unit would take the brunt of the Confederate Army's effort to bring the North to terms in the Civil War. General Robert E. Lee's Army of Northern Virginia invaded the north through Pennsylvania, threating Washington, D.C., from the west. Chamberlain's 20th Maine was part of the large Union army concentrated at Gettysburg in early July 1863. His youngest brother Tom was with him as a unit commander in the regiment. Another younger brother, John, a physician, had come to visit his brothers and stayed at the battlefield to treat the wounded in a field hospital.

At Gettysburg the regiment had 358 enlisted soldiers and 28 officers, mostly experienced. More than a hundred had joined from another regiment, the 2nd Maine Volunteers. These men were being held under guard as mutineers. They had refused to continue service when they were not allowed to return to Maine with their unit. They refused because they had been tricked into a long term of three years unlike the other members of the unit. Chamberlain was ordered to make them do their duty or shoot them. He had a difficult choice weighing how to treat rebellious soldiers but needing all the men he could get for the looming fight. He heard about the recruitment trick and poor treatment of the men—they had been imprisoned with no food and no one was interested in hearing their complaints. Chamberlain ordered that these men be fed and given proper clothing. He went to his commander and asked if he could handle the matter however he saw fit, and this discretion was granted. Rather than imprison or threaten the men, he told them he could not afford to guard them or treat them as "civilian guests." He said if they joined the fight he would treat them as soldiers, not prisoners. He promised that they would lose no rights by fighting and he "would see what could be done for their claim," which he did by writing in their behalf.[3] All but one or two of the men joined the regiment—in which they were dispersed to keep them apart— and they fought gallantly.

Chamberlain's forces knew a major engagement was likely. They had seen Lee's screening cavalry as they were marching north. While in a bivouac for the night the 20th Maine heard that the Confederate troops had struck the Union column at Gettysburg and driven it back. Chamberlain was ordered to form and march his regiment the remaining 16 miles to Gettysburg through the night. They reached Gettysburg in the morning, having had the chance for only an hour's sleep at the roadside. When they arrived the situation was very confusing. Chamberlain later reflected, "We were aware that other troops were coming up, on one side and the other; but we had no means of knowing or judging which side would take the offensive and which the defensive, or where the battle would begin."[4]

Soon Chamberlain's unit was directed toward a hill that was about 500 feet high, two miles away to the south, known as Little Round Top. It, together with a higher hill to the south, Great Round Top, gave a dominant view of the battlefield. The high ground was prized not only for its observational advantages but also for the superiority that could be gained for cannon fire from higher terrain. A road to the east, Baltimore Pike, led to Washington and the threatened capitol. Chamberlain was told to move his regiment into a defensive position on Little Round Top. He heard cannon fire in that direction and was ordered to head straight there, but due to battlefield conditions he instead led his unit first to the west of the hills, along a road. The regiment could see furious fighting in open areas nearby. Concerned that the Confederate troops were approaching and would seize the high ground, Chamberlain was ordered to rush the regiment to Little Round Top, and they ran there, where they encountered artillery fire and saw a large force headed for the base of the hills.

Little Round Top is a rocky hill with boulders. Even the smooth areas have rock fragments. As the regiment was mounting the hill they were under intensifying artillery fire. Chamberlain was with his two brothers and told them: "Boys, I don't like this. Another shot might make it hard for mother."[5] He had his brothers split up to lessen the chance they would all be killed with one shot. As the regiment was moving toward its defensive position, Chamberlain's brigade commander ordered: "I place you here! This is the left of the Union line. You understand. You are to hold this ground at all costs!"[6]

Chamberlain had everyone but the drummer boys and hospital attendants join the line of defense. He gave the deployment order "right by file into line," which enabled the men on the right, nearest the expected enemy assault, to be the first settled in position and able to load and fire. The line looked to the southwest toward Great Round Top. To the northwest the men could see the Confederate troops advancing and causing havoc. Chamberlain ordered his men to find the best cover possible behind rocks or trees.

The most difficult aspect of preparing for the assault was having enough men to hold the line while being prepared for the likelihood that the advancing Confederate troops would try to sweep around the end. Chamberlain ordered 40 men, commanded by an experienced veteran, Captain Morrill, to assume a detached position on the flank and be ready to respond if the attackers tried to go around. Chamberlain also sent out skirmishers beyond the lines who were experienced marksmen and could slow the advance. Chamberlain could tell that the Confederate troops were approaching when incoming artillery stopped. Mounting a rock he could see that the attackers were heading to try to turn the entire Union defensive line on his regiment's flank. He called his officers together and told them to keep up the fire at the front and to have every other man take side steps to the left. A flag was placed at the extreme left, and the men maneuvered in a way that doubled the width of the regiment's front. Chamberlain also put the troops in an obtuse angle, the left facing more toward the flank.

As Chamberlain said, when advancing Alabama troops met the Maine defenders, "The two lines met and broke and mingled in the shock. The crush of musketry gave way to cuts and thrusts, grapplings and wrestlings."[7] The fierce fighting continued with wave after wave of attackers, all repelled with heavy casualties on both sides. The Maine soldiers realized how dire the situation was but they also knew they had no choice but to continue to fight. Chamberlain noticed many instances of gallantry, such as when he saw a young soldier had returned who had been sent to the field hospital with a severe head wound. Chamberlain also saw his commander, Vincent, severely wounded at another part of the army's line. Vincent later died from his wounds.

Attacks on Chamberlain's position continued for three hours as the Union line grew thin. His troops were greatly outnumbered. Chamberlain noticed the fire from the line slackening and could see the soldiers' desperate expressions as they fired the last of their ammunition. When a lieutenant asked Chamberlain if he could move forward of the line and retrieve two wounded men from the field, Chamberlain decided that the best option was to use bayonets and charge ahead with hand-to-hand combat, rather than to wait in a defensive position for another assault. He had been wounded, his foot cut either from a shell fragment or a sharp rock, making it difficult for him to move up and down the hill. Nevertheless

Chamberlain walked calmly up and down the line, giving words of encouragement or caution.

As the exhausted soldiers ran out of ammunition Chamberlain stepped forward and shouted "bayonets"—an order to prepare to charge. The men understood their desperate situation as they moved forward, the line swinging into a sickle shape in a maneuver known as a "great right wheel." As the left of the line swung forward down the rocky hill using the force of gravity, the Confederate troops stopped their advance, and Morrill's detached company and the sharpshooters encountered the flanks of a retreating Confederate line. This caused the Confederate troops to bunch toward the center where there was fierce hand-to-hand fighting. Chamberlain himself met with a Confederate officer who fired a revolver almost in Chamberlain's face and then surrendered as Chamberlain put his saber to the man's throat. Other Confederate troops and commanders surrendered as the regiment continued downhill. The attack went on until the 20th Maine lined up with New York troops on its right, and the attack on Little Round Top had been repulsed. The Confederate troops soon began a retreat back to Virginia.

The 20th Maine suffered 125 men killed or wounded. The units that attacked his men lost 231. Chamberlain and his regiment were heralded for their steadfastness and the decisive stroke of the swinging charge. The commander of the 44th New York Regiment, Colonel James C. Rice, who fought alongside at Gettysburg, told Chamberlain "your gallantry was magnificent, and your coolness and skill saved us."[8]

Chamberlain went on to lead units in other important Civil War battles. He was wounded six times, twice almost fatally, and had five horses shot from under him. He commanded a brigade in assaulting Confederate trenches in Petersburg, for which Commanding General of the Army Ulysses Grant promoted him on the battlefield to brigadier general. Chamberlain continued a life of leadership after the war as president of Bowdoin College, governor of Maine, and a railroad executive.

Mayor Rudolph Giuliani and the World Trade Center Attacks[9]

Rudolph Giuliani was the youngest of five children. His parents were Italian immigrants. His father was a tailor and his mother a seamstress. He was surrounded by family members who were in law enforcement; four uncles and four cousins were police officers. He majored in political philosophy as a student at Manhattan College in the Bronx, commuting from his parent's house in an Italian-American section of Harlem. He became president of a fraternity and built its membership. After college he went to New York University Law School. He was interested in law enforcement, inspired by the example of Bobby Kennedy. As chief counsel of a Senate committee Kennedy publicly challenged corrupt union leadership, and as attorney general he was notorious for prosecution of powerful organized crime figures. After law school Giuliani clerked for the chief judge of the federal Southern District of New York, and then joined the U.S. Attorney's office as a federal prosecutor.

During five years as an assistant U.S. Attorney, Giuliani quickly advanced, rising to become the third highest ranking attorney in the office, heading units that prosecuted narcotics and corruption cases. He was involved in the investigation of corruption in the police department's internal investigating unit. The cases became the subject of books and movies. Giuliani also drew attention for his corruption prosecution of Congressman Bertram Podell, who was charged with receiving payments in exchange for obtaining a route for an airline. Podell claimed he received the payments for legitimate legal work. During cross-examination Giuliani handed Podell a reference book with listings of law firms. He asked Podell to point out the firm to which payments were made. No such firm was listed, which Podell had to concede, after which he pleaded guilty.

Giuliani later served in the criminal division of the U.S. Justice Department and with a private law firm. He then became the U.S. Attorney in New York City, an office with more than 100 attorneys. He focused on prosecution of organized crime leaders, and became known for doing extensive damage to the network. Giuliani also prosecuted high-level corruption within New York City government.

In 1989 Giuliani campaigned for mayor of New York City but was defeated by the Democrat David Dinkins, and he went into a private law firm practice. He ran again four years later and defied a long history of Democratic mayors when he defeated incumbent Mayor Dinkins. Giuliani thus became executive of one of the largest cities in the world, a financial center and home to diverse cultures and communities. The city employs 325,000, the most of any municipality in the country.

As mayor, Giuliani took immediate steps to implement his policy of controlling crime and making the city more livable. He pushed for hiring additional police officers and insulated the police, fire, and sanitation departments from budget cuts he otherwise urged to address city-wide deficits. Giuliani implemented what he described as the "broken windows" theory of addressing crime and decay. City services were directed to address such things as broken windows and graffiti, which according to this theory will reinvigorate communities and stem a tide of neglect and neighborhood deterioration. He also directed police to address "squeegee operators" who harassed commuters and visitors by wiping car windows with dirty rags and demanding payment for the "cleaning." If they were not paid they would sometimes kick the car door or do obscene things. When Giuliani's legal advisors told him that the "service" was not a crime for which someone could be arrested, he directed that the offenders be arrested instead for jaywalking. The nuisance was greatly curtailed, which was a conspicuous change in the public's perception of conditions on the street.[10]

Another aspect of Giuliani's efforts to make the city more hospitable was his vocal endorsement of anti-porn zoning legislation for Times Square. The change was associated with a renaissance of the area during Giuliani's administration. Giuliani also became known, and criticized, for aggressive efforts to remove individuals from the welfare rolls, speaking often about the need to respect even menial labor rather than seek public assistance.

New York City's management is a huge task and involves many departments, not all of which historically have worked well together. Giuliani sought to improve coordination by requiring leaders to attend regular meetings together. He wanted them talking with and listening to each other, which he believed also would make them more accountable. Giuliani was proud of holding meetings at which hard questions would be asked and responsive answers were expected. He said, "In any large organization, meetings are often derided as roadblocks to progress, set up by bureaucrats who would rather talk than act. In fact, my morning meetings have been extremely helpful to the reform agenda I set out to accomplish."[11] He also valued the benefit of having officials in the same room together because "socializing and simple daily contact helped prevent resentments from festering."[12]

While some saw in Giuliani an executive who could get things done, others saw an unfriendly, often combative side of the man. Carol Bellamy, former director of the Peace Corps who was a law school classmate of his, said, "I thought he picked many too many fights. There's a difference between being strong and fighting all the time. It seemed that if you could pick a fight or not pick a fight, he picked a fight."[13] Others described Giuliani as always craving being the center of attention. When police commissioner Bill Bratton resigned, Giuliani was accused by some of instigating the departure because Bratton received too much attention at Giuliani's expense. Fred Siegel, a campaign advisor to Giuliani, described this confrontation as "the biggest mistake of the Giuliani years. The problem was that they're the same person. Bratton is remarkably like Giuliani—quick mind, tough, fearless."[14] Herman Badillo, an influential New York attorney who had been a deputy mayor, described Giuliani this way: "He's a prosecutor by temperament and prosecutors tend to do outrageous things."[15]

One of Giuliani's projects that received much attention was building a $13 million emergency command center. It was located on the 23rd floor at 7 World Trade Center, part of the World Trade Center complex, connected by elevator walkway to the Twin Towers. Among the factors that led to selection of this site were that the building had security, it was close to the mayor's office, and it was near law enforcement agency offices. The command center had up-to-date computers, specialized display screens, sleeping accommodations, water and food, and antidotes in the case of a biological attack. It was to be in operation during hurricanes, snowstorms, and terrorist attacks. To focus attention the center had photos on a wall known as the "Hall of Horribles." They were of simulated emergency exercises, including a realistic-looking plane crash in Queens. One reason why Giuliani wanted a state-of-the-art emergency operations center was that he fully expected terrorists would attack the city. Several months before his election as mayor, terrorists detonated a large truck bomb below the North Tower of the World Trade Center, intending for it to crash into the South Tower. Six people were killed and more than a thousand injured. Six men were convicted in connection with the bomb. Despite fully expecting another serious attack, Giuliani later reflected, "We did not anticipate that airliners would be commandeered and turned into guided missiles; but the fact that we practiced for other kinds of disasters made us far more prepared to handle a catastrophe that nobody envisioned."[16]

On the morning of September 11, 2001, Mayor Giuliani was finishing breakfast with his counsel and a friend at a Midtown Manhattan hotel, when a member of his security detail told him a plane had hit the World Trade Center. Giuliani understood it to be a twin-engine plane civil aviation accident. He headed to the site because, as he said, "I made it my policy to see with my own eyes the scene of every crisis so I could evaluate it firsthand."[17] This was a practice he had learned when he was a prosecutor, from a detective as a way to appraise whether testimony seemed plausible based on physical circumstances. On his way to the crash site he was unable to reach the governor or the president's office because cell phone communications had been knocked out. He saw doctors and nurses in the street and realized there must be many injuries. When he noticed an explosion he assumed it was related to the already reported plane crash. It turned out to be a second plane, this one hitting the South Tower. When Giuliani saw a big flash of fire as he was heading toward Manhattan's southern tip, he realized it must have been a terrorist attack. Giuliani insisted on viewing the scene and getting a frank assessment from the fire commander.

As any mayor would realize, coordination with responder commanders is essential in a crisis. They must make difficult decisions about deployment of their rescuers and assets. Because New York City's emergency center was in the devastated area it was evacuated and unusable for command and control. Giuliani established two priorities from the start: setting up a working command center somewhere else, now that it was obvious the facility he had established was useless, and communicating with the people of the city about what was happening.

Giuliani met the police commissioner, Bernie Kerik, at the edge of the World Trade Center complex. As he was doing this he saw a man jump from the 102nd floor, and soon saw others leaping who preferred death over the flames and heat in the building caused by the jet fuel. Giuliani told Commissioner Kerik, "We're in uncharted waters now. We're going to have to make up our response."[18] Firefighters were heading up the stairs of the tower with heavy equipment to control the spread of the fire and rescue those below it. The fire department chief told Giuliani that people above the fire could not be rescued because firefighters could not get through from below and helicopter rescues were impossible. Fire Chief Peter Ganci, the highest ranking uniformed fire officer and a war veteran, advised moving people north away from the fire. Giuliani himself headed north a block away to where the police department had set up its temporary command center. Fire Chief Ganci was among those later killed in the building collapse.

Although Giuliani had been able to get information from the fire and police commanders, he knew of the importance of coordination for more than the response to the fires in the towers. He had to decide whether to establish one command post somewhere, or let the fire and police commands operate independently. He decided on two command posts. As he explained his decision, "The reason for this is that the departments were going to perform different tasks and had different requirements. The Fire Department had to lead the rescue and evacuation. The Police Department had to protect the rest of the city."[19] He said if the police had joined the fire department post "it would have been impossible for them to access the hardlines and necessary communications for the defense of the city."[20]

City officials commandeered a small office building to establish a temporary executive command, where deputy mayors and commissioners gathered. They used landline phones to contact the White House. Giuliani learned that the military was dispatched to protect New York City airspace from further attacks. He also learned from presidential staff that the country was being hit by a coordinated terrorist attack, including on the Pentagon, and the president was being kept in a protected location. The president's seclusion effectively made Giuliani the most visible public leader during much of the tumultuous day.

While in the office building with his staff Giuliani heard loud crashes and was told "the tower" was coming down. He thought this meant the radio tower on top of the building. The office building in which he was located was soon enveloped in gray smoke that looked like a nuclear cloud. When Giuliani and his staff tried to leave the building they discovered the doors were blocked. Two maintenance men eventually showed the way through a basement escape route. During this time Giuliani was out of contact. Landlines were dead and cell phones not working. The New York governor thought the mayor might have been killed during this time. Giuliani and about 20 of his group emerged just before 10:15 a.m., the South Tower now gone, and they were looking to establish communications.

On their way to a new command post, Giuliani's assistants organized the media for a live update. Giuliani's aides insisted that the media interviewers on site share their feeds with other media outlets. Giuliani let the public know that city leadership was in control and doing everything possible to protect the people. He said in a statement, "It's a horrible, horrible situation, and all that I can tell you is that every resource that we have is attempting to rescue as many people as possible. The end result is going to be some horrendous number of lives lost. I don't think we know yet, but right now we have to focus on saving as many people as possible."[21] His words conveyed pain and calm. On the way to a fire house as the next temporary headquarters, Giuliani was pushed by an aide to run to safety as the second tower began crashing.[22] Throughout that morning Giuliani controlled his physical reaction to the dangers, realizing the effect this image could have on the public. When the North Tower collapsed Giuliani was in the street and said loudly to others calmly to "keep going north."[23] Amazingly most everyone was evacuating toward the north in an orderly way.

When Giuliani arrived at the fire house at which they planned to set up a command post, the group had to break into the building because the firefighters were at the disaster scene. There Giuliani was able to talk with the governor and arrange for the National Guard to be called into the city. Giuliani also set a meeting with the governor at the police academy. He remained determined to be publicly visible. At one of his more conspicuous appearances, during an afternoon press conference together with the governor, Giuliani spoke softly and calmly and chose his words carefully when he said: "Today is obviously one of the most difficult days in the history of the city. The tragedy that we are undergoing right now is something that we've had nightmares about. We probably thought wouldn't happen. My heart goes out to all the innocent victims of this horrible and vicious act of terrorism. And our focus now has to be to save as many lives as possible."[24] When the media pressed for details about how many people were killed and injured, the mayor refused to give a specific figure, knowing it was too early to count and that giving a large number, as he suspected to be the case, could have a very strong emotional effect on the public. He said, "I don't think we want to speculate about that. The number of casualties," he continued, "will be more than any of us can bear ultimately."[25]

Mayor Giuliani made five trips during the afternoon back and forth to Ground Zero and visiting hospitals. He took strength from seeing the rescuers at the site. He said, "I would hug the guys who were working there, shake their hands and talk to them, and feel their determination revitalizing me, even as they told me how much the visits meant to them."[26] Police Commissioner Kerik later described Giuliani's presence during this time in this way: "He is almost like God. People are coming up to him crying, thanking him for being there. All they want to do is make him say it's gonna be okay. And that's exactly what he does."[27] At about 11 p.m. Giuliani sent his staff home to rest. He returned to the site for one more visit, and went home at 2:30 a.m. For about two more hours he was sleepless and read from a biography of Winston Churchill. Giuliani said he took inspiration from reading how the British had withstood German air assaults, and he saw the citizens of New York City reacting in a similar resilient manner.[28]

There were 2,606 victims killed in the towers, about half of whom were trapped above the impact. This number includes 343 members of the fire department and 71 law enforcement officers. As horrific as this loss was, the city was preparing that day for over 10,000 casualties. About 25,000 people were successfully evacuated from the site.

On the day after the attack Giuliani convened the city government at the Police Academy, beginning with his usual meeting with deputy mayors and commissioners and joined by Governor Pataki. The city leadership set to work on rescue operations, providing survivor assistance, arranging DNA collection to identify victims, and collecting and disseminating information about the missing. There were thousands of grieving families. The city established a family assistance center for over 20,000 people. The sanitation department began an operation for removal of over 100,000 truckloads of debris.

The city also immediately prepared for the possibility of another terrorist attack, possibly with anthrax, smallpox, botulism, or sarin gas. The mayor convened infectious disease experts and emergency services heads at a confidential meeting. Giuliani also directed attention to preventing reprisals aimed at the Arab community. He aimed to speak publicly in a way that linked the attacks with hatred in a broad sense, rather than involving any particular religion or group.[29] Giuliani also continued his focus on being a model of resolve in the public eye. A visible gesture occurred on the popular comedy show *Saturday Night Live* on September 29, where he appeared with city fire fighters and police officers to introduce the show. He combined an image of solemnity with a gesture of continuing with the happy things in life. He said, "It's up to us to face the future with renewed determination," which was reminiscent of the tone Winston Churchill maintained when England was under Nazi attacks. Later, Giuliani explained how he approached the balance between strength and humility this way: "Much of your ability to get people to do what they have to do is going to depend on what they perceive when they look at you and listen to you. They need to see someone who is stronger than they are, but human, too."[30]

Giuliani continued in office as mayor for a few months after 9/11, his tenure ending at the two-term limit. He was mostly portrayed heroically in the aftermath of the attack. As the editors of a collection of first-hand impressions of him put it, "Rudy Giuliani's actions that morning at ground zero not only brought some measure of assurance to his grief-stricken, traumatized constituents in the immediate aftermath of that defining tragedy, but in demonstrating his great personal courage, dedication, and leadership, he succeeded in shedding both the baggage of his long career and more recent, negative image to emerge to most people as a superhero to his city, the nation, and the world."[31]

After completing his mayoral term Giuliani was active in national politics. He was a candidate for the Republican nomination for president in 2008, but withdrew early after Senator John McCain became the clear favorite. Giuliani has remained active in politics and commentary, founded a security consulting business, and practices law.

Mayor Ray Nagin and Hurricane Katrina

Ray Nagin grew up in New Orleans with supportive parents. His father worked as a bricklayer, truck mechanic, and garment cutter, and moonlighted as a city hall janitor. Nagin's mother was a homemaker and worked at a store lunch counter. In high school he was captain of the basketball and baseball teams. He went to Tuskegee University on an athletic scholarship, where he earned a degree in accounting.

After college Nagin returned to New Orleans and was hired by Cox Communications, where he worked as a comptroller. He described the company as being in terrible condition when he joined, with books that were out of order and "borderline fraud."[32] He became vice president and general manager of the company's New Orleans operation. He was proud of improving customer relations, and used a live call-in show for customers to voice their problems. As he said, he honed his skills at "romancing the camera" and communicating "with angry, frustrated people."[33] He continued his professional education in an executive master of business administration program at Tulane. He also was involved as an investor and spokesperson in bringing a professional hockey team to New Orleans, convincing league officials to grant a franchise to the city.

In 2002 Nagin ran for mayor of New Orleans. He had been a registered Republican for most of his adult life and had supported Republican George Bush. He switched to Democrat shortly before seeking office. The Democratic Party historically dominated elections in New Orleans. He defeated Police Chief Richard Pennington in a run-off election. Pennington had been known for targeting corruption within the city's police department. Nagin himself campaigned as an anti-corruption and anti-patronage candidate, emphasizing the negative effects of corruption on economic development. He pointed to his work at Cox Communications in tackling irregular business practices.

After becoming mayor Nagin soon led conspicuous campaigns against what he said was corruption within a labyrinth of boards and commissions. He announced that 84 arrest warrants had been issued from an investigation of the city's car inspection and taxi licensing bureaus. He said the investigation revealed widespread graft in contracting and extensive fraud in federal housing contracts. As he described his effort, "Our initial focus was on bribery, inflated contracts, and other fiscal waste. Soon there were major busts and media events with a large number of arrests and public firings. My private sector background, initially seen as a weakness when I entered the mayor's race, prepared me well for other things I was about to uncover."[34]

Nagin had difficult relationships within his own political party, frequently clashing with the city council. In 2003 he supported a member of his party in the gubernatorial election but switched during the run-off to support the Republican, who was secretary of health and hospitals. Nagin later explained that he made his choice based on the candidates' responses to a letter he sent asking about their plans for New Orleans. The Democrat, Kathleen Blanco, who had been a leader in state tourism, won the election. The divide between Mayor Nagin and Governor Blanco became very public. The mayor had a low regard and open disdain for the governor's leadership. In his memoir he criticized her for entering her office "without any meaningful executive level experience," apparently by contrast to the mayor's view of the merits of his own business background.[35]

One of the main challenges facing any mayor of New Orleans is the possibility of a hurricane hitting this coastal city. It was built on swampland and marshes. The ground is higher nearer the river; the city is almost surrounded by water. It is the largest city in the country that lies below sea level. Protective levees are needed to retain flood waters, and a complex drainage system operates with more than 20 pumping stations and canals. The U.S. Army Corps of Engineers tried to prevent catastrophic flooding by enhancing the levee system, which had to be integrated with the city's own flood control facilities.

In 2004, as New Orleans prepared for Hurricane Ivan, 700,000 people were evacuated but about a quarter of the population, mostly the poor, did not leave. New Orleans was spared major problems when the hurricane changed direction. This may have given some false comfort. Evacuating a large city with limited routes away from the coast is a major undertaking. Success would depend not only on carefully orchestrated traffic patterns, in some cases reversing the usual direction, but also early warning of the impending storm. The city expects to need 72 hours to evacuate the population after the movement is begun.

The city was working on updating its evacuation plans in August 2005 when Katrina formed in the Gulf. As the storm approached New Orleans the mayor relied on a local weather reporter for a prediction about its course. Nagin said that the local figure "proved to have a more in-depth analysis and used different techniques in making predictions. We connected intellectually, and he also had a great sense of humor. I began to rely on his storm assessment over the course of the next few days more than any other weatherperson in the area."[36] On Friday afternoon, August 26, the National Hurricane Center changed its previous forecast that the storm would head for the Florida Panhandle, instead warning that it was aiming right at Mississippi and Alabama. Governor Blanco declared a state of emergency for Louisiana. The declaration triggered involvement by the Federal Emergency Management Agency and the deployment of some National Guard troops. On Saturday the governor requested that President Bush declare an emergency in Louisiana and he did so later that same day, authorizing federal assistance and funding.

On Saturday the storm continued to intensify and a mandatory evacuation order was issued in some Gulf coastal areas. In late afternoon Nagin issued a "Mayoral Proclamation of Hurricane Emergency" executive order for his city and began urging voluntary evacuation. His order gave the police chief authority to take command and suspend ordinances. He also gave public notice that the city would make the Superdome available as a shelter of last resort for evacuees with special needs. He did not order a mandatory evacuation.

On Saturday evening Nagin was having dinner with his family at a New Orleans restaurant. He had plane tickets for his family to go to Dallas early Sunday morning and stay there until the storm passed. Governor Blanco reached Nagin by phone at the restaurant and told him he should call Max Mayfield, director of the National Hurricane Center, to hear directly about the storm, the forecast of which had turned dramatically for the worse. Nagin says Mayfield told him: "I have never seen a storm or conditions like this. I am not sure what has been done, but you must get everyone out of the city as soon as you can!"[37] Maxfield recalls telling the governor and mayor that the storm was intense and could be devastating and catastrophic.[38] The mayor says that after speaking with Maxfield he called the city attorney and asked for formal papers to be papered for a mandatory evacuation order, and the mayor arranged a press conference for the next morning.

Sunday deceptively began as a beautiful day in New Orleans, while the storm approached with extreme 175 mile per hour winds. Katrina had become Category 5, the highest, which involves catastrophic damage to structures and high risk of injury or death from flying or falling debris. The National Weather Service warned that "most of the area will be uninhabitable for weeks ... perhaps longer" and there was the potential for "human suffering incredible by modern standards."[39] Nagin then appeared at a press conference with Blanco, the city council, and staff. He appealed to residents to evacuate, and about one million complied and left the area. The mayor made clear there was another option when he said he was opening the Superdome for refuge. He knew there were about 100,000 residents in the city without cars and no mass evacuation transportation was in place.

Soon there were 10,000 people in the Superdome. The city health director asked for volunteers to separate arrivals based on medical needs. Residents who could not evacuate or go to the shelters would be trapped in their homes. In media interviews the mayor advised residents to have an axe if they stayed home so they could chop their way through their roofs and be rescued. The mayor took his family to the airport.

To move residents to the Superdome the mayor's office was coordinating with Regional Transit Authority, a city controlled agency that managed bus and streetcar services. The office expected they could have up to 25,000 temporarily seeking shelter, but the facility was not equipped for the actual numbers. City leaders realized the scale of the shortages when Terry Ebbert, director of homeland security for the city, began trying to collect toilet paper for the facility. Instead of 300,000 packaged meals that the city requested from the Federal Emergency Management Agency, there were 40,000 on hand, and only five water trucks. The potential dangers were obvious to all as people continued to stream into the large structures that were poorly equipped for shelter.

The mayor went home Sunday night to collect some personal belongings. The weather was still deceptively calm. He returned to his office in city hall and prepared to move command to the Hyatt hotel across the street, from which the Superdome was visible. City hall was not expected to be able to withstand a major storm. The building was already swaying from the wind. City Homeland Security Director Ebbert objected to a backup plan to establish the emergency center at the Hyatt hotel because of its limited communications facilities. As Nagin described his response to the advice from Ebbert, "He was an ex–Marine who had gotten the Purple Heart award, so I looked him in the eyes and reluctantly said okay. I trusted him and his judgment, and I knew he would get his people out of harm's way if necessary."[40]

Nagin moved his office to the hotel, where the power company had backup power and secure telephone lines. The mayor used a 27th floor suite for private meetings and had a sleeping room on the 4th floor where other city offices were set up. These offices continued in operation throughout the storm even as some windows in the hotel were blown out. The emergency operations center also was relocated to the hotel after power failed in city hall.

Levees were breached and flooding began on Monday morning, and the city's emergency lines were overwhelmed with calls about flooding. Nagin reported that he drew on what he learned taking emergency preparedness courses in business when he retired to his suite to prepare a one-page, front and back, "action plan" to prioritize deployment of resources for rescue and recovery.[41] As he said, "As there was no manual to consult, I had to drum up all the management and technical strategies and skills that I had accumulated over the years. I knew I would be managing an unprecedented disaster that was unfolding all over my city, and with every passing minute things were quickly deteriorating. We needed a road map to get through this mess."[42] He said that his written plan later disappeared, but that he had "memorized it word for word."[43]

Nagin told police, firefighters, and National Guard to focus on rescue operations. The response from FEMA was delayed, which it attributed to awaiting coordination between state and local officials. Nagin called for buses to evacuate the Superdome, and from the Convention Center, which was also opened for shelter after the Superdome could not possibly hold anyone else. Meanwhile much of the city staff also was evacuated. Nagin reported that he tricked a city council member into leaving because he assumed she was staying "primarily for potential prestige due to an absolute love for being in front of a microphone or TV camera. She loved the spotlight almost as much as she liked being catered to. I immediately concluded that there would be no way that I could effectively concentrate on the many tasks confronting us if she stayed behind."[44]

Nagin also had a difficult relationship with his police superintendent, Eddie Compass. Nagin and Compass were childhood friends. Nagin appointed Compass to his post when Nagin's electoral opponent, former chief Pennington, resigned. During the crisis Compass contributed to public confusion by making public announcements repeating unsubstantiated allegations that people were being beaten and babies raped at the Convention Center. Compass also strangely reported that he had been nearly kidnapped at the Convention Center, which was never confirmed. Nagin later explained his feeling about Compass that "it was painfully evident that he had been sort of unraveling right before our eyes, but we were too busy to fully understand it."[45] During the emergency the mayor relied instead on Deputy Police Chief Riley for input about police operations. But to many in the public the police seemed leaderless and out of control.

As looting and roaming were shown on television some residents, and some police, established independent barricades and guard posts. Several members of the police department stormed a bridge and fired upon unarmed civilians, for which they were later prosecuted. Some police officers reported that they heard of an order to shoot looters and "take back the city," or "do what you have to do." Some say they refused to carry out this apparent order to use deadly force.

By Tuesday most of the city was under water. At this time Nagin signed a handwritten "Promulgation of Emergency Order" that directed the police, fire department, and the military to compel everyone's evacuation from the city. Those who had to implement the order were unclear about its meaning including whether they should use deadly force if necessary. Some officials urged people to leave, others forcibly removed residents.

FEMA's response continued to be delayed. The mayor took to communicating with text messages, drafted with aides and the mayor's name attached, which were distributed to the national media. This message, which he sent to accelerate the arrival of evacuation buses, and which he said "spread like wildfire," expressed great agitation: "This is a desperate SOS. Right now we are out of resources at the Convention Center and don't anticipate enough buses. We need buses. Currently the Convention Center is unsanitary and unsafe, and we're running out of supplies."[46] The mayor also gave radio interviews, lambasting the slowness of the federal government's rescue and evacuation efforts. He criticized the president for flying over the site on his way back to Washington from vacation. Nagin said he was "pissed" because the president's "fly over" failed to "do it justice." When a radio interviewer asked Nagin about reports that the state and federal government were awaiting proper requests for assistance, Nagin dismissed the need for such requests and asked why formalities should matter if they were not needed for emergencies such as a tsunami or the Iraq war.

The mayor praised one aspect of the federal response: the appointment of General Russel Honoré to command Joint Task Force Katrina, a combined operation between the U.S. Department of Defense and FEMA to organize the Gulf Coast relief efforts. During the interview in which Nagin loudly and angrily complained about state and federal government unresponsiveness, he added this: "Now, I will tell you this—and I give the president some credit on this—he sent one John Wayne dude down here that can get some stuff done, and his name is General Honoré. And he came off the doggone chopper, and he started cussing and people started moving. And he's getting some stuff done. They ought to give that guy—

if they don't want to give it to me—give him full authority to get the job done, and we can save some people."[47]

Lieutenant General Honoré, known to some as "The Ragin' Cajun," was an experienced Army officer and commander of the U.S. First Army at Fort Gillem, Georgia. His service included command of the 2nd Army Division in South Korea where his unit was involved with flood control during monsoon season. He planned and supported Department of Defense responses to hurricanes and flooding in the Gulf Coast region. The general instantly drew media attention after Hurricane Katrina for the authoritative manner in which he reacted to reporters' questions, insisting on a focus on clear communications with the public about the current situation. He said sternly, "Don't get stuck on stupid, reporters. We are moving forward. And don't confuse the people please. You are part of the public message. So help us get the message straight. And if you don't understand, maybe you'll confuse it to the people." Nagin praised the general's "can-do attitude" and reflected that his "presence and authoritative manner gave us all comfort that federal help had finally arrived and things would move faster."[48]

Governor Blanco asked the general to plan and coordinate evacuation efforts. The governor did not request that the federal government take control of the state's National Guard troops. Such a request would be necessary under federal law to shift from state to national control. Without the request not all units could be coordinated under a single command. President Bush proposed an arrangement in which General Honoré would have been made a member of the Louisiana National Guard with active-duty National Guard troops under his command. Governor Blanco rejected such an arrangement.

A focus of Nagin's frustration was the lack of transportation to evacuate people from the large shelters where conditions were dangerous. For a long while bus drivers refused to drive their vehicles into the city because of violent street conditions they heard about on television. The governor eventually directed the National Guard to drive the buses. During the crisis scary reports were broadcast about anarchy in the Superdome. Viewers worldwide were given the impression that police had entirely lost control. In reality the occupants broke into supplies and there was criminal behavior, but much exaggerated and sensationalized information was communicated to authorities and the public. Nagin made public statements that would contribute to public fear. For example, in his radio interview on Thursday, September 1, he said, "You have drug addicts that are now walking around this city looking for a fix, and that's the reason why they were breaking in hospitals and drugstores. They're looking for something to take the edge off of their jones, if you will. And right now, they don't have anything to take the edge off. And they've probably found guns. So what you're seeing is drug-starving crazy addicts, drug addicts, that are wreaking havoc. And we don't have the manpower to adequately deal with it."[49]

On Friday morning Nagin noticed buses starting to arrive in large numbers at the Superdome as he looked out his hotel window. He also noticed caravans of vehicles, troops, and supplies. Evacuations had begun by aircraft as well. The Superdome and the Convention Center were not cleared of sheltering residents until two days later. On Friday Nagin met with the president, governor, senators, congressmen, the National Guard chief, Secretary of Homeland Security Michael Chertoff, and FEMA Director Michael Brown, and they toured the area by helicopter.

During the second week after the storm, Nagin "announced a follow-up" order to his "original mandatory evacuation order." This one did not give residents any options. He said, "Everyone had to leave, and I wanted to put maximum pressure on anyone remaining in the city."[50] At that time there were over 20,000 active-duty personnel involved in relief operations in Mississippi and Louisiana, mostly air rescue and engineer units. Within two weeks 50,000 people were rescued, major levee work was taking hold, and pumping operations were progressing. Federal troops were involved in house-to-house searches and patrolled the streets. At one point 65,000 active and reserve forces, including from the 82nd Airborne and two Marine Expeditionary Units, were deployed to the area. Three weeks after the storm, power and water was restored to some of the unflooded neighborhoods and the French Quarter, central business district, Algiers, and parts of Uptown.

New Orleans was subjected to over $96 billion in damage as a result of Hurricane Katrina and its aftermath. Congress approved $52 billion in aid. At the storm's peak shelters housed 273,000 people. Seventy percent of occupied housing in the city was damaged by the storm and flooding.

While still in office Nagin continued his vocal and harsh criticism of federal and state authorities long after the recovery began. He publicly accused FEMA of being indifferent to the plight of the poor in New Orleans. In January 2006 he gave a speech on Martin Luther King Day described as the "Chocolate City Speech." Nagin said, "We as black people, it's time, it's time for us to come together. It's time for us to rebuild a New Orleans, the one that should be a chocolate New Orleans. And I don't care what people are saying Uptown or wherever they are. This city will be

chocolate at the end of the day." He said, "It's the way God wants it to be....
You can't have New Orleans no other way." "Chocolate City" was the title
of a 1975 song by Parliament, which mentions black leaders and the power
of majority black populations in cities. Nagin also made references connecting the wrath of the storm to God's punishment for the American
invasion of Iraq. He said, "God is mad at America. He sent us hurricane
after hurricane after hurricane, and it's destroyed and put stress on this
country.... Surely He doesn't approve of us being in Iraq under false pre-
tenses."[51]

Nagin was re-elected mayor in 2006, while two-thirds of the city's
population was still displaced from the storm. He served until the end of
his term limit, 2010, after which he formed a consulting business. Allegations of his involvement in corruption were reported in 2009, and in
2013 he was indicted for federal crimes. In 2014 he was convicted and
sentenced to ten years in prison. He was found guilty on 20 charges for
solicitation and receipt of payoffs during six years from multiple busi-
nessmen totaling hundreds of thousands of dollars, for rewarding bribers
with official contracts, for not paying taxes on hundreds of thousands of
dollars in income, and for lying to law enforcement.

Source of Strength in Crisis

Military leaders are trained to prepare their units for operations
under severe stress. In exercises decisions must be made after battle plans
and command relationships have been disrupted. Leaders expect that they
will have to deal with an enemy's surprises and that their units will suffer
casualties that will require individuals to exercise initiative and improvise.
They study how effective leaders have acted under the worst of circumstances and the tendencies that have been associated with success or failure.

Civil leaders do not focus on preparation for such extreme conditions.
They expect their responsibilities mostly to involve deliberate decision
making and incremental change. But as the experiences of Mayors Giuliani
and Nagin remind us, civil leaders can find themselves in situations that
involve war-like disruption and disorder. Their ability to exercise positive
influence in such circumstances necessarily will depend on abilities they
have developed through their range of other, more normal experiences.
As Mayor Giuliani said reflecting on his preparation for 9/11, "There's no
substitute for personal experience when it comes to dealing with problems.

That's particularly true in times of crisis, when there's less time to develop ideas and plans. Wisdom gained from one's own history provides a head start."[52]

Much of a leader's success in a crisis will depend on the person's character development and relationships already established. In this sense civil and military leaders are much the same. The day on which Colonel Chamberlain's regiment had to face a potentially overwhelming attack he had already done everything he could to understand the importance of remaining as calm as possible so he could make sound tactical decisions and give his troops the confidence to stick together and follow his direction. He also knew that his regiment's performance under fire depended on his relationships within the regiment and his subordinate leaders' ability to trust him and to inspire and rally others. The same is true of Mayors Giuliani and Nagin in their unexpected roles as leaders facing catastrophic circumstances. They had no time to consider how to act under pressure to inspire others, nor could they convince others for the first time that they should be trusted in their decision making. They had to act like leaders based on who they had become and what they had fostered.

Chamberlain, Giuliani, and Nagin each faced unique leadership challenges. Only Chamberlain was in command of an experienced military unit with developed command relationships, and only he of the three men had to make potentially fatal decisions while personally exposed to direct fire. Though Giuliani and Nagin were both mayors during a disaster in an urban and densely populated city, they were in very different environments within the community and with outside authorities and agencies. Despite the differences in these three leadership challenges, their decisions and behavior reveal valuable lessons about how a leader might be most effective in situations for which no one can truly anticipate how bad things will get. In particular their actions magnify three key aspects of leadership under fire: the leader's demeanor and its effect on others, the leader's decisiveness, and the extent to which the leader has trusted relationships with others.

Leadership Presence

Under normal circumstances leaders can influence others in many different ways. Some are effective with cheerful encouragement, others with brokered cooperation, and others with an example of commitment to a mission. A crisis amplifies a leader's influence through demeanor— or what can be called "leadership presence." Presence can give others confidence and keep them as calm as possible so they can act while in peril and make their own sound decisions that affect others. Leadership demeanor also involves how a leader communicates intent. A crisis requires simplicity, clarity, and persistence. An effective leader is aware that others need steady direction and a sense that they can ask for it.

Colonel Chamberlain is a legendary example of leadership presence. His situation at Little Round Top was dire; he must have sensed he was unlikely to survive the battle. In fact he was magically lucky. A Confederate soldier later wrote to Chamberlain that he had Chamberlain clear in his rifle sight twice during the battle but inexplicably did not pull the trigger either time.[53] But Chamberlain also knew that the unit's best chance was for him to keep his composure despite the dangers and despite what seemed to be overwhelming odds. His focus on the task at hand must have emboldened the members of his command.

Chamberlain's composure enabled him to make decisions that drew on his understanding of tactics, terrain, and the capabilities of his soldiers. When he deployed his regiment into a line to face the assault he used a formation that allowed those most likely to come under fire first to be already prepared with loaded weapons. This was done in the excitement of surrounding gunfire and on a chaotic battlefield. When ammunition was running out he could see that the only hope was a charge and that going downhill would be an advantage. The manner in which the line moved— whether it was by his design or simply by the way it unfolded—trapped the opposing forces.

Throughout the Battle of Gettysburg Chamberlain also kept attuned to the higher purpose at stake in the war and the importance of his unit's situation. Himself a volunteer in the cause, he was somehow able to inspire his fellow volunteers in the unit, as well as the mutineers whom he persuaded to join as the battle was about to begin. His personal courage and doggedness during the battle were an example for others to fight on even as the ammunition was depleted and assault waves were continuing.

In a crisis mayors do not personally face gunfire in the same sense as a battlefield commander, and their role does not call for them to put themselves in direct physical danger. They need to stay in the best position to gather information, make complex decisions, and communicate with other officials and the public. But like a military commander the nature of their visibility will have an effect on those whom they lead. Effectiveness may require them to overcome their fears and subordinate concerns about their own comfort and safety in order to embolden others.

Whether it was the peculiar circumstances of the way the attack on the World Trade Center unfolded, or his custom of wanting to see a scene first-hand, Giuliani's personal investment in the decisions he made was obvious to all. He understood the need to be visible and in contact with the police, firefighters, and the state and federal government. He was very intentional about showing that city government continued to operate, and he maintained a firm grip on the decision making process. Giuliani's demeanor on 9/11 proved to have a calming influence on others who had important responsibilities for dealing with the crisis. His aides, who themselves had to make difficult decisions and take action, were able to sense that Giuliani was able to listen, think clearly, and give needed direction. This must have given them greater strength to project a calming influence on their own assistants and personnel.

Giuliani's presence on the streets of Manhattan had a stabilizing influence when the situation could have become much worse under chaotic conditions. Many in the public remembered having a sense of solidarity with the mayor on that day. Giuliani was conscious and deliberate about how he showed his emotions in public. As he later wrote, "From my childhood days, I had trained myself to control my emotions when others become more emotional. My father had always told me to remain calm in a crisis. As others around me got excited, he said, staying deliberately calm would help me figure out the right answers. When a crisis occurred, it was my job to lead people through it."[54] As mayor of a major city that had been the subject of a truck bomb aimed at toppling the World Trade Center, he had actively considered his role if another attack occurred. It is an illuminating coincidence that he was reading about Winston Churchill at the time of 9/11. Churchill is remembered for rallying the people of England to survive relentless Nazi air attacks, and his radio announcements of courage and defiance are legendary. In Giuliani's actions and words on 9/11, he echoed Churchill's famous quote, "Success is not final, failure is not final; it is the courage to continue that counts."

Giuliani realized that the people of New York City, and the nation and the world, were watching the mayor on the scene and taking from him clues about the extent of the risk to themselves. With President Bush being kept away from danger for several hours on 9/11, the mayor became the key figure for the world to get a sense of the reach of the terrorist attack, which was intended to cause terror in the hearts of others. Giuliani kept a focus on the immediate need to control the disaster and try to rescue victims, rather than contributing to fright and confusion.

An important aspect of Giuliani's way of communicating was how he spoke publicly about the scale of the loss being suffered in the city. He was conscious that both his gestures and words could have a strong effect on emotions especially of those who knew victims. The media were soon pressing him for "body counts" about how many were lost in the buildings. Giuliani was told that there could be tens of thousands of deaths. He was committed not to add to the misery or generate fear with use of loaded language or horrific imagery. Instead he carefully struck a balance of acknowledging grief without intensifying it by saying the city had lost "more than any of us can bear." A study of the public's reaction to the mayor's public statements on 9/11, measured by the emotional tone of e-mail messages that were exchanged in the area on that day, shows that Giuliani's choice of words and his tone caused a dramatic decrease in sadness and an increase in anger aimed at the terrorists.[55] Giuliani communicated with the public in a way that encouraged resolve rather than contribute to a sense of helplessness.

Giuliani's focus on mission enabled him to control his own emotions. He was not personally insulated from the horrors that were occurring. He saw people jumping from the towers, lost friends and advisors, and was appropriately concerned about other attacks on the city's tunnels, bridges, and landmarks. Several times he had to suppress his personal grief. He recalled one moment when it was particularly difficult for him not to break down. After he finished speaking at a press conference with commissioners a reporter asked whether the speakers had heard about a phone call made by a woman on the plane that crashed in Pennsylvania saying that hijackers were slitting the passengers' throats with box cutters. Giuliani was personal friends with both the woman, Barbara Olsen, and the man she called, her husband, Solicitor General Ted Olsen. Giuliani later said it took all he had to restrain himself from an emotional outburst in public, but he knew that he had to do it.[56]

Mayor Nagin got his perspective from a hotel room and helicopter overflights. He was not at the shelters during the crisis. His communications with city officials came mostly from meetings in the hotel from which city government was operating. From these vantage points Nagin was in a difficult position for exerting a calming influence, either through visibility or a sense of shared danger. He was deliberate in how he presented himself but his goal in communication during the days of crisis was very different than Giuliani's. He aimed at influencing outside authorities to send relief and did this through the media by directing anger at other public officials. This may have been an understandable choice to make considering the urgency of the situation and the apparent unresponsiveness of state and federal authorities. But it also caused Nagin to exacerbate frustration and heighten emotions. The people of New Orleans may have been well served if these public complaints did in fact accelerate the response. At the same time, the furious and frustrated tone of the city's leader contributed to a sense of helplessness within government and the community.

Many who found themselves in the midst of flooding and disorder in New Orleans felt that they had been left alone, especially as word spread that the police had lost control of the situation. Nagin did not have the first-hand knowledge from which he could personally speak to address sensational media reports about widespread violence, and in fact contributed to a sense of anarchy. During his radio interview Nagin spoke of roaming drug addicts who were looting to fund their habits. The public impression that such statements fueled had an effect that went beyond morale; it also impaired rescue operations. Bus drivers and relief workers feared lawlessness in the city, which contributed to the delays in evacuation. Emphasizing disorder also could not have quelled the secessionist citizen groups that formed their own armed security units, nor could it have discouraged the lawlessness of renegade police officers.

No one knows for sure if rescue and relief operations would have been more effective in New Orleans if the mayor had not assumed an angry and hostile tone. We also do not know if the governor, police chief, or others would have responded differently if Nagin had given a better impression of being in control of the situation. We can see, however, that in any crisis a leaders' demeanor can influence others for better or worse.

Decisiveness

In a crisis situation leaders' decisions may involve choices with severe consequences, and the process for making them is accelerated. They may have to make these decisions based on limited and conflicting information. Maybe all of the choices seem bad. But the decisions must nonetheless be made—others need direction. Common sense and research tell us that if a leader seems too hesitant or confused—or hostile to bad news or tough questions—those who need direction are likely either to act independently or seek different leadership.[57]

Colonel Chamberlain had to make decisions on which his unit's survival depended. Even before his unit was in battle he had to figure out what to do with mutineers assigned to him. He approached the problem in a way that resulted in a strengthening of his line rather than a distraction. As the battle began he had to give immediate instructions to deploy his soldiers in terrain he was seeing for the first time, and then redeploy them as the unit suffered casualties and the enemy revealed its tactics. As his unit ran out of ammunition and faced annihilation, he was able to cause his men to mount a charge that saved the day. In retrospect we can wonder whether Chamberlain really had much choice in these critical moments. Unquestionably, however, he influenced his men to act as a unit toward a single purpose when hesitancy, confusion, and helplessness could easily have overwhelmed Chamberlain and his regiment.

Mayor Giuliani also had many important decisions to make on 9/11 that could not await much consultation or deliberation. He immediately had to commit to an approach for communicating with the public about ongoing danger and the city's responses. He had to make decisions about command centers and responder coordination, and deploy assets to the site and at other potentially threatened locations. He also had to make decisions about requesting security and rescue assistance from state and federal authorities. Through all of this he kept in mind the bigger picture and the importance of showing that city government was functioning, which he did with a resilient demeanor and carefully worded public statements.

Giuliani struck an effective balance between giving confidence that he was in control while enabling other leaders to make on-the-ground decisions about the deployment of responders and resources. The same kind of strength of purpose that caused him difficulties in other circumstances served him well during the crisis. As Mark Green, a former member of the city's administration, said, Giuliani is "a guy with a lawyerlike ability to calmly elicit and pull together facts, arrive calmly at conclusions, and convey them to the public."[58] The many who depended on Giuliani were served well when Giuliani was able to employ this ability in a situation more dire than a lawyer could expect to encounter.

Mayor Nagin also found himself having to make momentous decisions under intense pressure with no good options. In deciding about evacuation as the storm intensified and changed its direction toward the city, he had to weigh a number of heavy factors including the costs and dangers of moving many thousands of people away from the city and providing for their temporary relocation, against the potential catastrophic consequences of leaving people stranded. No reasonable person would have wanted the responsibility thrust on Nagin to make this choice and there is some unfairness in using hindsight to conclude he should have heeded the warnings earlier. But hindsight does show that the situation suffered from the way in which he made decisions and communicated them.

Nagin gave conflicting signals as danger approached. He urged the public to leave but also told them shelter was available at the Superdome. This indecisiveness proved to be costly. The U.S. House of Representative's report on the response to Hurricane Katrina concluded that "the failure to order a mandatory evacuation until Sunday, the decision to enforce that order by 'asking people' who had not evacuated to go to checkpoints for bus service, and then using that bus service to take people only as far as the Superdome did not reflect the publicly stated recognition that Hurricane Katrina would 'most likely topple [the] levee system' and result in 'intense flooding' and 'waters as high as 15 or 20 feet,' rendering large portions of the city uninhabitable."[59] As a result more than 70,000 people who remained in the city had to be rescued from dangerous conditions.[60]

Nagin also had the leadership responsibility to make decisions about deployment of the city's resources and coordination among departments. Internally he deferred to his director of emergency operations in the choice of an operations center, which initially stayed in city hall while Nagin moved to the hotel. As conditions worsened in the city Nagin's view was from a distance that required him to rely on information that proved to be exaggerated and unreliable. His lines of communication with police were severed, and he was unable to exert control as he heard reports about renegade police vigilantes. The decisions he made—or failed to make—early in the crisis were part of an irreversible sequence that resulted in his loss of control.

Indecisiveness also may have proved costly in communications with the state and federal agencies. The governor's decisions about federal troops and the deployment of state resources contributed to delayed relief and disorder. Nagin did not make the kind of prompt and direct requests that likely would have contributed to a better focus on the clear decisions that had to be made. When asked by a reporter about whether he had made the proper requests to get state and federal assets, he dismissed such requests as unnecessary in hyperbolic language combined with angry criticisms of others for failing to act. Effective leadership may require putting aside assignment of responsibility and expression of even the most legitimate complaints about bureaucracy.

The troubles Nagin experienced during the disaster contrast sharply with his own assessment of the leadership demonstrated by General Honoré. Nagin applauded the general's "presence and authoritative manner."[61] With his contrasting approach Honoré quickly set a tone of seriousness and attention to mission. He established order in the rescue and evacuation operations, causing others to begin to work together. He was able to be decisive in a way that was missing from leadership prior to his arrival. The traits Honoré exhibited were those he had been taught and had applied as an experienced military commander and were welcomed among those who looked for steady direction.

Trusted Relationships

Leaders cannot sustain a high performing organization by themselves. No single person can be expert in all aspects of the organization's functions. Success requires subordinate leaders who have that expertise and who can exercise effective leadership within their subunits. Organizational leaders need to develop trusted relationships with and among others in the organization. They must keep everyone collaborating with a focus on the mission.

The importance of a web of trusted relationships becomes critical in crisis situations in which resources are overwhelmed and for which there is no standard operating procedure. Military commanders know full well that they must be able to depend on subordinate leaders in the chain of command to provide honest information and make sound decisions about deploying their people and assets consistent with the leader's direction and example. The military intentionally organizes and trains based on this reality, developing a chain of command with leaders at each link who can exercise control in a coordinated way. Colonel Chamberlain was part of this kind of command structure and tradition. He had clear lines of communication for interrelated unit movements, something that is of paramount importance to an army at war. He was instructed to deploy his regiment to the right spot at the right time, and he gave further direction about how his subordinate commanders should place their troops to accomplish the larger purpose. His immediate grasp of what was needed for coordination was essential for success.

Of course the dynamics of leadership relationships outside the military are different in important ways. Key subordinate units may operate largely independently and not be part of the same kind of well-established chain of command as with military units. Relationships may be affected by political and territorial considerations, within the units and within the larger organization of which they are a part. Still as with a military unit a civil affairs leader's effectiveness can depend on how well trusted relationships have been developed within and beyond the organization. The responses to the 9/11 attacks and Hurricane Katrina showed this to be true.

On 9/11, Giuliani made contact with the governor and the president's office as soon as he could after he was isolated due to collapsing buildings. He was able to arrange for military air cover and rapid deployment of state and national assets. Resources from others states and the federal government were coordinated for additional security, evacuation of Lower Manhattan, and rescue and recovery. The responsiveness should not be a surprise given the nature of the region as a financial, commercial, and industrial center, and the potential magnitude of the global terrorist threat. Giuliani also maintained effective communications with his department leaders for deployment of city resources. He had a staff with him as he moved from location to location in search of a suitable command center, and was able to communicate with commissioners and deputies for deploying their resources to fight the fire, organize rescue operations, establish order, and provide security. His staff also immediately began coordinating with hospitals to care for the injured and quickly attended to such things as arranging for the lighting needed at the site for around-the-clock rescue operations.

Aware of the importance of a coordinated response Giuliani's early focus appropriately was on having an operational central command and giving direction to the fire and police departments. He decided on separate commands because he determined that their primary functions were separate. As he saw it, the fire department had to focus on rescue and the police department on security. In making this decision Giuliani considered the dynamics of these departments, which sometimes put them in competition for influence and resources. The fire department, for example, relied heavily on individual station command.

Although the city had conducted joint readiness exercises in preparation for a disaster, at the time of 9/11 the ability of the police and fire departments to work together had continued to be a matter of concern. Giuliani's decision to have separate command centers on that day has been criticized for the way it limited the responders' ability to share information and coordinate their efforts. Some question whether so many firefighters would have been trapped in the collapsing buildings had they received more timely and complete information including what the police helicopters could see from above. The 9/11 Commission found that effective decision making was hampered by problems in coordination and communication among unit commanders and their units.[62] Some of this was attributed to the inability to use the new emergency response center at the World Trade Center, and the unexpected disruption of the communication system when cell towers and phone lines were destroyed in the fire and building collapse. The experience highlights that command relationships and communications are most important when decisions must be made quickly and based on limited and conflicting information.

Two journalists emphasized the communication difficulties on 9/11 above all else in their analysis of Giuliani's leadership. They wrote, "We rely on our leaders to behave well in such a moment, to set an example of calm and compassion. But we do not expect them to manage the intricacies of the rescue operation. For that, we hope there are men and women throughout the government who have been preparing and training just so that if a crisis comes, they can operate on instinct, yet automatically make the proper decisions. If the mayor of New York had made sure that the city's emergency headquarters was securely located and had put in place communications and command systems that worked, he would have been of greater service on 9/11—even if he had spent the whole day cowering under his desk."[63] The mayor does bear responsibility for the decisions in which he was involved regarding how best to prepare for emergency command and communications. Whether he should be blamed because the joint command center was built at a location that would be attacked is another matter. But contrary to the journalists' light measure of Giuliani's words and actions on the day of the crisis, we cannot know what else might have happened had Giuliani been "cowering" rather than providing the public with decisive and calm leadership on 9/11. The journalists' critical rear view of one aspect of the city's response, and the mayor's role in preparation that might have hampered it, gives insufficient weight to the many other aspects of his exemplary leadership that had such an impact during the crisis.

Mayor Nagin's situation also was unprecedented as the flood waters rose in New Orleans and urgently needed help from state and federal authorities were not being delivered. In his case some important internal relationships quickly failed, including with his key subordinate leader for security in the city—the chief of police. Although Nagin had selected the chief based in part on a personal relationship he found the chief to be unreliable in the kind of situation in which trust is most important. Without effective leadership the police lost control, and individual misconduct exacerbated the public's sense of abandonment. Failures in communication and control between the mayor and key figures affected other aspects of the city's response and how the various departments performed under the extreme conditions.

External relationships also were crucial for dealing with the flooding and displacement in New Orleans. Nagin focused on making public criticism to pressure the federal and state officials to deploy more resources. Much has been said about deserved blame at all levels of government. The governor has been fairly criticized for a slow response with state resources and for her refusal to release the National Guard units to federal authorities. FEMA and other federal agencies have been fairly criticized for a late and initially inadequate response with rescue and security forces. But the mayor ultimately at least shares responsibility for the dysfunctional relationships and hostile communications he had with those who could have done more and done it more quickly to address the situation. He had a distrustful and combative relationship with the governor, a key figure for a mayor's ability to muster resources beyond the limited means at the city's disposal. When coordinated action was needed he argued with her about what the response should be and accused her of politically related sabotage. He also did not have, and did not establish, working relationships that might have affected FEMA's responsiveness. The importance of clear lines of communication with those who can deploy state and federal resources should have been readily apparent to the mayor of a city that depends on a flood control system that is susceptible to hurricanes. The arrival of General Honoré highlighted the mayor's inability to affect others' actions. Nagin welcomed the general as someone who could "get some stuff done" and urged that full authority be given to him. The general stepped into a leadership void. His command presence, quick decision making, and ability to communicate within all levels of government proved to be a turning point.

* * *

Chamberlain, Giuliani, and Nagin were in unprecedented situations that called for tough decisions, clear direction, and exemplary inspiration that would influence others to do extraordinary things. In how they met the challenges we can see the importance of a leader's influence on others before, during, and after a crisis. Humans have amazing capacity to unify under the worst of circumstances. They do not expect their leaders to be perfect or to make the problems disappear. But they will be better off if they can sense their leaders' trust in themselves and in others. While there is no sure way to prepare for leadership that guides through challenging situations, the military necessarily strives to develop this in its leaders and its learning and experience are a fertile ground for study.

CHAPTER 4

Adaptable Military Leadership Methods

Contrary to popular impression the military's leadership methods are not purely derivative of its combat orientation or an authoritarian culture. Many of its methods are simply interpersonal dynamics based on experience and reflection. Veterans looking to serve in leadership positions beyond the military often are surprised at how the methods they learned are nowhere to be found even when their suitability is obvious. They are even more surprised to find widespread prejudice against even the possibility that these methods could be relevant. Often they confirm to themselves that this prejudice is mistaken, because when they do employ what they learned in the military, modified to fit the circumstances as they were taught they should do, it tends to work.

What follows is a sampling of leadership methods employed in the military that can be adapted to be effective in other contexts. They may already exist in any given organization in some form, either as a result of institutional approaches or because they are a consequence of natural leadership ability. But everyone can be reminded about or learn from approaches that have proved successful over time. The ways a method can best be adapted depend on several factors.

Public service organizations and the leadership cultures within them are diverse—much more so than in the military. Leadership methods within them must fit the public mission and internal dynamics. What works in one organization is not necessarily the same as what would work in another. Some have essential similarities with the military in mission and structure, such as in law enforcement and other public safety units. Leaders in these organizations often have military experience on which they draw. In other organizations leaders must contend with professionals or officials who largely function independently and have little incentive to respond to authority or influence, such as in commissions or boards and in academic environments. In these contexts leaders cannot expect others to respond as much to their personal influence or to be as receptive to efforts to align with others in the organization. The methods outlined here are among those that are most likely to apply in some meaningful way to any public organization, though the challenges of implementing them may vary.

A second important aspect in adapting military leadership experience to other contexts is the additional obvious reality that most public organizations do not have the military's clear lines of authority. Regardless of how well veterans understand this, they are likely to be surprised by how much less respect for authority there is within most organizations in which they will work after service. The difference exists at all levels. Individuals naturally feel less bound to follow the leadership's direction or stated intent. In group settings and personal exchanges individuals are less likely to feel accountable for expressed disagreement and some do not hesitate to show disrespect or contempt without fearing consequences. But this difference in perceived authority does not render the military's leadership methods irrelevant. Leadership as taught and applied in the military is based on the premise that formal authority has only limited usefulness. Methods are aimed at how to exercise influence in the absence of this authority.

A third reality in considering how military experience applies to other contexts is that even though the military has well developed leadership practices, training, and accountability, the military is large and dispersed and its personnel have a wide range of strengths and weaknesses. Military leaders can have very different responsibilities and experiences and their learned practices do not necessary reflect what they were taught. Many veterans emerge with a wealth of leadership experience that could not be duplicated elsewhere. They have finely tuned abilities and insights that are readily transferrable to any responsible position. Others may have had much more limited responsibilities. Some also may have embodied the "Peter Principle," attributed to education scholar Laurence J. Peter, that responsible people are promoted based on their success at their current position and tend to rise to the level of their incompetence. Some may have been entirely unsuccessful in learning or applying what they were taught; they may have been toxic leaders who misused the command authority with which they were entrusted. The important point for purposes of valuing military leadership experience is that as sound as the practices may be, in any context their successful implementation depends on human factors. There should be no pretense that everyone in the military successfully learned and applied what was taught, but neither should the value of this education and experience be overlooked because it is not always entirely manifested.

The adaptation of military leadership methods may in some ways seem contradictory to leadership teachings in public administration and workshops and the literature on which they are based. This is partly due to the singularity of emphasis in public service teaching, much of which is a reaction to perceptions about leadership failures beginning in the 1970s. Public administration leadership scholars reacted to problems with leaders who were disconnected from the public interest and what should inspire those in service. So emerging leaders were urged to do things like involve others within the organization in decision making and spend more time thinking about them as whole human beings. These are valuable lessons. But effective leadership in practice is complex and involves many other considerations that are not addressed with this emphasis. Today there is no less of a need for guidance based on experience about how to handle daily leadership challenges in the field.

Veterans who join public service organizations are likely to be familiar with these leadership methods and may have had direct experience with variations that were part of their responsibilities in service. An organization gains if veterans and their supervisors and colleagues share perspectives. Leadership in any public service is essentially the same, and any well-developed method may be effective if appropriately adapted to the circumstances. Unfortunately veterans should not expect such an open-minded reception. They are more likely to encounter back-handed dismissal stemming from a simplistic and mistaken assumption that military leadership does not apply to other contexts, which is a natural consequence of what has been taught for many years. For many veterans the notion of having to camouflage their association with military leadership seems contrary to how they learned and lived it. Real leaders are direct and sincere about their intent. They also would expect that other leaders who disagreed with an approach would share their own views reasonably and tactfully and in the spirit of doing what is best to accomplish the mission. But the cold reality is that methods learned in the military are more likely to find a place if presented for the practical realities and logic on which they are based and not packaged as a "military" approach. Veterans should also keep in mind that their own experiences were not perfect, and they should not feel a need to prove they know more than others.

Veterans can hurt their own cause if they expect they will be greeted with only praise and others will subordinate their own knowledge and experience. A large part of why many in American society for so long have felt so positively about veterans who returned from war and deployment was the veterans' humility about their sacrifice and courage. Much in American culture has changed, including public perception of those who have served, especially among those who influence public policy. Veterans who let their abilities speak for themselves are most likely to be welcomed and able to apply what they learned.

A final important reminder that applies to all leadership development is that success depends on willpower. No method will work unless the leader is committed to doing it right even when the going gets tough. This can mean acknowledging that initial efforts were flawed and methods need to be modified. It also can mean doing what comes at a personal cost. But with a determined, flexible, and honest mindset, military leadership techniques can be highly effective regardless of where anyone thinks they were learned.

Cultivate Integrity

"Leaders of integrity consistently follow clear principles. The Army relies on leaders of integrity who possess high moral standards and are honest in word and deed. Leaders are honest to others by not presenting themselves or their actions as anything other than what they are, remaining committed to truth."

—U.S. Army, *Army Values*

No trait is more important to effective leadership than integrity. No trait is more difficult to embed in an organization's culture —it must be pure because there is no such thing as "almost" having integrity. It is something that is easy to proclaim and to portray publicly with hollow words and gestures. But the essence of integrity is what people do when no one is watching and no one will know. To paraphrase Jane Addams, it is not making an exception of yourself. In today's organizations there is a tendency to claim the banner of high ethical standards without doing the hard work of embodying it personally and embedding it in the organization's culture.

For many reasons integrity is essential for effective leadership in public service. As a practical matter acting with integrity avoids trouble for the leader and for the organization. Those who act unethically or at the limits of what is allowed expose themselves and their organizations to accusations and legal trouble that can be costly in many ways. Accusations require investigation and explanations, and can lead to a path of hide-and-seek mentality, with leaders diverting their efforts to public perceptions rather than to their mission. Questions about integrity also undermine the organization's credibility in its public affairs, including in performing its functions and receiving public support with resources, further distracting the leader and the organization from the mission.

Integrity has always been considered part of public leadership. Representative democracy is based on a premise that individuals can be trusted to act responsibly and without harming the public interest. As a leader with an impeccable reputation for honesty, George Washington was the model for both military command and civilian executive leadership. As he famously said of himself, "I hope I shall always possess firmness and virtue enough to maintain (what I consider the most enviable of all titles) the character of an honest man." Even Washington did not take integrity in himself for granted.

In public perception Washington's model is fading from memory. Ignominious instances of dishonest and self-serving behavior have engendered widespread public distrust. Political leaders now seem to speak only through carefully contrived, overly simplified sound bites written by others; the public rarely sees a person who, though flawed as all human beings are, is essentially good and dedicated to service above self. Recent studies give reason to be concerned that the behavioral trend is in the wrong direction. A 2011 sociological study of youths 18 to 23 years old depicted young people who mostly do not consider moral positions or the assumptions that underlie them, do not think through the logical implications of moral positions, and are unable to have a constructive discussion with people who have different moral beliefs.[1] The study concluded that "fully one in three (34 percent) of the emerging adults we interviewed said that *they simply did not know what makes anything morally right or wrong.* They had no idea about the basis of morality."[2] Another third of the emerging adults studied had no objective reference or basis for what they professed to be right or wrong.[3] Those in any generation who are submerged in narcissistic social media and guided by shallow trends are unlikely to have the interest or attention span to consider ultimate truths.

Integrity in public service—more commonly described as "ethics"— has become a central theme for leadership theorists, especially since the Watergate era. While they agree on the importance of trust there is little evidence that such ethereal discussions have caused any improvement in personal integrity in practice. A leader needs to face the reality that most people have a shallow or even cynical view about personal integrity and most likely expect not to be part of a culture in which individuals really are held to high standards. Leaders therefore must go against the tide to create a culture of integrity within their organizations.

Leaders can have no credibility in this battle unless they set an impeccable example for emulation within their organization. They should always be sincere in deeds as well as in words, never lightening the seriousness of this commitment. Those who make the right choices should be acknowledged, especially when it might not be in the best personal interest. If a breach occurs then others in the organization should know, within the bounds of legal confidentiality and professional courtesy, that it will not be overlooked.

By their example leaders can influence the organizational culture—that shared system of values and rituals that are enforced with social sanctions as well as formal authority. Studies of employees in American businesses show that co-worker culture is a powerful influence on ethical choices, and perceptions about top managers are the most important factor for countering tolerance of ethical breaches within an organization.[4] This should be no surprise. Members of an organization who know that the leaders have uncompromising ethical standards also sense that integrity will be expected of them as well. Those with personal integrity will value being part of such an organization and be inhospitable to threats to an ethical culture. Conversely, when leaders speak of integrity and advertise its importance, but act in ways that do not demonstrate a personal commitment, members of the organization will be more inclined to go close to the line and maybe go over it, especially if they see others nearby doing the same.

Integrity also translates into trust. Members of an organization can be inspired to be courageous in situations in which integrity is at risk by knowing that their leaders do not comprise and will value others' dedication to making the right choices.

In public service integrity must go beyond abstaining from unethical conduct. It must also animate effort toward accomplishing the public service mission. Raising integrity beyond empty words can start with treating the oath of office as a solemn expression of service above self. Leaders should be bold and confident about expressing this nonnegotiable commitment, and not only when questions arise.

Integrity also is related to discipline: the state of acting according to what is best in the long term and not according to immediate desires. Disciplined leaders are present and reliable. They follow through on their promises. They do not ask others to do what they would not do themselves. They maintain order in their affairs to avoid confusion and distractions and they insist that others in the organization do the same. Simply put, discipline keeps the focus on what matters. Performance reviews should consider these various aspects of integrity, and examples should be noted when the right choices are being made.

Leaders also must confront the widespread sense that public leaders are uncaring and self-serving people who avoid public scrutiny. As a matter of fact this is an over-generalization and unfair to the many who fulfill their public service pledges working in government offices and other public service organizations. More than 14 million people work in local governments alone and most of them are trusted neighbors. They honor the public's trust by carrying out their responsibilities faithfully. Unfortunately the temptation of personal gain causes some to violate their oaths for personal gain and this is what makes the headlines.

Too often integrity is equated with mere legal compliance. Since the Watergate Era federal and state governments have enacted codes that subject officials to detailed conflict of interest rules and require disclosures of financial interests. The federal executive branch has rules about conflicts of interest, procurement and contracting, gifts and travel, outside employment, hiring of relatives, use of government property and information, political activities, and disclosure of financial interests, among other things. State governments also now have ethics offices that collect financial disclosures and monitor compliance and laws that apply at least to elected and appointed officials at the state level. Some states also have restrictions that apply to local officials. Legislators usually are not governed by the same ethics laws as other public officials and employees, but they are subject to statutes specifically aimed at legislative activity. Typical among such statutes are prohibitions against voting on matters in which legislators have a direct interest, campaign-finance restrictions, financial disclosure requirements, and restrictions on dealing with lobbyists. Enforcement is largely retained by the legislative bodies themselves, usually a committee of legislators. Lobbyists at the federal and state level are subject to laws requiring them to register and declare their affiliation and to file reports about gifts and other matters. Other public officials are subject to various ethical codes, including judges and attorneys.

Despite these every-expanding rules deemed to prohibited conduct, leaders must not leave ethics to the regulators. The body of ethics laws would not keep expanding if not for worsening public discomfort with the state of public integrity. Even strict compliance does not equate to a culture of ethics. The rules are lengthy and complex yet riddled with exceptions. There are strict laws about individual contributions to political candidates yet political action committees and corporations dominate the campaigns; state officials must file detailed disclosures of personal finance with state ethics committees but those committees barely have the resources to inspect the records without any meaningful use of the information.

The technical ethics rules can actually be traps for those who use common sense rather plumb the details before every step they take. Some experts argue persuasively that enacting detailed proscriptive rules is doomed to ineffectiveness and may be counterproductive. In their insightful book *The Appearance of Impropriety*,[5] Washington, D.C., attorney Peter Morgan and law professor Glenn Reynolds argue that rather than cause more ethical behavior the codes have laid traps of inconsequential violations that can be used by the unscrupulous against the well-intentioned. According to the authors, "The Ethics Establishment has produced rules, regulations, and fanfare galore. But the average citizen, while not familiar with the intricacies of the rules, can plainly see that the ethics emperor is naked: Government is not appreciably more ethical than it was."[6] They argue that to promote more ethical conduct leaders need to focus on the substance of what people are doing and why they are doing it and not just how it might look.

Morgan and Reynolds have several more basic rules for creating an ethical culture that goes beyond merely a matter of appearances. Their rules strike chords that would resonate throughout military leadership training. One is to "seek out and encourage the reporting of bad news."[7] More commonly in public service organizations leaders look to put a positive spin on everything and avoid disclosures about questionable ethical behavior. Members of the organization tend to have a sense that the leadership does not want bad news to be reported. This suppresses the ethics discussion and creates shadows in which questionable behaviors can thrive. The authors also recommend that organizations "keep it crunchy,"[8] by which they mean having consequences for bad choices. An example they give is how putting bumper stickers on commercial vehicles with a toll free number for reporting bad driving proves to be more effective at encouraging safe driving than seminars for drivers. The authors conclude that "in almost any setting, organizational structures in which someone has to take responsibility for results, and in which results are obvious, produce better behavior than those in which responsibility is diffused, and results are difficult to measure."[9] Taking responsibility for your actions is a leadership principle stressed in the military.

Morgan and Reynolds also urge keeping the "eye on the ball" by paying attention to indications of real virtue as shown by intent and effort, rather than only to compliance with inconsequential rules that can be satisfied strategically.[10] They point out that leaders need to reflect on their own true intent as well. As they say, "If we all take responsibility for acting ethically, we must ask not just, was the act in question actually *wrong*? Or, what were its motive and result? We must also ask *ourselves*, why am I making this particular accusation, and at this particular time? What do I stand to gain? And others should ask such questions as well."[11]

Leaders should not undercut an ethical culture with cynicism or by making light of ethical violations. As Morgan and Reynolds say, "don't call virtuous people chumps."[12] In the same vein leaders must not countenance a workplace attitude in which everyone considers small breaches to be acceptable either because "everyone does it" or "no one gets hurt." Small indiscretions add up to a self-serving culture. Things such as spending excessive work time on personal matters, using office supplies for personal use, and detours in reimbursed travel, as common as they may be, undermine an ethical culture and mission focus. Morgan and Reynolds conclude their wise advice by noting that "if you focus on appearances, you will fail even at that."[13] The ethical culture must be deep and firm to shield it from collapsing from below.

Keep the Focus on the Mission

> "We are a team, disciplined and well-prepared, committed to mission accomplishment."—U.S. Navy, *Navy Ethos*

A public service organization exists to accomplish a mission beyond its members' personal interests. Most organizations have a mission statement and talk about it on occasion, a conversation that usually involves aspirational declarations of doing big things exceptionally. The message is a good one, but to an effective leader a mission is more useful if it can be grasped by all as a clear goal toward which efforts should be directed. It may be simple and specific, or complex and broad, and it might change over time, as long as it sets a visible course at which everyone can aim their efforts and to which leaders can point as they exercise their influence. There are a number of dynamics that can cause leaders to lose sight of this essential orientation.

Anyone in a leadership position can encounter what might seem to be a choice between what is best for accomplishment of the mission and what might be best for personal advancement. Realism requires acknowledging that people who have leadership responsibilities likely also are interested in their own career advancement. This reality becomes misaligned with effective leadership when the temptations for personal advancement are not in sync with the mission. When faced with this divergence, both military and other public service leaders are bound by their oaths and the responsibilities they assumed to make choices in only one way: what is in the public interest. The military is explicit in its leadership doctrine and training about this. Although many public organizations similarly speak of the priority of mission on occasion, the preeminence of the mission usually is not the centerpiece when questions arise about how decisions should be made and efforts oriented.

There also is a tendency within public organizations for leaders to confound dedication to their mission of public service with preserving and enhancing the standing of the organization. Accomplishment of the public mission can be hard to define and difficult to measure. Few public organizations can look to market feedback in the way business and industry use it for a sense of whether they are on the right track. Instead most public organizations are considered to be a necessity and not expected to turn a profit or otherwise appeal to consumers. They will exist and they will be funded. Their leaders have incentives always to portray themselves and their organizations as doing everything well, and to claim that they can do it even better, as long as they can get a bigger share of the budget. These dynamics can substitute organizational self-promotion for mission focus.

Political realities also can interfere with an organization's focus on its mission. Leaders in public service organizations usually depend on external approval for their positions—voters or appointing executives or bodies. For some political survival can be the paramount concern within the organization. For example, some government agency heads have a staff member within the unit who serves chiefly as a political advisor. This person tracks the popularity ramifications of decisions and the way to best communicate publicly about them, and may internally act as a kind of henchman when someone within or outside the organization threatens the carefully constructed image. This looming presence can be a serious obstacle to subordinate leaders' efforts to focus decision making on the mission. The henchman's involvement may even run counter to the real public service interest. It can be disillusioning and get ugly. Promising careers have been squandered as a result of choices that had to be made between what will be rewarded and what is right. Effective leadership requires being alert to these realities and making decisions in the public interest while avoiding unnecessary trouble with personal agendas.

Mission focus can be blurred for far less sinister reasons. For example, increasingly the rhetoric in public service equates effective and visionary leadership with bringing "change" to the organization. Influential public administration leadership scholars advise students that "leaders *envision the future by imagining exciting and ennobling possibilities.* You need to make something happen, to change the way things are, to create something no one else has ever created before."[14] Few of these scholars would give serious thought to the less fervid tone of political theorist Russell Kirk, who advised us to recognize "that change and reform are not identical, and that innovation is a devouring conflagration more often than it is a torch of progress."[15] Certainly the ability to see the need for change and to lead through it is an essential aspect of effective leadership. But effective leadership also involves not assuming that things *must* be changed, that success is measured by how much it occurs, or that leaders must leave a personal mark on their organizations. Effective leadership also can be preserving what is good about a well-functioning organization. The departing leader who is being replaced may have been very successful at positioning the organization and developing its personnel and highly respected within the organization including by the senior remaining leaders. To announce a need for change before understanding the organizational dynamics can disrupt what should be preserved and spoil the chance to develop effective relationships. It is simply illogical—and foolhardy—always to assume that the best approach is to change whatever there is. In fact effective leadership may mean resisting the impulse that change is always good for its own sake or that what is forecast as a future trend should always be pursued.

Another message ringing within the modern mantra that change is always good is a cultural infatuation with treating any new version of technology as an exciting improvement that must be quickly adopted. Of course leaders must be aware of changes in the environment in which their organization functions and anticipate how these changes create new opportunities and pose new threats. Some technological trends have fundamentally changed how we communicate and interact with each other and only a very rare organization would be immune from having to respond by shifting operations and capabilities. Being adept at such things as data collection and analysis, web-based applications, social media, and mobile access may be essential to individual competence and require a new focus in mission. But the public service mission is still what matters and the technology is relevant only to the extent it contributes to better accomplishing that mission. Technology initiatives can introduce unexpected challenges that quickly consume an organization. Effective leadership in the modern environment requires not succumbing to unthinking assumptions that can put information technology in the organizational driver's seat.

These are only some of the distractions that can pull a leader off course from pursuit of the organization's mission. There is no alarm mechanism that goes off when the organization begins to drift. Instead leaders must be relentless in insisting that the mission be part of the decision making process, be alert to misalignment between the mission and effort and resource allocation, and have the difficult conversation when there needs to be a reminder. The most effective leaders have the character and clarity of purpose to cause others within the organization to see the way through a maelstrom of distractions.

Cultivate Taking Responsibility

"Seek responsibility and take responsibility for your actions."
—U.S. Marine Corps, *Leadership Principle*

Achievements and failures often can be attributed to particular decisions or a series of decisions, but indecisiveness also can result in the organization's mission drift. Effective organizational decision making requires clarity about who makes the decision and who has the responsibility for its outcome. Most people naturally want to have a say in decisions that affect them. They also naturally want to express an opinion when someone else's decision might negatively affect them. The military principle to seek responsibility and take responsibility for actions urges leaders to want decision making authority but connects that privilege to personal responsibility. Taking responsibility involves accountability for results and an obligation to reflect on decisions that were made so better decisions can be made in the future. This is essential for personal growth and for the organization's improvement.

Business and industry typically have built-in rewards and punishments for decisions made contrary to the organization's best interest, particularly when the outcome is an obvious monetary cost to investors. This kind of accountability is not common in other public service organizations. Appearances are paramount in politics, and politicians can be expert at avoiding blame for their unpopular or detrimental decisions, and may be adept at attributing bad outcomes to others' failures to cooperate or unexpected circumstances. The nature of public service also enables managers to put the blame on others or on external causes. They can point to their lack of direct control over decision making, limited authority, and the inherent limitation on organizational resources. They also may be able to plead that they must accommodate the interests of many stakeholders and that there are many other practical reasons why they are not the ones who should be held responsible—even if they would be quick to take credit if things went well.

Connecting decision making to responsibility strengthens leaders and their organizations. Paul Rogers and Marcia Blenko of Bain & Company, a global organizational consulting practice, surveyed executives at 350 large companies about what makes an organization effective. They found that "making good decisions and making them happen quickly are the hallmarks of high-performing organizations."[16] They also found that "even in companies respected for their decisiveness, however, there can be ambiguity over who is accountable for which decisions."[17] Ineffective decision making can result from a number of factors. They include a lack of understanding about who can make decisions, counterproductive competition within the organization for authority, and centralization of authority disconnected from those who are responsible for implementing the decision.

Effective leaders are able both to be clear about who has decision making authority and to create an environment in which everyone who will be involved in implementing the decision will feel invested in it. Others should not presume themselves finished with responsibility just because a decision was made by someone else even if they expressed disagreement. There can be difficulty understanding the important difference between wanting and listening to concerns and thinking individuals can remain part of the organization without earnestly working to implement a decision that has been made. Once the decision is made no one should be trying to impair its implementation. Everyone is responsible for doing their part for success. As the Rogers and Blenko study concluded, "Clear accountability is essential: Who contributes input, who makes the decision, and who carries it out? Without clarity, gridlock and delay are the most likely outcomes. Clarity doesn't necessarily mean concentrating authority in a few people; it means defining who has responsibility to make decisions, who has input, and who is charged with putting them into action."[18] Those who feel they will be held accountable for putting a decision into action will naturally care more about the decision when it is made.

One reason some leaders in public service organizations may be disinclined to take responsibility for decisions is the modern trend of striving to give the appearance of dispersed authority. Even when the organizational chart has one person at the top, leaders are urged that decisions will be better made and better implemented if always made "collaboratively." They form committees with representatives of various constituencies at which everyone is encouraged to comment. In gatherings and on electronic bulletin boards they invite everyone to express their opinions, which often are offered casually and are therefore easily ignored in the end.

Seeking the advice of others within and beyond the organization is part of effective leadership and can result in better informed decisions and a broader sense within the organization of a personal stake in the outcome. But in reality decisions rarely are put to a vote; someone makes or guides them, often with only the appearance of collaboration. Often on reflection those who were invited to express opinions knew ahead of time what the decision would be. The organizational leadership was looking for "buy-in" for a course that had already been set. Trying to give an appearance of inclusivity can have the effect of making everyone feel less accountable. Rather than putting so much effort into making decisions look like they are collective, organizations should strive to be clear and conspicuous about decision making authority, and connect it to a sense of responsibility.

Public service leadership education often sounds a very different mantra about decision making. It equates leadership with facilitation, "flattening" organizations, and encouraging everyone to eschew authority and "lead from the middle" in a way that makes everyone feel equally empowered. "Top-down" management is discredited as failing to realize that today's work force does not care about who is in charge and only cares about doing the work. This kind of thinking is valuable to the extent it is a reminder that effective leadership rarely is dictatorial and group members tend to perform best when they have been part of the decision making process and feel their insights are welcome and their contributions are valued. But welcoming and valuing input is different than making everyone feel they can have their way. Striving always to lead only "from the middle" is more likely to result in the absence of effective influence, with the untoward effect of disassembling the group from needed direction and generating counterproductive frustration.

Avoidance of responsibility within groups is not peculiar to public service. It is a basic human tendency, which social psychologists call the principle of "diffusion of responsibility." This is how researchers describe it: "If the decision is made by one person, that person will worry about whether the decision he or she makes will be a bad one, because he or she will feel responsible for the poor decision. Also, others will hold that person responsible and criticize and perhaps punish that person. On the other hand, suppose that it is a group that is making a decision about what action will be taken. Again, intuitively, each individual participating in a group decisionmaking process will feel that he or she would not be so responsible for the joint decision outcome if the decision comes out poorly. After all, the decision would not have been made if others didn't agree with it. 'So I was not really so dumb because everybody thought it was the right decision.'"[19]

Contrary to the modern assumption that larger groups make for better decisions, there is an optimal number of individuals involved in a decision that will maximize their satisfaction with the outcome. Research shows this to be about five. As the group gets larger individuals must compete to be heard. Discussions then tend to be dominated by a few, or a small subgroup, who are not necessarily the most competent to contribute meaningfully to the discussion or guide its course. As social psychologists J. Richard Hickman and Neil Vidmar found in a landmark study of group decision making, "Consistent with the findings of previous studies, there was more dissatisfaction with group processes as size increased. The larger the group size, the more members complained that the group was *too* large for effective task performance. Larger groups were seen as being highly competitive, as having considerable disagreement, and as showing disunity. Members reported feeling that some individuals talked too much in the larger groups and that they themselves felt inhibited from expressing their feelings."[20] As groups are expanded individuals also are more likely to feel free to offer viewpoints or make suggestions merely to be heard or to make an impression, which they would not make if they felt they would be held accountable.

Also contrary to popular impression putting decisions before large groups does not usually lead to the expression of more varied perspectives. Abundant research shows how readily individuals instead will conform to group pressures, including the famous Asch experiment. Social psychologist

Solomon Asch studied groups of seven to nine in which a subject was asked if drawn lines were of equal or different lengths, when one was obviously longer than two others that were equal. More than a third of the subjects said the lines were all the same length when everyone else in the room had been instructed to give this false opinion. Subjects' readiness to contradict their own senses depended on the size of the group. When only one other person in the group gave the false opinion, the subject was not influenced, but when just two others gave it, the subject agreed with the false answer almost 14 percent of the time. Asch found "the tendency to conformity in our society so strong that reasonably intelligent and well-meaning young people are willing to call white black."[21] Conformity is not exclusively a youthful tendency. The Asch and other experiments show that social expectations and pressure can have a powerful influence on opinions and give the false impression that there is greater merit when more people agree. The danger, as Asch noted, is that "consensus, to be productive, requires that each individual contribute independently out of his experience and insight. When consensus comes under the dominance of conformity, the social process is polluted and the individual at the same time surrenders the powers on which his functioning as a feeling and thinking being depends."[22]

The negative effects of diffused responsibility can be lessened with a clearly defined process in which participants know who makes the decisions. Being clear does not mean decisions should be made in silos or that there should be no tolerance for errors in judgment. It does mean putting individuals in a position of feeling that they should say what they mean and that the decisions they make, or to which they contribute, have consequences.

Creating a sense of responsibility for decision making also requires a process for reflecting on choices that were made as the outcome unfolds. The tendency within public organizations, however, is to move onto the next decision and not look back. When something goes well everyone cheers the outcome and forgets that there still may be lessons learned in how the details evolved. When something goes wrong blame usually is attributed to limited resources or unexpected developments, and the official narrative is that no one saw it coming. Those who did see it coming feel uncomfortable saying so in retrospect, or if they do say anything their voices are subdued and soon forgotten.

One technique for instilling better decision making accountability is to follow a practice similar to the military's "after-action" review. An after-action review is conducted as soon as possible after an event and involves as many participants as possible. Everyone who had responsibility is expected to respond to frank, open-ended questions that seek feedback for both strengths and weaknesses. It is not a self-congratulatory exercise as commonly occurs in many organizations. The goal is to link performance to future operations. In public service honest self-criticism seems reserved for only when something has gone terribly wrong, such as after 9/11 or Hurricane Katrina. But the exercise is worthwhile after any major endeavor.

Honest self-criticism requires looking beyond generalities for ways to measure success, including whenever possible the use of comparative data. Greater reliance on data for management decisions is a trend within the field of public service. It is sometimes called "evidence-based management." With this approach decision makers actively seek the best available and most current empirical information to inform themselves about their options and the most likely outcomes from choices that are available to them. For instance, with a technique called "performance measurement" organizations define a desire outcome that can be depicted in ways tied to data, and then they compare actual outcomes to the targets. This approach focuses attention on what is being measured and gives a more tangible picture of achievement than the usual self-descriptions of just claiming to be "the best" or anecdotal information exchanged at the water cooler. It also cuts through the natural tendency of internal divisions to report based on comparisons only to their own self-referential benchmarks or their own prior performance assessments.

Using objective evidence is one way to cut through generalities and see the connections between decisions and performance. But metrics are not a substitute for effective leadership. No matter how much data are available, or how sophisticated the spreadsheets and charts can be made to look, it all is of little benefit if it is answering the wrong questions. Famed statistician John Tukey said, "It is better to have an approximate answer to the right question than an exact answer to the wrong one."[23] Infatuation with statistical analysis can put the proverbial cart before the horse, causing leaders to worry more about "the numbers" than what is essential for success such as focus on a compelling mission and giving priority to the front lines.

What organizations need to do, therefore, is be ever-vigilant about the realities of their decision making process. This requires consideration of all the various components that comprise the process and the ways in which they might be improved. The Bain study about effective decision making suggested reflecting on the following questions to assess how well the organization is doing and how it can make its process better:

- Were the decisions right?
- Were they made with appropriate speed?
- Were they executed well?
- Were the right people involved, in the right way?
- Was it clear for each decision who would recommend a solution, provide input, have the final say, and be responsible for following through?
- Were the decision roles, process, and time frame respected?
- Were the decisions based on appropriate facts?
- To the extent that there were divergent facts or opinions, was it clear who had the authority to make the decision?
- Were the decision makers at the appropriate level in the company?
- Did the organization's measures and incentives encourage the people involved to make the right decisions?[24]

Any honest review that asks these questions is likely to reveal ways in which decision making was flawed and can be improved. What is most important for effective leadership is having a climate within the organization in which the difficult questions are asked and honestly answered. Too often within public service the process for making decisions seems invisible and the lines of responsibility lead back only to a murky discussion that in retrospect seemed foreordained.

Have Other Honest Eyes and Ears

"I have a duty to report any indicators that may hurt my wingman."—U.S. Air Force, *Wingman's Creed*

Effective leadership depends on intimate knowledge about the capabilities, performance, welfare, and morale of the organization's members. No matter how caring leaders are, they can be consumed by their own responsibilities. The heavier the responsibilities the more likely it is that the leader will lose touch with what the others in the organization are actually doing and whether everyone is pulling in the same direction. To avoid isolation leaders must turn to others to be trusted eyes and ears. This will not just happen on its own regardless of everyone's best intentions.

Military organizations are intentionally hierarchical in the sense they have a clear delegation of authority and responsibility. Military leaders also are fully aware of the danger this creates for losing touch with what is happening at the line and becoming insensitive to subordinates' welfare and morale. The risk is greater as the organization gets larger or more complex. In small, direct leadership situations the leader and the unit members are in constant contact and the leader should be attuned to the abilities and status of the unit members. As the command expands the organizational leadership is more disconnected, particularly when there are intervening unit commanders. Those at the top of the organizational chart must rely heavily on subordinate commanders to convey information about the readiness and challenges on the front lines. Unfortunately the human tendency is for subordinate leaders to want to portray matters within their responsibility in the best possible way. This is particularly true of those who are self-absorbed or lack the integrity to report negative information. Organizational leadership must be alert for these tendencies and the many other ways in which they can lose touch. Organizations that deny being hierarchical are not immune from the tendency of those who exercise leadership influence to isolate themselves from the realities of how people are doing their work. They may become oblivious to the signs or even ignore them for the sake of maintaining a collaborative appearance.

The military employs several methods aimed at expanding a leader's view by involving others for whom this is their primary role. These additional eyes and ears watch the leader's blind spots and keep lines of communication open with those who are carrying on the work within the organization.

One feedback channel that is common in the military that cuts through the chain of command is to assign a very experienced enlisted individual whose primary responsibility is to be the commander's eyes and ears with those on the front line. This individual is a senior noncommissioned officer, such as a sergeant major or master chief, who has credibility throughout the ranks based on having lived through what they are experiencing. In some units the title is "command sergeant major." For example, there will be a command sergeant major in an infantry battalion, which has several hundred members organized into four subordinate units. A similar role can be found in other types of military units that have more than one level of command, such as divisions, wings, and sections. The command sergeant major can detect serious matters about which the organizational leader needs to know, as well good signs that should be brought to the leader's attention. The command sergeant major also is a trusted advisor to the rank and file, able to communicate the commander's intent in understandable terms, put things in perspective, and convey a sense that someone with a direct line to the leadership knows and cares.

There likely is no one equivalent to a command sergeant major in most public service organizations, either in experience or in working relationships. But an organization may have someone who has extensive first-hand knowledge of the organization's core work and a sound basis for rapport with those who currently deal with the daily challenges of doing it. Organizational leaders can benefit from the counsel of someone who has this kind of credibility, a voice for those who are not regularly heard.

Executives in public service often have a confidant in the inner circle as an informal advisor, who gives frank and plain advice free of personal interest. For example, during the years when Franklin Roosevelt was pressing his New Deal reforms, he would test his ideas on Gus Gennerich, a former police officer and the president's personal bodyguard. Roosevelt called him his "ambassador to the man on the street."[25] Gennerich died just before Roosevelt submitted his unpopular and doomed Supreme Court-packing plan to Congress, and some historians wonder if Gennerich's absence was a factor in what probably was Roosevelt's worst error in political judgment.[26] Wise and experienced public figures often tap into the advice of others who have daily contact with the public and are inclined to speak freely, such as cab drivers and health care providers.

The leader's trusted advisor must be someone with the kind of experience that gives credibility for understanding challenges currently faced in the field. The advisor should have a direct relationship with the organizational leader and be able to act as a sounding board for the leader's ideas. The advisor must feel safe giving honest opinions without retribution or an expectation that the advisor will be compelled to reveal sources of information. For this to be so the leader must sincerely want this kind of relationship. A leader who is not comfortable with bad news or unflattering opinions takes the risk not only of an oversight or misjudgment that could have been avoided, but also of becoming isolated from the rest of the organization.

To get a sense of morale and any issues that are below the surface, the advisor needs to visit the field independently and informally, to ask questions and look for signs of discontent or worse trouble. An experienced trusted advisor also can provide important guidance to subordinate leaders, who may lack the experience to work their way through problems that the advisor has seen before.

An advisor of this sort must have the kind of experience and demeanor that invites honest feedback, including complaints that are made in good faith. Everyone must understand the advisor's purpose and trust the intent. Neither organizational leadership nor the advisor can violate that trust.

An untrustworthy advisor will either be secluded from honest feedback, or, worse, hurt morale. The advisor also must work not to become just another residential member of the executive suite, appearing only at luncheons and facilitated "brainstorming" sessions. The view from such a perch is too near sighted.

Other types of team members perform a vital trusted advice function. One is a "wingman," a term first used to describe a pilot who flies to the side and slightly behind the lead aircraft in a formation. The wingman keeps an eye on the leader's blind spots and watches for threats that might otherwise escape notice. The wingman might spot something wrong with the lead pilot's aircraft, or notice an enemy plane or missile approaching from the side, below, or above. The lead pilot might not have the wingman in sight and must trust that the wingman will be there, alert for dangers and opportunities, and unhesitant to bring them to the leader's attention. In combat the wingman is an extension of the flight leader for the purpose of accomplishing the mission.

Pilots are not alone in having blind spots. Every leader has them. They are not only areas that cannot be seen visually; they also are limitations in perception about what is happening both within and outside the organization. Focusing on the tasks at hand, the leader might not realize how decisions are affecting morale and organizational performance. Or the leader, committed to making a new program successful, may not be seeing that it is not working as intended. Or the leader may need to hear that there could be a reason to change personally to be more effective. A wingman can broaden perspective about all of these tendencies.

Many organizational leaders form a kind of trusted relationship with a senior manager or assistant who is expected to give confidential advice but who becomes a colleague in a "we versus them" pairing, focused more on peer support than effective organizational leadership. A wingman is not a bodyguard or political advisor, or a confidant who runs interference for the leader's personal or political agenda. To the contrary; a wingman with an eye on the mission should be a counterweight against diversions for personal agendas.

Another type of advisor who can broaden perspective in some types of organizations is an ombuds. The word "ombudsman," now sometimes called "ombuds," originated in Scandinavian countries referring to a government official who investigated complaints about wrongful acts of public officials. Today many different kinds of organizations have an ombuds, including some military units. For example, a Navy ombuds is a volunteer appointed by the commanding officer to serve as an information link between command leadership and service member families. This gives the commander a direct connection to families whose concerns may not be communicated through the service members. An ombuds is a voice and does not have disciplinary authority. Someone in this role may be especially appropriate for organizations that tend to have members or constituents who feel they are shut off from the decision makers by bureaucratic intermediaries. An ombuds can avoid or resolve disputes through informal assistance, as well as bring perspective to the leaders about issues that need to be addressed for the long term.

Each of these types of advisors can extend the organizational leader's vision and hearing. Whether or not individuals are formally assigned such roles, leaders should consider how others within the organization can be employed to help counter the natural tendency to get burrowed in heavy responsibilities and lose contact with what is happening among those who ultimately control how well the organizational will accomplish its mission.

Keep Everyone Attuned to the Front Lines

"Give the field priority."—U.S. Coast Guard, *Leadership Principle*

Effective leadership requires empowering those who carry out the mission to make decisions about how it is to be done. As organizations grow in size and complexity they tend to install institutional controls that require decisions to be made centrally. They impede field decision making and innovation by insisting that decisions first be studied on an organizational level and only implemented when plans can be developed for organization-wide implementation. Centralizing decision making might deploy additional expertise and resources not available to the front lines, and bring beneficial regularity and uniformity. It also can stultify innovation and frustrate front line units that are hamstrung from acting on their more immediate and intimate understanding of what is needed. To give the field priority an organization needs to work to overcome these tendencies.

Contrary to the often-held presumption that the military prepares its leaders only for authoritarian rule, it teaches that those who are being led should be able to understand what needs to be accomplished and why—the mission and the commander's intent—and whenever possible left to figure out the best way to do it. This may not result in the most uniformity, and it may leave room for mistakes in judgment. But such risks can be outweighed in the long run by the increased responsiveness and innovation associated with energizing individuals to look for ways to do things better. And when those on the front lines feel empowered they also are more likely to develop their own leadership and commitment and apply it toward organizational success.

To empower the field an organizational leader must do more than just step away and let things take their course. The field gets priority for a reason: so that *the organization* can accomplish its mission. Toward this end the front lines must understand when innovation is appropriate and when it is not, and when it is, how best to share this information within the organization. Organizational leaders must remain continually personally involved to create and nurture this type of culture. They must keep themselves apprised of the challenges in the field and how they are being addressed. They must find the resources and cut through barriers when necessary to implement change, and follow through to ensure that successful innovation is spread throughout the organization.

Giving priority to the field is made more difficult by the natural tendency to confuse individual perspectives about the importance of work with the extent to which that work truly contributes to accomplishing the organization's mission. Complex organizations involve subunits and individuals who work within professional specialties who can get insular perspectives. For example, organizations typically have web designers and programmers to maintain an Internet presence, hardware experts and troubleshooters to keep essential equipment working, human resources specialists to hire and manage employees and comply with reporting requirements, facilities and logistic mangers to supply space and supplies, and business support personnel to handle accounts and reports. Often these support specialists operate in spaces away from field operations and communicate directly only within their own units. Increasingly their exchanges with the field are through remote communications and fill-in forms—they rarely see the real faces of those who depend on their services while they are working, much less interact with the clients or members of the public being served. Support units also tend to look only at internal measures of their own productivity and tailor their practices to those measures rather than how well they support the field.

To be able to give meaningful direction that aligns everyone with the field, organizational leaders must know what is going on throughout the organization including in the support units. Much of this knowledge can be acquired through observation and more by asking questions. Too often organizational leaders simply defer to others within the organization, especially with highly technical functions. They should instead insist that everyone responsible for functions be able to communicate about what they do and the challenges they face, and how well their efforts support the organization's mission.

An important part of keeping everyone regardless of function attuned to the front lines is clarity about what makes the organization distinctive as a whole. Each of the military branches has a wide range of individual specialties and functional units, many of which do not involve combat operations and may be the same as specialties and functions found in organizations unconnected to the military. For instance, each branch has medical personnel, supply chain managers, computer programmers, human resource managers, police officers, and just about every other kind of expertise that could be found in any public organization or business. But each of the branches also is persistent in trying to maintain everyone's focus on the essence of its existence. Everyone orients their activities with this in mind. The Army keeps everyone attuned to the solider, the Navy to sea power, the Air Force to air power, and the Coast Guard to public safety and saving lives. The Marine Corps, which has a vast array of specialties including such things as air wings, signals intelligence, shipping terminals, and public affairs, singularly keeps its focus on rapid response combined arms warfare, the foundation of which is the infantry that will meet the enemy. Only a few percent of Marines are infantry specialists— only about 12 percent of the officers. To keep everyone's focus on the needs of the front lines the Corps ensures that everyone has a sense of what it is to be in the infantry. Everyone learns basic infantry skills and tactics regardless of future specialization; everyone goes to the rifle range every year regardless of whether they ever expect to use a rifle in combat. While few public organizations have a mission that can be stated as simply as the Marine Corps does, they all have a reason to exist on which everyone is to orient their efforts. This should be kept in the forefront of everyone's thinking regardless of specialty.

Trust and *Verify*

> "Leaders need to learn how to observe subordinates and provide developmental feedback."—U.S. Army, *Leader Development Principle*

Effective leaders establish and maintain trust with the members of their organizations. They enable subordinate leaders to exercise initiative even when there is a calculated risk involved. But only a foolhardy leader has blind trust; the trust should be based on confidence gained through observed ability and performance. The trust also should be continually verified.

Leaders are responsible for the performance of everyone in the organization and should remain personally invested in all that happens. Verification is not mistrust; it can be seen as a chance for everyone to inform the leader about successes, share insights about how leadership and support units could be more supportive, and spread successes and ideas throughout the organization. Knowing that there will be verification also is an incentive to address weaknesses, knowing that they will come to light and questions will be asked about what is going to be done to improve.

Public affairs leadership theory notes the importance of trusted relationships and warns of the dangers of relying only on the power that accompanies authority. But when trust is emphasized apart from verification a barrier can be formed that removes the leader from essential involvement and feedback. It can also create a dynamic in which attempts at verification are perceived as a lack of trust, which further isolates the leader from understanding what is really happening within the organization. To reverse this dynamic a leader should make verification an accepted part of the trusted relationship and not a perceived contradiction of it.

The military's approach to leader verification includes regular inspections. Most people who think of military inspections think of unforgiving drill instructors in theatrical portrayals of basic training. A stressful inspection in which fine details are examined and every flaw is emphatically pointed out has its place in instilling discipline and teaching attention to detail. It conveys the importance of pursuit of perfection in an environment in which there is a potential high cost of even slightest discrepancies. But inspections are not only of this sort. The military uses inspections also to check on preparedness in the field and give leaders feedback so they can make decisions about actions necessary to improve the organization. They also give leaders the opportunity to be visible and convey their commitment to preparedness and welfare.

The military teaches that the purpose of any inspection should be connected to mission accomplishment and the overall capability of the organization. With it the leader receives first-hand information that is factored into the decision making process about how to improve the organization, looking at both strengths and weaknesses. The unit being inspected should be measured based on a recognized standard and understandable expectations. The leader takes an objective look and asks probing questions, especially the difficult ones. The questions should be open-ended, to get to the heart of the unit's status and its challenges. Whenever appropriate the feedback is memorialized in a report. Issues that are detected are examined for root causes and solutions. Opportunities that are uncovered become part of an action plan for further development and sharing throughout the organization. The leader follows up on what is learned in the inspections, and, when corrective action was necessary, ensures that it occurs. With this approach inspections become a very valuable part of an integrated and long-range plan for continuous improvement.

Most public service organizations would not respond well to the notion of military-style inspections. Leaders in most organizations typically rely on what is said at staff meetings and written periodic reports for information from the front lines. This flow of information is important in its own way but typically does not involve looking past the natural tendency to highlight achievements and attribute difficulties to lack of resources, others' shortcomings, or unavoidable consequences. This tendency can only be pierced with a process in which the organization's leaders get a first-hand perspective with a probing, direct inquiry.

Some form of inspection can be useful even for work that does not involve obviously tangible things for examination. There may be no physical "workplace" to visit for many kinds of work that today are important to organizational success. But there should be ways to examine the nature of anyone's work and productivity first-hand, and to have an in-person exchange to discuss it. Leaders should be wary of anyone within the organization who claims not to be able to convey the nature and importance of the work in a way that the leader can understand.

While the leader's personal view should be tailored to the nature of the unit's functions, there are basic questions that are likely to be relevant in any inspection context. The Marine Corps identifies five questions that an inspector should ask:

- What do you do?
- How do you do it?
- How are you doing at it?
- How do you know?
- What are your challenges?[27]

The answers to these questions should reveal both strengths and weaknesses.

Of course something akin to an inspection is not the only way organizational leaders can see for themselves how the members of their organization are doing. There are other methods for digging deeper into the organization beyond what its members naturally would want to portray. These include audits, benchmarking, and outside peer review.

Auditing is a time-tested method of having an expert from outside the organization examine a state of affairs and provide a report. Audits are best known as a way to ensure that internal accounting is accurate, complete, and according to applicable industry standards. It can also be used to check on how resources are being used as a way to prevent waste or fraud. Auditing can be seen in a more general sense as a way to have someone credible take a fresh, unbiased look at how things are being done. In this sense the goal is not as much to prevent wrongdoing as to ask questions about what is working well, how something might be done better, and what resources would be needed to make changes. When properly approached the subjects of the audit can see it as a way to get and give feedback, consider alternatives, and communicate to the leadership through an objective voice. This is more likely to happen when auditing is known to be part of the organization's overall plan of accountability and communication, rather than only becoming a topic when there is a sense that leadership is suspicious about possible wrongdoing.

Peer review is a similar way to get another perspective on strengths and weaknesses. The military uses a form of peer review when someone from outside a unit conducts an inspection or reviews an exercise and reports on performance and readiness. Universities use it for program accreditation. With this procedure in any organization someone who practices in the same field is engaged to visit the organization, review its records, and talk to individuals to find out what is going well and, most importantly, what might need improvement. This is a technique also sometimes employed in professional practices, such as in medicine and law.

In instances when performance is in question, an outside reviewer's comments can be extremely valuable. An outside reviewer also can add new insights about internal cultures because the peer reviewer does not share the same sense of "this is how we've always done things." Peer review has limited value when leaders cannot resist the tendency to reject criticism as merely a failure to understand the special nature of the organization. There should be a commitment to discuss the results openly and honestly and to consider an action plan to address weaknesses.

Benchmarking is another way to examine internal operations with external reference. It involves comparing performance information to measurable standards within the field or with organizations that perform similar functions. One such technique is known as "best-practice benchmarking," which was developed in large businesses by which the procedures of others within the industry are examined for ways to improve. Another form of benchmarking is to compare performance statistics to those of other units that perform similar functions. To be effective the benchmark must be a relevant comparison of an important function. The comparison is aimed at identifying possible ways to improve. It must be constructed in a way in which unfavorable comparisons cannot simply be dismissed by faulting the comparison. Organizational leadership should insist on an actual plan for improvement based on the results, and follow up on that plan.

These and other methods for obtaining insight and feedback offer potentially valuable ways to let light pierce the bubble of self-image and confirmation bias. None of these methods is likely to be well received unless the organization's culture includes an understanding that there is always room for improvement and that honest feedback should not be feared. Improvement comes from being true to yourself, to paraphrase Shakespeare, and being true to yourself usually means being willing to be made uncomfortable. Any such momentary truthful insight will be most valuable to the organization if the leader is involved directly in the discovery and in decisions about the actions to be taken based on that insight.

Meet with a Purpose

"Ensure that training is meaningful, and that the purpose is clear to all members of the command."—U.S. Navy, *Leadership Principle*

The way that organizational leaders meet with subordinate leaders and others in the organization, and the way subordinate leaders and other members of the organization meet with each other, often is handled in a way that is at one of two ends of a spectrum. There may be only ad hoc meetings convened to announce changes, otherwise leaving the members of the organization in informational silos. Or at the other end of the spectrum, there are routine meetings that seem to bloat in number and duration until they become a dreaded and wasteful consumption of time and deadening to the spirit.

Dysfunctional leadership environments often can be attributed to a lack of communication with leadership and across functional areas, resulting in destructive territorialism. Organizational decision makers should meet both regularly and as needed but always with a purpose known to everyone involved. Those who have leadership responsibilities within the organization should update organizational leadership and each other about developments, invite others' input, and listen about how others might be affected. Being in a room together with contemporaneous exchanges of viewpoint, and sensing demeanor and tone, gives perspective and can build a sense of teamwork in a way that cannot be replicated with communications by smart phone and computer screen. Contemporaneous virtual meetings can be useful, especially when the organization's members work apart, but taking the time and making the effort to be together requires commitment and minimizes distractions—provided everyone puts away their devices at the meeting. As the saying goes, everyone should "be in the room."

These benefits of meetings can only be achieved if the convening leader insists that they only occur when there is a clear purpose and runs them so that everyone gets a sense that their time is being well spent. The purpose should be communicated in advance; any decisions to be made should be clearly identified so the participants can inform and prepare themselves. During the meetings the participants should speak from knowledge and say what they mean, and discussions should remain on task.

Even with best intentions meetings can get off track quickly, accomplishing nothing except to give the floor to participants who enjoy making others listen to them. Too often meetings are held regularly with no decisions to be made, and participants have no real sense that they have any responsibility for the nature of their participation. In public service organizations the meeting's convener usually does not try to intervene to keep discussions on task and reports and comments precise, fearing being perceived as too heavy handed. Some who should be at the meetings then try to avoid them, preferring to spend their time more productively; others welcome them as a way to idle time away.

One method that the military employs, and that is rarely used in other contexts, is an impromptu gathering with a learning purpose mindset known as the "school circle." Veterans especially remember these from basic training, but they are also used in other training and field environments. A leader calls everyone together into a semi-circle and immediately makes clear a purpose relevant to the circumstance in which it is convened. It can involve a brief lecture or demonstration, or an exchange with an opportunity for questions, but is always kept tightly focused. The tone is entirely or mostly serious, but calm. In the military the relaxed atmosphere of a school circle often contrasts with the stress otherwise created in training exercises or in the field, which helps set a tone that the purpose of the meeting is to learn.

All organizations can benefit from leaders calling such spontaneous gatherings to focus on a particular challenge or learning point. It might seem awkward at first but with the right tone it can be an opportunity to sharpen attention and a way for supervisors to get important feedback from those who are carrying on the work. It should always have a clear purpose and kept focused to avoid becoming an annoyance or joke. Brief learning meetings can serve the added purpose of getting leaders out into the field, where challenges can be uncovered and innovation can surface. This is also a way for the members of the organization to get a sense that leaders care about continuous learning and improvement.

Regardless of a meeting's specific purpose its utility depends on how the participants communicate with each other. The climate should be one of honest exchange and focus on the organizational mission. A strategy being urged within public service leadership education to overcome interpersonal barriers is to encourage open and positive communications and receptiveness and to discourage critical or questioning attitudes. For instance, in group discussions members may be urged not to follow someone's comment with "yes, but," but instead always with "yes, and," accepting what the speaker is saying and integrating it into the next statement. This is intended to build creative collaboration rather than have exchanges stultify due to the natural tendency to want to express independent or contrarian views. A similar approach now being encouraged is to outlaw expressions of any "what ifs" when discussing a possible decision that involves change. This is meant to have exchanges that focus on possibilities and avoid getting mired in negativity caused by the tendency to worry about why something will not work. Techniques such as these can be useful in the right circumstances, such as when the goal is to make a point of overcoming resistance to change, or to explore previously unrecognized creative possibilities. The danger of such enforced artificiality, however, is that an insistence on always being positive falsifies the exchange and relieves the participants from accountability for what they say. Meetings can become farcical or just result in more meetings built on an unrealistic foundation created by pretended agreement. An enforced emphasis on always being positive also tends to isolate those who have valuable criticism because they fear they will be excluded for not being a "team player."

Unless a meeting explicitly is intended to be an exercise in positive thinking, leaders should insist on thoughtful and truthful participation that is intended to be constructive. Part of effective leadership is being able to set the right tone for getting to the point, and this sometimes requires the courage of tactfully curtailing or redirecting participation. This might require uncomfortable separate conversations, but once participants can see what is expected they should adjust their approach accordingly to the organization's benefit.

Give Honest Individual Feedback

"The completion of an accurate and timely fitness report is one of an officer's most critical responsibilities."—U.S. Marine Corps, *Commandant's Guidance*

Having a sincere interest in others' personal and professional welfare is both a human virtue and a leadership principle. Everyone in an organization should have a sense that they have an important role in a team that works together to accomplish the mission. Sounds simple but it is not easy. Effective leaders know that individuals respond to feeling they are part of something important and are appreciated. So effective leaders take the time and make the effort to understand everyone's work and its challenges. They ask for input about ways to make changes for improvement, and they encourage others to grow in responsibility. Good things happen when the members of an organization want to be there and to make it even better.

The military expects leaders to give continuous, honest feedback to the members of their commands, evaluate their performance, and support their potential for advancement. This includes regular, formal evaluations that record what has been observed and recommended steps for continued growth. Everyone in a leadership position receives instruction and guidance on the importance of providing this feedback. The evaluations are reviewed up the chain of command, and reporting officers are evaluated on how well they carry out this duty. The system is not foolproof; naturally different commanders can have different standards for performance and different degrees of concern and diligence, and the process creates tension and justifiable concern about the effects of unthoughtful or unfair evaluations. But the weight that the military gives to the evaluation process is an important part of its emphasis on leadership development.

Public service organizations tend not to have a performance evaluation program that gives the kind of regular and honest feedback that the military requires. The unfortunate tendency today is to treat everyone as a high achiever and spread accolades and awards throughout the organization, believing that this is what lifts spirits. There can be competition for how much hyperbole is used to announce even routine accomplishments—words such as "incredible" and "superstar" may be used when referring to something in fact wholly believable and expected. The same kind of inflated language can be used to describe effort. Leaders might portray the members of their organization as working "tirelessly" and always with a "full plate," and proposals for new funding typically note there is no "capacity" for taking on more without it. Celebrating successes is certainly an important part of leadership; few people want to toil unnoticed and unappreciated. But the advice in a popular public administration leadership text to "put celebrations on your calendar"[28] can be taken too literally, if the celebration becomes an expected back-patting session with no connection to real effort or achievement.

When performance evaluations are unrealistically positive or merely formulaic, as they often are in organizations, they lose their value both to the organization and the individual being evaluated. As the Commandant of the Marine Corps instructs on the fitness report form, "Inflationary markings only serve to dilute the value of each report."[29] The same is true of other kinds of inflated performance reward systems including such things as "employee of the month" awards that seem disconnected to effort and achievement. Those who receive unearned praise or prizes should know the truth and not be inspired by them, and those who see them given without merit get no real incentive to do greater things. Trivializing rewards is lost opportunity to reward the best performers meaningfully and to encourage others to improve.

The organization's leaders, and the others involved in administering the process, must give useful guidance and supervise the process to fend off bias and favoritism. To be effective a performance review process must be perceived as fundamentally fair and honest throughout the organization. This can only happen if the evaluators are fair and honest themselves. Comments should encourage initiative, creativity, and taking reasonable risks. Fairness requires understanding that mistakes can be made and everyone has room for improvement. But fairness also means telling the truth when someone needs to try harder or do better. This is the more difficult part of leadership. Giving compliments is easy and feels good. Giving criticism can be emotionally difficult for everyone concerned, and doing it effectively requires courage, tact, and the ability to convey sincere concern. Evaluations must not be used as a substitute for discipline— whenever possible no one should learn about shortcomings when it is too late to fix them before they become part of a permanent record. Problems should be addressed when they arise with guidance given about the needed corrective action. The goal is not to punish; the hope always is to enable the person to see more clearly and either make the changes necessary for success within the organization, or consider whether there would be a better fit elsewhere.

Addressing performance issues is difficult but there is a cost to the organization when leadership does not seem to have the courage to deal with them. In many organizations leaders strive to deal with incompetency or misconduct quietly. They will remove the individual from a responsible position often trying to conceal the problem within the organization. They may even offer incentives to resolve the situation quietly. This may be done as a courtesy to avoid the indignities of public knowledge about the problems, as well as to minimize the chance of a hostile reaction or legal complications based on how the events are portrayed. But often the performance failure that is being concealed is in fact obvious to everyone in the organization. Those who worked with the individual likely are intimately aware of it. Although individual situations need to be handled carefully and with courtesy and respect, and with due regard for legal risks, leaders lose credibility when they go too far and give the impression that those who cause problems get more attention and better treatment than those who quietly perform well. Others in the organization could wonder whether effort really matters.

In the military everyone always gets regular feedback. A proper evaluation contains observations about performance and makes suggestions for growth, and if there is need for correction that has not been made it is noted. The evaluation looks at four general areas:

Mission accomplishment. A performance evaluation is an opportunity to review how well someone's responsibilities and performance of them are attuned to the organization's mission. This emphasizes the importance of commitment to unit success above personal reward. Too often individual priorities stray from the core mission, and when they do energy, time, and resources are not put to the best use. An assessment of mission accomplishment should review previously stated objectives and refine them as guidance for future effort.

Knowledge and skill. Reviewing the state of professional knowledge and skill is an opportunity to emphasize the importance of continuous development through training, education, and reflection on experience. Knowledge includes general intellect as well as specialized knowledge pertaining to individual responsibilities. The organization should value demonstrated ability to think clearly and analytically and exercise sound judgment, traits that can only be developed through more than formal education. The evaluation also should consider demonstrated skill in performing specialized functions and identify opportunities for acquiring additional expertise.

Character. A performance evaluation should include an explicit discussion about the importance of integrity within the organization as demonstrated by such things as personal conduct, reliability, and self-discipline. Integrity can be demonstrated by having the courage to be honest and take responsibility. Character also involves interactions with others in the organization, as demonstrated by treating them with respect, being supportive, and showing concern for their professional success and personal well-being.

Leadership. Anyone with leadership responsibility should get regular feedback on demonstrated ability to influence others while sustaining motivation and morale. Leadership considerations include how well the individual develops individuals and teams, focuses members on the mission, sets an example in effort and demeanor, and exhibits concern for others' wellbeing and development. Communication skills also are part of leadership assessment, which require giving clear instructions to others, inviting their input, and being receptive to their suggestions.

This may seem like a long and wide net to cast in a performance review, especially compared to the experience in most organizations. The approach can be tuned finely to suit the organization but should always be intended to give honest, constructive feedback. It should not be reduced to going through motions, or reduced to filling out forms with boxes and scales that are formulaically completed. It needs to be a serious and honest effort to articulate expectations, consider how well they are being met, and outline a path for growth.

Insist That Everyone Pulls Their Weight

> "While it is important to meet overall accession goals, it is more important to access the right individuals and skills to provide field commanders trained troops to accomplish the mission."—U.S. Air Force, *Personnel Policy*

An organization's ability to accomplish a challenging mission in the public interest depends on cooperative effort by everyone in the organization. Leaders are responsible for inspiring this effort in others and enabling them to contribute to the best of their ability. At the same time leaders must ensure that everyone is working toward the same end and address instances in which this is not the case. Ignoring the reality that even the best performing and most effectively led organization can have individuals who are toxic and should be corrected is either ignorant or intentionally blind.

Leaders must cut through appearances and see actual productivity and effort. This only happens if the leader does all the things that effective leaders should do, such as keeping everyone focused on the mission, maintaining a culture of integrity, and giving honest feedback. Those who are reliable and hard-working should be noticed, suitably rewarded, and given opportunities for growth, and not just expected to carry the load of the organization. The other part of the equation—and the harder part—is paying attention to those who are not pulling their weight.

The military intentionally creates dynamics that tend to illuminate serious nonperformance issues and generate attention to them. These dynamics include clear lines of supervisory responsibility and accountability and a relentless emphasis on reliability and teamwork. Most public service organizations do not have these dynamics and they are unlikely to be as intolerant of non-performers. They also are inclined to avoid the risks and difficulties of corrective action or termination. This disinclination can be very costly to the organization in more ways than the obvious loss of productivity and redirection of others' effort. Managers tend to work around uncooperative or unproductive workers by following the adage "When you want something done give it to a busy person." Productive people tend to be well organized and diligent. They aggressively tackle tasks and stick with them until they are complete. They have a good sense of how long something will take when they agree to do it. They also tend not to complain about being busy. They are unfairly taxed and naturally frustrated when leaders tend always to give the heavy work to them and avoid those who are slower, more disorganized, or unreliable.

Effective leadership requires caring about the welfare of everyone in the organization, wanting them to excel, and giving them the chance to do so. The leader needs to be attuned to each individual's situation. Leaders who are sufficiently involved throughout their organization, and who have developed subordinate leadership throughout it, should be aware of issues as soon as they begin to arise. At that point the expectations should be made clear and expressed directly but tactfully. The leader must also notice, however, if the problem continues or worsens and have the courage to confront it. When handled correctly this outcome should be no surprise to someone who from the start was dealt with honestly, directly, and supportively.

For some effective leadership means acknowledgment and support, for others it means constructive criticism or clearly articulated required changes. The reality may also be that some people are not fit for the organization, or they may be fit but have decided that they are unwilling to make the necessary effort on which others can rely. Recognizing that corrective action is sometimes needed does not require becoming boorish, petty, or insensitive to special circumstances. Everyone in the organization should be willing to make adjustments to support someone who is experiencing health or personal challenges, and they will do so if they feel they are part of a team to which everyone is committed. But leaders have the heavy responsibility of noticing when something else is going on.

Although dealing with situations in which individuals are not carrying their own weight is unpleasant and requires attention to legal considerations, the costs to the organization are likely worse if such situations are left to fester. There can be a positive jolt within the organization when a problematic situation is addressed. The reality is that knowing there are consequences for poor performance or lack of effort is an incentive to do better and work harder. Those who have shouldered more than their fair share of the weight as a result of someone else's choices will see that there can be justice within the organization. They will more highly value being part of it when membership is only accorded to those who earn it.

Cultivate Leadership Throughout

> "Good leadership develops through a never-ending process of self-study, education, training, experience, observation, and emulation."
> —U.S. Coast Guard, *Leadership Development Principle*

The military considers leadership development to be everyone's responsibility. Regardless of seniority everyone is expected to strive to advance in their own leadership ability and ready themselves for stepping into more demanding roles at any time. Leadership ability is essential to career progression; each next assignment likely will involve a more complex unit, probably of larger size with more subordinate commanders, and with different functions and challenges. In this progression there is relentless accountability in performance reviews by senior commanders both in daily contact and periodic formal evaluations. But the responsibility for leadership development is not purely personal. The military also stresses that every leader is responsible for developing the leadership ability of others within their units so they are prepared for additional responsibilities and career advancement. Performance evaluations are explicit about this responsibility to mentor others and give them opportunities to become better leaders themselves.

Leadership development is not just a matter of growth in personal ability of the leader. It is essential for organizational success. A culture of leadership unleashes talent and encourages initiative and innovation. Those who think of themselves as leaders tend to reach for responsibility and feel more of a personal stake in the organization. Treating everyone as someone expected to develop as a leader can create a vibrant organization.

The key is tying leadership development to the organization rather than an abstract notion. A study by the worldwide management consulting firm McKinsey & Company found that successful companies recognize the importance of leadership development and spend billions annually on programs for their people, but these investments commonly fall short by failing to correlate leadership training with the organization's mission and performance.[30] The report concluded, "Companies can avoid the most common mistakes in leadership development and increase the odds of success by matching specific leadership skills and traits to the context at hand; embedding leadership development in real work; fearlessly investigating the mind-sets that underpin behavior; and monitoring the impact so as to make improvements over time."[31] These conclusions reinforce the importance of not expecting people to become better leaders by simply talking about it or sending them to workshops. Instead leadership development must be embedded in the organization's operations and culture.

Unlike the military, in which leadership training and education are continuous and personal development is relentlessly assessed, in other public service leadership development tends to be sporadic or left to individual initiative. Some federal and state governments, university-based institutes, and other public service environments have formal workshops or continuing education programs for leadership studies. These programs may enable participants to draw on their work experience or submit reports from the field that reflect on their learning. They can be valuable to those who participate in them. But given the limited access to these programs, more is likely to be learned about leadership in public service through direct experience, especially in assignments that present new challenges. In his article *How Leaders Are Grown*, Ray Blunt suggests these types of job experiences that produce leadership learning:

- a change in the scope of a job;
- a job that requires a "fix it" opportunity;
- a job that needs to be started from scratch;
- line to staff or staff to line switches (including headquarters to field); and
- projects and tasks that require new skills or learning but where the individual remains on the job.[32]

There are risks involved in making these kinds of assignments. But when an organization has a culture of leadership development, its leaders are willing to take those risks and give others a chance to feel the weight of responsibility and learn how to influence others, including in difficult circumstances.

Assignments made with leadership development in mind are not a matter of throwing others into positions as a kind of sink-or-swim gauntlet. They are prepared for the role and remain in contact to receive advice from more experienced leaders. But the leadership responsibility must be real—both for the person given the assignment and for those with whom that person interacts. Supervisors must resist the natural tendency to delegate responsibility without authority and to pull back as soon as things go differently than expected. The military expects assignments to be made with the purpose of giving such experiences. This is rarely the case in other public service organizations.

Another important part of a continuous leadership development mindset is a sense that all leaders should think of themselves as a mentor to others for their leadership development. A mentor subordinates self-interest for the benefit of someone else's growth. As Ray Blunt advised would-be mentors in *How Leaders are Grown*, "Remember, it's not about you. It is about the people you are mentoring. This is not a power trip or recognition that you know best what is right for another or that you want this person to champion your cause within the organization.... Your role is to serve the learning needs of another by building and sustaining a long-term relationship whose objective is to help the other person grow, learn, and reach his or her potential. To do this you give up some of yourself, including your time, for building toward the future."[33]

The most important aspect of mentoring is setting an example. Talking about leadership is of little use if those in authority do not act the part. The example must demonstrate such essential leadership traits as integrity and taking responsibility. Reasonable people do not expect perfection from a leader, but they do expect leaders to do what they say and to be willing to make decisions in the organization's best interest. Successful leaders can remember examples they have seen of both highly effective and highly toxic leadership. They will strive to emulate the effectiveness and avoid the toxicity. They also should consider how others will recall their own example.

Mentoring also includes making the effort to share approaches to current leadership challenges. Leaders should provide context for their decisions and about their own relevant experiences on which they are drawing. A mentor's counsel can be particularly helpful for learning leadership practices that involve a delicate balance between personal performance and influence of others in the unit. Someone given new responsibilities likely has earned the opportunity by doing something particularly well and will want to continue to do so. But in a leadership role those interests may become secondary to responsibilities that require attention and effort to be spent elsewhere. This change in orientation is a common difficulty in a number of respects.

One such challenge for which a mentor's counsel can be particularly helpful is learning how to find the right balance of supervision and delegation. New leaders want everything to go well and will naturally want to do more things themselves than they should. But effective leaders need to develop a sense of responsibility in their subordinates and so must delegate responsibility and give the freedom to figure out the best way to do things themselves. Effective leaders also must resist the natural tendency to pretend to delegate responsibility while in reality micromanaging performance. This can be especially difficult for new leaders, who want to avoid any risk of things going wrong and probably have strong opinions about exactly how to do them. One insight that an experienced mentor likely can share is that entrusting others, while involving some discomfort, can have a better outcome not only for the development of those entrusted but also because the organization becomes more capable in the long run.

At the same time, a mentor can show that leadership not only involves the heavy responsibility of influencing others but also the obligation to continue to develop personal technical and tactical proficiency. New leaders can be consumed by the new challenge of supervising others and lose sight of their own development. By example and with advice an experienced mentor can reinforce the importance of continuous learning and the need for curiosity about new developments in the field.

Another aspect of the leadership transition for which a mentor's counsel can be especially helpful is figuring how to act like a leader while still maintaining effective relationships with the other members of the unit. This can be particularly difficult when the new leader has been promoted from within. New military officers usually have the benefit of advice from senior noncommissioned officers to deal with the challenge of being the least experienced yet the one in charge. Such counsel is not likely available to someone in other public service. Still, more experienced mentors can help with avoiding the polar problematic tendencies of either being too friendly and causing later problems when difficult decisions must be made, or being too authoritarian and damaging the necessary trusted relationship. Advice and support can be especially helpful when something goes wrong or corrective action is required in a newly formed supervisory relationship. New leaders faced with these situations naturally feel personal turmoil about having to act in ways that seem hurtful to those affected. Experience teaches that such situations can be unavoidable and a leader must have the courage to confront them for the good of the organization, but must do so with equanimity, judiciousness, and tact.

Mentoring also involves a leader's responsibilities for transition after departure. Leaders who care about their organizations want to do everything possible to assist a successor. The military has frequent transitions in leadership, both as a regular progression and change of command and, in times of war, as an accelerated necessity. Commanders are therefore expected to think beyond their own tenure when they train their units and assign responsibilities. They also are expected to establish and document internal procedures that can be quickly grasped by a successor. This orientation highlights that effective leadership means a commitment to the organization that is not switched off the minute someone else bears the primary responsibility. How much someone cares about the organization, and those who are committed to it, reflect both personal integrity and the embodiment of the other leadership traits.

* * *

These are some leadership methods that can be effective when used in the right context. They are not "tools" to be used when leadership is otherwise lacking. Their effectiveness is interrelated with a commitment to influencing others for the right reasons.

Real leaders are guided by what a leader *ought* to do to inspire others to accomplish the organization's mission. They do not make decisions based on what will make them popular within their organization, with their colleagues, or in the public eye. Sometimes this requires difficult decisions to be made that others do not like, or that come at a cost. But leaders ought to inspire others to *want* to be led and do not forget that everyone has feelings and hopes. They assume others are essentially good and capable and give them the chance to be both.

Real leaders do not try to prove they made the right decision in the past by making more decisions with that goal in mind. They strive to make the best possible choices to accomplish the mission based on available information, understanding that in any difficult situation there will be unavoidable uncertainties and differing opinions about it. They are decisive, but they also are always rethinking what they ought to do. If they make a mistake they live up to it and do what they can to correct it. Reasonable people do not expect their leaders to be perfect. They should expect them to try to do the right thing and to be honest about the choices they have made.

Character is what gives someone the strength to do what ought to be done. There is no finer example of how real leadership depends on character than George Washington, who held the most powerful and esteemed positions both in war and peace. More than anything else he was known to be guided by ideals beyond his own personal interests. He miraculously held an army together in desperate circumstances to fight for an ideal. He relinquished power and convinced others to do the same. To the framers of a constitution he embodied the idea of a citizen executive in a government designed to protect personal liberties. After fulfilling that role he again stepped away from power, returning home as soon as someone else was ready to assume his responsibilities.

No one can give us a clearer historical perspective of Washington's influence than John Marshall, who was Chief Justice of the United States during the nation's formative years. At a time when political leaders were dividing along party lines, and many feared the federal government would fail, Marshall wrote ingenious opinions that built a viable constitutional framework. Like most of the founders he had known military service and had personal experience with Washington—they served together at Valley Forge, and Marshall first ran for the House of Representatives at Washington's urging. He became the close confidant of the second president, John Adams, and Adams appointed him to the U.S. Supreme Court when the country faced its first challenge in a transition of power from the Federalist Adams to the Republican Thomas Jefferson. This made Marshall the first Supreme Court justice to serve in all three branches of the federal government. He was a great leader in his own right. As was written of him in a study of his central role in history, "He had a gift for bringing people along and making them feel at ease, and an instinct for finding the center and common ground."[34]

Marshall wrote only one book: a five-volume biography of Washington, a few years after Washington's death. He was given special access to the entire collection of Washington's correspondence and other records of his career and private life. What Marshall found is a powerful statement of Washington's leadership and the integrity that was its foundation. Marshall wrote that he could not find in Washington's papers "a single case from which even an enemy would infer that he was capable, under any circumstances, of stooping to the employment of duplicity."[35] He said of Washington, "Endowed by nature with a sound judgment, and an accurate discriminating mind, he feared not that laborious attention which made him perfectly master of those subjects, in all their relations, on which he was to decide: and this essential quality was guided by an unvarying sense of moral right, which would tolerate the employment, only, of those means that would bear the most rigid examination; by a fairness of intention which neither sought nor required disguise; and by a purity of virtue which was not only untainted, but unsuspected."[36]

Washington's example has faded from discussions about leadership. Only a generation or so ago his memory was honored in annual holiday celebrations and his portrait was in every school. Today his name is virtually unmentioned during what has become a generic "President's Day." His shadow has faded into the background in public perceptions of public leaders. This is a tragic loss. Washington showed that the same traits and principles that can inspire an army in the field also can inspire a nation to have justified faith in its civil leadership. At its core the nature of this inspiration is simple; it is an untainted dedication to do the right thing. All effective methods of leadership, in the military and in other public service, flow from this truth.

Immutable
Leadership Principles

L eadership involves exercising influence to accomplish a mission through personal traits, words, and actions. Growth in leadership ability comes from self-discipline, learning, reflection, and adaptability. Leaders will never arrive at a simple formula for effectiveness that can be applied uniformly. What is most needed depends on the people who are to be led and the circumstances encountered in the battlefield, workplace, or community environment. But experience shows that effective leadership for a higher purpose can be traced to core, immutable leadership principles, including the following:

- Maintain focus on a well-defined and *compelling mission,* aligning actions and decisions with it even when doing so is unpopular or not in your short-term personal interest.
- *Be trustworthy,* sharing reliable information and only making promises intended to be kept.
- *Always act like a leader,* keeping in mind your responsibility is to guide and inspire regardless of the circumstances.
- *Demonstrate sincere interest* in the professional success and personal welfare of everyone in the organization.
- *Be knowledgeable* about all functions within the organization and expert in its core functions, demonstrating ongoing commitment to learning.
- *Approach problems analytically,* reflecting on possible fallacies, considering alternative perspectives, and looking for patterns and solutions that are not readily apparent.
- *Be decisive* and prepared to adapt after a decision has been

made, always collecting information and perspective whenever possible, but not courting endorsement.

- *Assign, promote, and discipline based on merit,* demonstrating just assessment and a willingness to have difficult conversations when improvement is necessary.
- *Develop leadership in others* throughout the organization, encouraging initiative and responsibility and demonstrating a willingness to address bureaucratic barriers and entrenched cultural resistance.

Recommended Leadership Development Reading

Collins, Jim. *Good to Great: Why Some Companies Make the Leap ... and Others Don't.* New York: HarperCollins, 2001.

Department of the Army. *Army Leadership*, ADRP 6–22 (2012).

Donnithorne, Larry R. *The West Point Way of Leadership: From Learning Principled Leadership to Practicing It.* New York: Doubleday, 1993.

Freedman, David H. *Corps Business: The 30 Management Principles of the U.S. Marines.* New York: HarperBusiness, 2000.

Gardner, John W. *On Leadership.* New York: The Free Press, 1990.

Phillips, Donald T., and James M. Loy. *Character in Action: The U.S. Coast Guard on Leadership.* Annapolis: Naval Institute Press, 2003.

Rees, James C. with Stephen Spignesi. *George Washington's Leadership Lessons: What the Father of Our Country Can Teach Us About Effective Leadership and Character.* Hoboken, NJ: John Wiley & Sons, 2007.

Roth-Douquet, Kathy and Frank Schaeffer. *AWOL: The Unexcused Absence of America's Upper Classes from Military Service—and How It Hurts Our Country.* New York: HarperCollins, 2006.

Taylor, Robert L., William E. Rosenbach, and Eric B. Rosenbach eds. *Military Leadership*, 6th ed. Philadelphia: Westview Press, 2009.

U.S. Air Force. *Leadership and Force Development*, Air Force Doctrine Document 1–1 (2011).

U.S. Marine Corps. *Leading Marines*, MCWP 6–11 (2014).

Chapter Notes

Chapter 1

1. Boris Groysberg, Andrew Hill, and Toby Johnson, "Which of These People Is Your Future CEO? The Different Ways Military Experience Prepares Managers for Leadership," *Harvard Business Review* (November 2010).

2. *Ibid.*

3. *Ibid.*

4. Korn/Ferry International, *Military Experience & CEOs: Is There a Link* (2006), 1, http://www.kornferry.com/institute/190-military-experience-and-ceos-is-there-a-link.

5. David D. Van Fleet and Gary A. Yukl, *Military Leadership: An Organizational Behavior Perspective* (Greenwich, CT: JAI Press, 1986), 20.

6. 10 U.S.C. § 502.

7. 5 U.S.C. § 3331.

8. Mark R. Rutgers, "The Oath of Office as Public Value Guardian," *American Review of Public Administration* 40(4) (2010), 429–30.

9. *Ibid.*, 434.

10. *Ibid.*, 428.

11. Trui P.S. Steen and Mark R. Rutgers, "The Double-Edged Sword: Public Service Motivation, the Oath of Office, and the Backlash of an Instrumental Approach," *Public Management Review* 13(3) (2011), 356.

12. John A. Rohr, *To Run a Constitution: The Legitimacy of the Administrative State* (Lawrence: University Press of Kansas, 1986), 192.

13. *Ibid.*

14. Montgomery Van Wart, *Leadership in Public Organizations*, 2d ed. (Armonk, NY: M.E. Sharpe, 2012), 328.

15. James Thomas Flexner, Washington: *The Indispensable Man* (New York: Little, Brown, , 1979), 177.

16. George Washington, "Newburg Address," *The History Place, Great Speeches Collection* (March 15, 1783), http://www.historyplace.com/speeches/washington.htm.

17. Richard Brookhiser, *Founding Father: Rediscovering George Washington* (New York: The Free Press, 1996), 103.

18. Pierce Butler to Weedon Butler, May 5, 1788, *The Records of the Federal Convention of 1787*, ed. Max Farrand, vol. 3 (New Haven: Yale University Press, 1911), 301.

19. George Washington, "Farewell Address," *Papers of George Washington*, University of Virginia, http://gwpapers.virginia.edu/documents/washingtons-farewell-address/.

20. Al Kaltman, *Leadership Lessons from General Ulysses S. Grant* (Paramus, NJ: Prentice Hall, 1998), 136.

21. H.W. Brands, *The Man Who Saved the Union: Ulysses S. Grant in War and Peace* (New York: Doubleday, 2012), 633.

22. *Ibid.*, 632–33.

23. *Ibid.*, 633.

24. Brands, *The Man Who Saved the Union*, 636.

25. "Suspension of the Writ of Habeas Corpus," *New York Herald*, September 18, 1863, in Public Opinion vol. 4, 378.

26. Ulysses S. Grant, "Farewell Address," *A Compilation of the Messages and Papers of the Presidents, 1789–1897*, ed. James D. Richardson, vol. VII (Washington, D.C.:

Government Printing Office, 1898), 399–400.

27. Stephen E. Ambrose, *Eisenhower Vol. 1: Soldier, General of the Army, President Elect 1890–1952* (New York: Simon & Schuster, 1983), 133.

28. *Ibid.*, 271.

29. *Ibid.*, 271–72.

30. Dwight Eisenhower, "Farewell Address," *100 Milestone Doc*uments, U.S. National Archives, http://www.ourdocuments.gov/doc.php?flash=true&doc=90.

31. George Washington, "Farewell Address," *Papers of George Washington*, University of Virginia, http://gwpapers.virginia.edu/documents/washingtons-farewell-address/.

32. H. Norman Schwarzkopf, with Peter Petre, *General H. Norman Schwarzkopf: The Autobiography: It Doesn't Take a Hero* (New York: Bantam Books, 1993), 96–97.

33. *Ibid.*, xiii.

34. *Ibid.*, 502.

35. Michael Hastings, "The Runaway General," *Rolling Stone*, June 22, 2010.

36. Military demographics are reported in U.S. Department of Defense, *2013 Demographics: Profile of the Military Community* (2013).

37. Korn/Ferry International, *Military Experience and CEOs: Is There a Link* (2006), 8, http://www.kornferry.com/institute/190-military-experience-and-ceos-is-there-a-link.

38. *Ibid.*

39. Congressional Research Service, *Membership of the 114th Congress: A Profile* (2015), 8.

40. Donald N. Zillman, "Where Have All the Soldiers Gone II: Military Veterans in Congress and the State of Civil-Military Relations," *Maine Law Review* 58 (2006), 138.

41. Center on the American Governor, *Fast Facts About American Governors* (2015), http://governors.rutgers.edu/on-governors/us-governors/fast-facts-about-american-governors/.

42. U.S. Census Bureau, *Statistical Abstract of the United States: 2012, Table 520: Veterans by Selected Period of Service and State* (2010).

43. U.S. Census Bureau, *How Do We Know?, A Snapshot of Our Nation's Veterans*.

44. U.S. Office of Personnel Management, *Employment of Veterans in the Fed-*eral *Executive Branch Fiscal Year 2012* (2013), 2.

45. *Ibid.*, 3.

46. U.S. Census Bureau, *How Do We Know?, A Snapshot of Our Nation's Veterans*.

47. 38 U.S.C. § 4212.

48. Howard Kurtz, "College Faculties a Most Liberal Lot, Study Finds," *Washington Post*, March 29, 2005, C01; Scott Jaschik, "Moving Further to the Left," *Inside Higher Ed* (October 24, 2012), https://www.insidehighered.com/news/2012/10/24/survey-finds-professors-already-liberal-have-moved-further-left.

49. Mark Shields, "Bellicose Hypocrites," *Washington Post*, November 2, 1990, 25.

50. Mark Shields, "Why Liberals Should Back the Return of the Draft," *Star Banner*, June 20, 2006, 6A.

51. Kathy Roth-Douquet and Frank Schaeffer, *AWOL: The Unexcused Absence of America's Upper Classes from Military Service—and How It Hurts Our Country* (New York: HarperCollins, 2006).

52. *Ibid.*, 32.

53. *Ibid.*, 42.

54. *Ibid.*, 43 (emphasis in original).

55. *Ibid.*, 50.

56. *Ibid.*, 41 (emphasis in original).

57. *Ibid.*

58. Peace Corps, *Peace Corps Today*, http://www.peacecorps.gov/today/.

59. Alison Lighthall, "Ten Things You Should Know About Today's Student Veteran," *Thought & Action* (Fall 2012), 80.

60. *Ibid.*, 88.

61. Dennis Jacobs, "The Military and the Law Elite," *Cornell Journal of Law and Public Policy* 19 (2009), 206.

62. Karen Hough, "'Yes, But'—The Evil Twin to 'Yes, And,'" *Huffington Post*, November 11 2014, http://www.huffingtonpost.com/karen-hough/yes-but-the-evil-twin-to-_b_5669640.html.

63. David L. Cooperrider and Diana Whitney, *A Positive Revolution in Change: Appreciative Inquiry* (San Francisco: Berrett-Koehler, 2005).

64. James H. Toner, *Morals Under the Gun: The Cardinal Virtues, Military Ethics, and American Society* (Lexington: University Press of Kentucky, 2000), 19.

65. U.S. Department of Defense, *2013 Demographics, Profile of the Military Community*, 22.

66. David R. Segal and Mady Wechster Segal, "America's Military Population," *Population Bulletin* 59 (December 2004), 37.

67. *Ibid.*, 23.

68. *Ibid.*, 28.

69. Sebastian Junger, "Why Veterans Miss War," *TED Talks*, January 2014, https://www.ted.com/talks/sebastian_junger_why_veterans_miss_war?language=en.

70. Montgomery Van Wart, *Leadership in Public Organizations*, 2d ed. (Armonk, NY: M.E. Sharpe, 2012), 95.

71. Charles Moskos, "Our Will to Fight Depends on Who Is Willing to Die," *Wall Street Journal*, March 20, 2002, http://www.wsj.com/articles/SB1016587423567462560.

72. *Ibid.*

73. Gretel C. Kovach, "Marine Corps Study Says Units with Women Fall Short on Combat Skills," *Los Angeles Times*, September 12, 2015, http://www.latimes.com/nation/la-na-marines-women-20150912-story.html.

74. Efraim Benmelech and Carola Frydman, *Military CEOs*, National Bureau of Economic Research (January 2014), 22, http://www.nber.org/papers/w19782.

75. *Ibid.*, 24.

76. *Ibid.*, 34.

77. John W. Gardner, *On Leadership* (New York: The Free Press, 1990).

Chapter 2

1. Larry Donnithorne, *The West Point Way of Leadership: From Learning Principled Leadership to Practicing It* (New York: Doubleday, 1994), 6 (emphasis in original).

2. *Leadership: The Warrior's Art*, ed. Christopher Kolenda, 2d ed. (Carlisle, PA: Army War College Foundation Press, 2001).

3. Nathaniel Fick, *One Bullet Away: The Making of a Marine Officer* (New York: Houghton Mifflin, 2005), 24.

4. Jim Collins, *Good to Great: Why Some Companies Make the Leap ... and Others Don't* (New York: HarperCollins, 2001).

5. *Ibid.*, 13.

6. *Ibid.*, 51.

7. Donald T. Phillips and James M. Loy, *Character in Action: The U.S. Coast Guard on Leadership* (Annapolis: Naval Institute Press, 2003), 18–19, 25. Coast Guard official doctrine refers to the Phillips and Loy book for its statement of leadership. U.S. Coast Guard, *Doctrine for the U.S. Coast Guard*, Publication 1 (2014).

8. Headquarters, Department of the Army, *Army Leadership*, ADRP 6–22, 1–1 (2012).

9. *Ibid.*, 7–16.

10. *Ibid.*, 6–9 to 6–10.

11. *Ibid.*, 3–3.

12. Donnithorne, *The West Point Way of Leadership*, 114.

13. U.S. Marine Corps, *Leading Marines*, MCWP 6–11 (2014).

14. U.S. Navy, *Core Values*, http://www.navy.mil/navydata/nav_legacy.asp?id=193; U.S. Naval Academy, Naval Service Training Command, *Officer Professional Corps Competencies Manual* (2014), II-1; U.S. Marine Corps, *Leading Marines*.

15. U.S. Marine Corps, *Leading Marines*, 1–7.

16. U.S. Marine Corps, *Leading Marines*; Toraiheeb Al Harbi, *Navy Definitions of Leadership and LMEWT/NAVLEAD Competency Clusters Compared to Selected Leadership Theories* (master's thesis, Naval Postgraduate School, 1995), 38–40.

17. U.S. Marine Corps, *Leading Marines*, 2–4.

18. *Ibid.*, 2–6; Toraiheeb Al Harbi, *Navy Definitions of Leadership*, 38.

19. U.S. Air Force, *Leadership and Force Development*, Air Force Doctrine Document 1–1 (2011), 22.

20. *Ibid.*, 26.

21. *Ibid.*, 35–36.

22. *Ibid.*, 27.

23. *Ibid.*, 28–31.

24. Donald T. Phillips and James M. Loy, *Character in Action*, 149.

25. *Ibid.*, 13.

26. *Ibid.*

27. *Ibid.*, 15.

28. *Ibid.*, 45.

29. *Ibid.*, 46–47.

30. *Ibid.*, 33–129.

31. *Ibid.*, 111.

32. Headquarters, Department of the Army, *Leader Development*, FM 6–22 (2015), 1–1.

33. Headquarters, Department of the Army, *Army Leadership*, 7–10.

34. *Ibid.*

35. Peter G. Northouse, *Leadership: Theory and Practice*, 6th ed. (Thousand Oaks, CA: Sage Publications, 2013), 4.

36. Network of Schools of Public Policy,

Affairs, and Administration, *NASPAA Annual Accreditation Data Report 2013–2014* (September 2015), 3–5.

37. *Ibid.*, 8.

38. Institute of Education Sciences, National Center for Education Statistics, *Graduate Degree Fields* (2015), https://nces.ed.gov/programs/coe/indicator_ctb.asp.

39. Montgomery Van Wart and Kevin O'Farrell, "Organizational Leadership and the Challenges in Teaching It," *Journal of Public Affairs Education* 13(2) (2007), 439–50.

40. *Ibid.*, 442.

41. *Ibid.*, 442–43.

42. Isabel Briggs Myers and Mary H. McCaulley, *Manual: A Guide to the Development and Use of the Myers-Briggs Type Indicator* (Palo Alto, CA: Consulting Psychologists Press, 1990).

43. *Ibid.*, 1.

44. Leadership Practices Inventory (LPI) Assessments: A Leader's First Step Toward Achieving the Extraordinary, John Wiley & Sons, http://www.leadershipchallenge.com/professionals-section-lpi.aspx.

45. Van Wart and O'Farrell, "Organizational Leadership and the Challenges in Teaching It," 446.

46. Edward de Bono, *Six Thinking Hats* (Boston: Little, Brown, 1999).

47. Van Wart and O'Farrell, "Organizational Leadership and the Challenges in Teaching It," 442.

48. *Ibid.*

49. *Ibid.*

50. *Ibid.*

51. Lloyd A. Blanchard and Amy K. Donahue, "Teaching Leadership in Public Administration," *Journal of Public Affairs Education* 13(3/4) (2007–2008), 480.

52. *Ibid.*, 480–81.

53. Terry Newell, Grant Reeher, and Peter Ronayne, *The Trusted Leader: Building the Relationships that Make Government Work*, 2d ed. (Washington, D.C.: CQ Press, 2011).

54. Ray Blunt, "How Leaders Are Grown: The Lessons of Example and Experience," in *The Jossey-Bass Reader on Nonprofit and Public Leadership*, ed. James L. Perry (San Francisco: John Wiley & Sons, 2010), 38.

55. *Ibid.*, 38–54.

56. *Ibid.*, 39.

57. *Ibid.*, 40.

58. Montgomery Van Wart, "Public-Sector Leadership Theory: An Assessment," in *The Jossey-Bass Reader on Nonprofit and Public Sector Leadership*, ed. James L. Perry (San Francisco: John Wiley & Sons, 2010), 92–93.

59. CMS Alliance to Modernize Healthcare Federally Funded Research and Development Center, *Independent Assessment of the Health Care Delivery Systems and Management Processes of the Department of Veterans Affairs* (2015), 53.

60. Montgomery Van Wart, "Public-Sector Leadership Theory: An Assessment," 78–79.

61. John W. Gardner, *On Leadership* (New York: The Free Press, 1990).

62. *Ibid.*, xi.

63. *Ibid.*, 9.

64. *Ibid.*, 1.

65. *Ibid.*, 48–54.

66. *Ibid.*, 53.

67. *Ibid.*, 54.

68. *Ibid.*, 162.

69. *Ibid.*, 162–170.

70. *E.g.*, John W. Gardner, "The Tasks of Leadership," in *The Jossey-Bass Reader on Nonprofit and Public Sector Leadership*, ed. James L. Perry (San Francisco: John Wiley & Sons, 2010), 11–24.

71. Larry C. Spears, *The Understanding and Practice of Servant Leadership* (paper, Servant Leadership Research Roundtable, Regent University School of Leadership Studies, 2005), https://www.regent.edu/acad/global/publications/sl_proceedings/2005/spears_practice.pdf.

72. Douglas McGregor, *The Human Side of Enterprise* (New York: McGraw-Hill, 1960).

73. *Ibid.*, 22.

74. James MacGregor Burns, *Leadership* (New York: Harper & Row, 1978).

75. *Ibid.*, 2.

76. *Ibid.*, 3.

77. *Ibid.*, 425–26.

78. Montgomery Van Wart, "Public-Sector Leadership Theory: An Assessment," 79.

79. *Ibid.*

80. *Ibid.*, 79–80.

81. Peter G. Northouse, *Leadership: Theory and Practice*, 58.

82. *Ibid.*, 59.

83. *Ibid.*, 60.

84. *Ibid.*

85. For example, see the Ethics & Compliance Initiative's long-running and extensive surveys of ethical behavior perceptions

across all industries in more than 450 organizations, such as those reported in Ethics & Compliance Initiative, *National Business Ethics Survey* (2014).

86. James M. Kouzes and Barry Z. Posner, *The Leadership Challenge*, 5th ed. (San Francisco: John Wiley & Sons, 2012).

87. *Ibid.*, 34.

88. Montgomery Van Wart, *Leadership in Public Organizations*, 2d ed. (Armonk, NY: M.E. Sharpe, 2012), 201.

89. *Ibid.*, 201–18.

90. *Ibid.*, 203.

91. *Ibid.*, 204.

92. *Ibid.*, 205–06.

93. *Ibid.*, 207–11.

94. Robert K. Greenleaf, *Servant Leadership: A Journey into the Nature of Legitimate Power and Greatness* (New York: Paulist Press, 1977), 27.

95. Peter G. Northouse, *Leadership: Theory and Practice*, 232–33.

96. *Ibid.*, 232.

97. *Ibid.*, 245 (a sample form of "servant leader questionnaire").

98. Martin M. Chemers, *An Integrative Theory of Leadership* (Mahwah, NJ: Lawrence Erlbaum Associates, 2009).

99. *Ibid.*, 151.

100. *Ibid.*, 172–73.

101. *Ibid.*, 28.

Chapter 3

1. Chamberlain's life and actions in the war are described in Joshua Lawrence Chamberlain, *The Passing of the Armies: An Account of the Final Campaign of the Army of the Potomac Based upon Personal Reminiscences of the Fifth Army Corps* (New York: G.P. Putnam's Sons, 1915); Joshua Lawrence Chamberlain, *Through Blood & Fire at Gettysburg* (Gettysburg, PA: Stan Clark Military Books, 1994); Edward G. Longacre, *Joshua Chamberlain: The Soldier and the Man* (Conshohocken, PA: Combined Publishing, 1999); and Alice Rains Trulock, *In the Hands of Providence: Joshua L. Chamberlain and the American Civil War* (Chapel Hill: University of North Carolina Press, 1992).

2. Chamberlain, *The Passing of the Armies*, 19–20.

3. Chamberlain, *Through Blood & Fire*, 11.

4. *Ibid.*, 5.

5. *Ibid.* 9.

6. *Ibid.*, 10.

7. *Ibid.*, 16.

8. Trulock, *In the Hands of Providence*, 155.

9. The attacks on 9/11 and the response are described in National Commission on Terrorist Attacks upon the United States, *The 9/11 Commission Report* (2004). Giuliani describes his mayoralty and actions on 9/11 in Rudolph W. Giuliani, with Ken Kurson, *Leadership* (New York: Hyperion, 2002).

10. Giuliani, *Leadership*, 42.

11. *Ibid.*, 34.

12. *Ibid.*, 36–37.

13. Deborah Hart Strober and Gerald S. Strober, *Giuliani: Flawed or Flawless* (Hoboken, NJ: John Wiley & Sons, 2007), 125.

14. *Ibid.* 138.

15. *Ibid.*, 133.

16. Giuliani, *Leadership,* 63.

17. *Ibid.*, 4.

18. *Ibid.*, 7.

19. *Ibid.*

20. *Ibid.*

21. *Ibid.*, 16.

22. *Ibid.*, 14.

23. *Ibid.*, 18.

24. Recording of Press Conference, Rudolph Giuliani and Governor George Pataki, http://www.authentichistory.com/2001–2008/1-911/1-timeline1/20010911_1438_Giuliani-Pataki_Press_Conference-audio.html.

25. *Ibid.*

26. Giuliani, *Leadership,* 353.

27. James W. Cortada and Edward Wakin, *Betting on America: Why the U.S. Can Be Stronger After September 11* (Upper Saddle River, NJ: Prentice Hall, 2002), 202.

28. Giuliani, *Leadership*, 26.

29. *Ibid.*, 359.

30. *Ibid.*, xii–xiii.

31. Strober and Strober, *Guiliani*, 259.

32. Nagin, *Katrina's Secrets*, 19.

33. *Ibid.*

34. *Ibid.*, 24.

35. *Ibid.*, 40.

36. *Ibid.*, 37.

37. *Ibid.*, 46.

38. Select Bipartisan Committee to Investigate the Preparation for and Response to Hurricane Katrina, *A Failure f Initiative, Final Report of the Select Bipartisan Committee to Investigate the Preparation for and Response to Hurricane Katrina* (2006), 70.

39. *Ibid.*
40. Nagin, *Katrina's Secrets*, 55.
41. *Ibid.*, 77–78.
42. *Ibid.*, 76.
43. *Ibid.*, 77.
44. *Ibid.*, 97.
45. *Ibid.*, 262.
46. *Ibid.*, 176.
47. *Ibid.*, 188–89.
48. *Ibid.*, 163.
49. *Ibid.* 192–93.
50. *Ibid.* 273.
51. New Orleans Mayor Ray Nagin Gave this Speech Monday During a Program at City Hall Commemorating Martin Luther King Jr., January 17, 2006, http://www.nola.com/news/t-p/stories/011706_nagin_transcript.html.
52. Giuliani, *Leadership*, xiv.
53. Chamberlain, *Through Blood & Fire*, 21.
54. Giuliani, *Leadership*, 361.
55. Mitja D. Back, C.P. Albrecht, and Boris Egloff, "The Emotional Timeline of September 11, 2001," *Psychological Science* 21(10) (2010): 1417–19.
56. Giuliani, *Leadership*, 23–24.
57. Robert L. Hamblin, "Leadership and Crises," *Sociometry* 21(4) (1958).
58. Strober and Strober, *Giuliani*, 269.
59. Select Bipartisan Committee to Investigate the Preparation for and Response to Hurricane Katrina, *A Failure of Initiative, Final Report of the Select Bipartisan Committee to Investigate the Preparation for and Response to Hurricane Katrina* (2006), 111.
60. *Ibid.*
61. Nagin, *Katrina's Secrets*, 163.
62. National Commission on Terrorist Attacks Upon the United States, *The 9/11 Commission Report* (2004), 390.
63. Wayne Barrett and Dan Collins, *Grand Illusion* (New York: HarperCollins, 2006), 356.

Chapter 4

1. Christian Smith, Kari Christofferson, Hilary Davidson, and Patricia Snell Herzog, *Lost in Transition: The Dark Side of Emerging Childhood* (Oxford: Oxford University Press, 2011).
2. *Ibid.*, 36 (emphasis in original).
3. *Ibid.* 37.
4. Ethics & Compliance Initiative, National Business Ethics Survey (2014).
5. Peter W. Morgan and Glenn H. Reynolds, *The Appearance of Impropriety: How the Ethics Wars Have Undermined American Government, Business, and Society* (New York: The Free Press, 1997).
6. *Ibid.*, 98.
7. *Ibid.*, 201.
8. *Ibid.*, 202.
9. *Ibid.*
10. *Ibid.*, 203.
11. *Ibid.*, 205 (emphasis in original).
12. *Ibid.*
13. *Ibid.*, 206.
14. James M. Kouzes and Barry Z. Posner, *The Leadership Challenge*, 5th ed. (San Francisco: John Wiley & Sons, 2012), 18 (emphasis in original).
15. Russell Kirk, *The Conservative Mind: From Burke to Santayana* (Chicago: Henry Regenery Co., 1953), 8.
16. Paul Rogers and Marcia Blenko, "Who Has the D? How Clear Decision Roles Enhance Organizational Performance," *Harvard Business Review* (January 2006), 2.
17. *Ibid.*
18. *Ibid.*, 8.
19. John Darley, "Diffusion of Responsibility," *Encyclopedia of Social Psychology*, ed. Roy F. Baumeister and Kathleen D. Vohs (Thousand Oaks, CA: Sage Publications, 2007).
20. J. Richard Hackman and Neil Vidmar, "Effects of Size and Task Type on Group Performance and Member Reactions," *Sociometry* 33(1) (March 1970), 43 (emphasis in original).
21. Solomon E. Asch, "Opinions and Social Pressure," *Scientific American* 193(5) (November 1955), 34.
22. *Ibid.*
23. David Salsburg, *The Lady Tasting Tea: How Statistics Revolutionized Science in the Twentieth Century* (New York: Holt Paperbacks, 2001), 231.
24. Rogers and Blenko, "Who Has the D?," 9.
25. Franklin Roosevelt to Eleanor Roosevelt, December 3, 1936, *F.D.R.: His Personal Letters, 1928–1945*, vol. I (New York: Duell, Sloan and Pearce, 1950), 635.
26. Jeff Shesol, *Supreme Power: Franklin Roosevelt vs. The Supreme Court* (New York: W.W. Norton, 2010), 472.
27. Inspector General of the Marine Corps, *Marine Corps Inspector General Program Inspections Guide* (2009), 3–3–1.

28. Kouzes and Posner, *The Leadership Challenge*, 323.

29. USMC Fitness Report (1610), NAVMC 10835 (Rev. 7–11).

30. Pierre Gurdjian, Thomas Halbeisen, and Kevin Lane, "Why Leadership-Development Programs Fail," *McKinsey Quarterly* (January 2014), http://www.mckinsey.com/global-themes/leadership/why-leadership-development-programs-fail.

31. *Ibid.*

32. Ray Blunt, "How Leaders are Grown,"

in *The Jossey-Bass Reader on Nonprofit and Public Leadership*, ed. James L. Perry (San Francisco: John Wiley & Sons, 2010), 39.

33. *Ibid.*, 45.

34. Cliff Sloan and David McKean, *The Great Decision: Jefferson, Adams, Marshall, and the Battle for the Supreme Court* (New York: Public Affairs, 2009), 152.

35. John Marshall, *The Life of George Washington*, vol. V (Philadelphia: C.P. Wayne, 1807), 777.

36. *Ibid.*, 779.

Bibliography

Al Harbi, Toraiheeb. *Navy Definitions of Leadership and LMEWT/NAVLEAD Competency Clusters Compared to Selected Leadership Theories.* Master's thesis, Naval Postgraduate School, 1995.

Ambrose, Stephen E. *Eisenhower Vol. 1: Soldier, General of the Army, President Elect 1890–1952.* New York: Simon & Schuster, 1983.

Asch, Solomon E. "Opinions and Social Pressure." *Scientific American* 193(5) (November 1955): 31–35.

Back, Mitja D., C.P. Albrecht, and Boris Egloff. "The Emotional Timeline of September 11, 2001." *Psychological Science* 21(10) (2010): 1417–19.

Barrett, Wayne, and Dan Collins. *Grand Illusion.* New York: HarperCollins, 2006.

Benmelech, Efraim, and Carola Frydman. *Military CEOs, National Bureau of Economic Research* (January 2014). http://www.nber.org/papers/w19782.

Blanchard, Lloyd A., and Amy K. Donahue. "Teaching Leadership in Public Administration." *Journal of Public Affairs Education* 13(3/4) (2007–2008), 461–85.

Blunt, Ray. "How Leaders are Grown: The Lessons of Example and Experience." In *The Jossey-Bass Reader on Nonprofit and Public Leadership*, edited by James L. Perry, 38–54. San Francisco: John Wiley & Sons, 2010.

Brands, H.W. *The Man Who Saved the Union: Ulysses S. Grant in War and Peace.* New York: Doubleday, 2012.

Brookhiser, Richard. *Founding Father: Rediscovering George Washington.* New York: The Free Press, 1996.

Burns, James MacGregor. *Leadership.* New York: Harper & Row, 1978.

Butler, Pierce. Pierce Butler to Weedon Butler, May 5, 1788. In *The Records of the Federal Convention of 1787*, ed. Max Farrand, vol. 3. New Haven: Yale University Press, 1911: 301.

Center on the American Governor, *Fast Facts about American Governors* (2015). http://governors.rutgers.edu/on-governors/us-governors/fast-facts-about-american-governors/.

Chamberlain, Joshua Lawrence. *The Passing of the Armies: An Account of the Final Campaign of the Army of the Potomac Based upon Personal Reminiscences of the Fifth Army Corps.* New York: G.P. Putnam's Sons, 1915.

_____. *Through Blood & Fire at Gettysburg.* Gettysburg, PA: Stan Clark Military Books, 1994.

Chemers, Martin M. *An Integrative Theory of Leadership.* Mahwah, NJ: Lawrence Erlbaum Associates, 2009.

CMS Alliance to Modernize Healthcare Federally Funded Research and Development Center. *Independent Assessment of the Health Care Delivery Systems and Management Processes of the Department of Veterans Affairs* (2015).

Collins, Jim. *Good to Great: Why Some Companies Make the Leap ... and Others Don't*. New York: HarperCollins, 2001.

Congressional Research Service. *Membership of the 114th Congress: A Profile*. 2015.

Cooperrider, David L., and Diana Whitney. *A Positive Revolution in Change: Appreciative Inquiry*. San Francisco: Berrett-Koehler, 2005.

Cortada, James W., and Edward Wakin. *Betting on America: Why the U.S. Can Be Stronger After September 11*. Upper Saddle River, NJ: Prentice Hall, 2002.

de Bono, Edward. *Six Thinking Hats*. Boston: Little, Brown, 1999.

Darley, John. "Diffusion of Responsibility." *Encyclopedia of Social Psychology*, ed. Roy F. Baumeister and Kathleen D. Vohs. Thousand Oaks, CA: Sage Publications, 2007.

Donnithorne, Larry. *The West Point Way of Leadership: From Learning Principled Leadership to Practicing It*. New York: Doubleday, 1994.

Eisenhower, Dwight. "Farewell Address." *100 Milestone Documents*, U.S. National Archives. http://www.ourdocuments.gov/doc.php?flash=true&doc=90.

Ethics & Compliance Initiative. *National Business Ethics Survey* (2014).

Fick, Nathaniel. *One Bullet Away: The Making of a Marine Officer*. New York: Houghton Mifflin, 2005.

Flexner, James Thomas. *Washington: The Indispensable Man*. New York: Little, Brown, 1979.

Freedman, David G. *Corps Business: The 30 Management Principles of the U.S. Marines*. New York: HarperBusiness, 2000.

Gardner, John W. *On Leadership*. New York: The Free Press, 1990.

_____. "The Tasks of Leadership." In *The Jossey-Bass Reader on Nonprofit and Public Sector Leadership*, ed. James L. Perry, 11–24. San Francisco: John Wiley & Sons, 2010.

Giuliani, Rudolph W., with Ken Kurson. *Leadership*. New York: Hyperion, 2002.

_____. Recording of Press Conference, Rudolph Giuliani and Governor George Pataki. http://www.authentichistory.com/2001-2008/1-911/1-timeline1/20010 911_1438_Giuliani-Pataki_Press_Conference-audio.html.

Greenleaf, Robert K. *Servant Leadership: A Journey into the Nature of Legitimate Power and Greatness*. New York: Paulist Press, 1977.

Grant, Ulysses S. "Farewell Address." In *A Compilation of the Messages and Papers of the Presidents, 1789–1897*, ed. James D. Richardson, vol. VII. Washington, D.C.: Government Printing Office, 1898: 399–400.

Groysberg, Boris, Andrew Hill, and Toby Johnson. "Which of These People Is Your Future CEO? The Different Ways Military Experience Prepares Managers for Leadership." *Harvard Business Review* (November 2010).

Gurdjian, Pierre, Thomas Halbeisen, and Kevin Lane. "Why Leadership-Development Programs Fail." *McKinsey Quarterly* (January 2014). http://www.mc kinsey.com/global-themes/leadership/why-leadership-development-programs-fail.

Hackman, Richard J., and Vidmar, Neil. "Effects of Size and Task Type on Group Performance and Member Reactions." *Sociometry* 33(1) (March 1970) 37–54.

Hamblin, Robert L. "Leadership and Crises." *Sociometry* 21(4) (1958): 322–35.

Hastings, Michael. "The Runaway General." *Rolling Stone* (June 22, 2010).

Hough, Karen. "'Yes, But'—The Evil Twin to 'Yes, And,'" *Huffington Post* (November 11 2014), http://www.huffingtonpost.com/karen-hough/yes-but-the-evil-twin-to-_b_5669640.html.

Inspector General of the Marine Corps. *Marine Corps Inspector General Program Inspections Guide* (2009).

Institute of Education Sciences, National Center for Education Statistics. *Graduate Degree Fields* (2015). https://nces.ed.gov/programs/coe/indicator_ctb.asp.

Jacobs, Dennis. "The Military and the Law Elite." *Cornell Journal of Law and Public Policy* 19 (2009): 205–12.

Jaschik, Scott. "Moving Further to the Left." *Inside Higher Ed* (October 24, 2012). https://www.insidehighered.com/news/2012/10/24/survey-finds-professors-already-liberal-have-moved-further-left.

Junger, Sebastian. "Why Veterans Miss War." *TED Talks* (January 2014). https://www.ted.com/talks/sebastian_junger_why_veterans_miss_war?language=en.

Kaltman, Al. *Leadership Lessons from General Ulysses S. Grant.* Paramus, NJ: Prentice Hall, 1998.

Keskel, Kenneth. "The Oath of Office: A Historical Guide to Moral Leadership." *Air & Space Power Journal* 16(4) (Winter 2002): 47–57.

Kirk, Russell. *The Conservative Mind: From Burke to Santayana.* Chicago: Henry Regenery Co., 1953.

Kolenda, Christopher, ed. *Leadership: The Warrior's Art,* 2d ed. Carlisle, PA: Army War College Foundation Press, 2001.

Korn/Ferry International. *Military Experience & CEOs: Is There a Link* (2006). http://www.kornferry.com/institute/190-military-experience-and-ceos-is-there-a-link.

Kouzes, James M., and Barry Z. Posner. *The Leadership Challenge,* 5th ed. San Francisco: John Wiley & Sons, 2012.

Kovach, Gretel C. "Marine Corps Study Says Units with Women Fall Short on Combat Skills." *Los Angeles Times* (September 12, 2015). http://www.latimes.com/nation/la-na-marines-women-20150912-story.html.

Kurtz, Howard. "College Faculties a Most Liberal Lot, Study Finds." *Washington Post* (March 29, 2005).

John Wiley & Sons. *Leadership Practices Inventory (LPI) Assessments: A Leader's First Step Toward Achieving the Extraordinary* (2016). http://www.leadershipchallenge.com/professionals-section-lpi.aspx.

Lighthall, Alison. "Ten Things You Should Know About Today's Student Veteran." *Thought & Action* (Fall 2012): 80–89.

Longacre, Edward G. *Joshua Chamberlain: The Soldier and the Man.* Conshohocken, PA: Combined Publishing, 1999.

Marshall, John. *The Life of George Washington.* Philadelphia: C.P. Wayne, 1807.

McGregor, Douglas. *The Human Side of Enterprise.* New York: McGraw-Hill, 1960.

Morgan, Peter W., and Glenn H. Reynolds. *The Appearance of Impropriety: How the Ethics Wars Have Undermined American Government, Business, and Society.* New York: The Free Press, 1997.

Moskos, Charles. "Our Will to Fight Depends on Who Is Willing to Die." *Wall Street Journal* (March 20, 2002), http://www.wsj.com/articles/SB1016587423567462560.

Myers, Isabel Briggs, and Mary H. McCaulley, *Manual: A Guide to the Development and Use of the Myers-Briggs Type Indicator.* Palo Alto, CA: Consulting Psychologists Press, 1990.

Nagin, C. Ray. *Katrina's Secrets* (2011).

_____. New Orleans Mayor Ray Nagin Gave This Speech Monday During a Program at City Hall Commemorating Martin Luther King Jr., January 17, 2006. http://www.nola.com/news/t-p/stories/011706_nagin_transcript.html.

National Commission on Terrorist Attacks upon the United States. *The 9/11 Commission Report* (2004).

Network of Schools of Public Policy, Affairs, and Administration. *NASPAA Annual Accreditation Data Report 2013–2014* (September 2015).

Newell, Terry, Grant Reeher, and Peter Ronayne. *The Trusted Leader: Building the Relationships that Make Government Work*, 2d ed. Washington, D.C.: CQ Press, 2011.

New York Herald. "Suspension of the Writ of Habeas Corpus," September 18, 1863, in *Public Opinion* 4, 378 (1894).

Northouse, Peter G. *Leadership: Theory and Practice*, 6th ed. Thousand Oaks, CA: Sage Publications, 2013.

Phillips, Donald T., and James M. Loy. *Character in Action: The U.S. Coast Guard on Leadership.* Annapolis: Naval Institute Press, 2003.

Rees, James C., with Stephen Spignesi. *George Washington's Leadership Lessons: What the Father of Our Country Can Teach Us About Effective Leadership and Character.* Hoboken, NJ: John Wiley & Sons, 2007.

Rogers. Paul. and Marcia Blenko. "Who Has the D? How Clear Decision Roles Enhance Organizational Performance." *Harvard Business Review* (January 2006).

Rohr, John A. *To Run a Constitution: The Legitimacy of the Administrative State.* Lawrence: University Press of Kansas, 1986.

Roosevelt, Franklin. Franklin Roosevelt to Eleanor Roosevelt, December 3, 1936. In *F.D.R.: His Personal Letters, 1928–1945*, vol. I. New York: Duell, Sloan and Pearce, 1950: 635.

Roth-Douquet, Kathy, and Frank Schaeffer. *AWOL: The Unexcused Absence of America's Upper Classes from Military Service—and How It Hurts Our Country.* New York: HarperCollins, 2006.

Rutgers, Mark R. "The Oath of Office as Public Value Guardian." *American Review of Public Administration* 40(4) (2010): 428–44.

Salsburg, David. *The Lady Tasting Tea: How Statistics Revolutionized Science in the Twentieth Century.* New York: Holt Paperbacks, 2001.

Schwarzkopf, Norman H., with Peter Petre. *General H. Norman Schwarzkopf: The Autobiography: It Doesn't Take a Hero.* New York: Bantam Books, 1993.

Segal, David R., and Mady Wechster Segal. "America's Military Population." *Population Bulletin* 59 (December 2004).

Select Bipartisan Committee to Investigate the Preparation for and Response to Hurricane Katrina. *A Failure of Initiative, Final Report of the Select Bipartisan Committee to Investigate the Preparation for and Response to Hurricane Katrina* (2006).

Shesol, Jeff. *Supreme Power: Franklin Roosevelt vs. The Supreme Court.* New York: W.W. Norton, 2010.

Shields, Mark. "Bellicose Hypocrites." *Washington Post* (November 2, 1990).

_____. "Why Liberals Should Back the Return of the Draft." *Star Banner* (June 20, 2006).

Sloan, Cliff, and David McKean. *The Great Decision: Jefferson, Adams, Marshall, and the Battle for the Supreme Court.* New York: Public Affairs, 2009.

Smith, Christian, Kari Christofferson, Hilary Davidson, and Patricia Snell Herzog. *Lost in Transition: The Dark Side of Emerging Childhood.* Oxford: Oxford University Press, 2011.

Spears, Larry C. *The Understanding and Practice of Servant Leadership* (paper). *Servant Leadership Research Roundtable.* Regent University School of Leadership Studies, 2005. https://www.regent.edu/acad/global/publications/sl_proceedings/2005/spears_practice.pdf.

Steen, Trui P.S., and Mark R. Rutgers. "The Double-Edged Sword: Public Service

Motivation, the Oath of Office, and the Backlash of an Instrumental Approach." *Public Management Review* 13(3) (2011): 343–61.

Strober, Deborah Hart, and Gerald S. Strober, *Giuliani: Flawed or Flawless.* Hoboken, NJ: John Wiley & Sons, 2007.

Taylor, Robert L., William E. Rosenbach, and Eric B. Rosenbach, eds. *Military Leadership,* 6th ed. Philadelphia: Westview Press, 2009.

Toner, James H. *Morals Under the Gun: The Cardinal Virtues, Military Ethics, and American Society.* Lexington: University Press of Kentucky, 2000.

Trulock, Alice Rains. *In the Hands of Providence: Joshua L. Chamberlain and the American Civil War.* Chapel Hill: University of North Carolina Press, 1992.

U.S. Air Force. *Leadership and Force Development.* Air Force Doctrine Document 1-1 (2011).

U.S. Army, Headquarters, Department of the Army. *Army Leadership,* ADRP 6-22, 1-1 (2012).

_____. *Leader Development,* FM 6–22 (2015).

U.S. Census Bureau. *Statistical Abstract of the United States: 2012, Table 520: Veterans by Selected Period of Service and State* (2010).

U.S. Coast Guard. *Doctrine for the U.S. Coast Guard,* Publication 1 (2014).

U.S. Department of Defense. *2013 Demographics: Profile of the Military Community* (2013).

U.S. Marine Corps. *Fitness Report* (1610), NAVMC 10835 (Rev. 7–11).

_____. *Leading Marines,* MCWP 6–11 (2014).

U.S. Navy. *Core Values* (2009), http://www.navy.mil/navydata/nav_legacy.asp?id= 193.

_____, Naval Service Training Command. *Officer Professional Corps Competencies Manual* (2014).

U.S. Office of Personnel Management. *Employment of Veterans in the Federal Executive Branch Fiscal Year 2012* (2013).

Van Fleet, David D., and Gary A. Yukl. *Military Leadership: An Organizational Behavior Perspective.* Greenwich, CT: JAI Press, 1986.

Van Wart, Montgomery. *Leadership in Public Organizations,* 2d ed. Armonk, NY: M.E. Sharpe, 2012.

_____. "Public-Sector Leadership Theory: An Assessment." In *The Jossey-Bass Reader on Nonprofit and Public Sector Leadership,* ed. James L. Perry, 73–107. San Francisco: John Wiley & Sons, 2010.

_____, and Kevin O'Farrell. "Organizational Leadership and the Challenges in Teaching It." *Journal of Public Affairs Education* 13(2) (2007): 439–50.

Washington, George. "Farewell Address." *Papers of George Washington,* University of Virginia, http://gwpapers.virginia.edu/documents/washingtons-farewell-address/.

_____. "Newburg Address." *The History Place, Great Speeches Collection* (March 15, 1783). http://www.historyplace.com/speeches/washington.htm.

Zillman, Donald N. "Where Have All the Soldiers Gone II: Military Veterans in Congress and the State of Civil-Military Relations." *Maine Law Review* 58 (2006): 135–56.

Index

193